Integrated E-learning

It is ... oach
used ... pro-
gran ... these
new ... ns of
lear

Thi ... that
e-le ... ves a
new ... l and
org;

A p ... and
case

Inte ... esign,
dev

Wir ... at the
inte ... Open
Uni ... ector
of t

Open and Flexible Learning Series

Series Editor: Fred Lockwood

Activities in Self-Instructional Texts, Fred Lockwood
Assessing Open and Distance Learners, Chris Morgan and Meg O'Reilly
Changing University Teaching, Terry Evans and Daryl Nation
The Costs and Economies of Open and Distance Learning, Greville Rumble
Delivering Digitally, Alistair Inglis, Peter Ling and Vera Joosten
Delivering Learning on the Net: The Why, What and How of Online Education, Martin Weller
The Design and Production of Self-Instructional Materials, Fred Lockwood
Developing Innovation in Online Learning, Maggie McPherson and Miguel Baptista Nunes
E-Moderating, Gilly Salmon
Exploring Open and Distance Learning, Derek Rowntree
Flexible Learning in a Digital World, Betty Collis and Jef Moonen
Improving Your Students' Learning, Alistair Morgan
Innovation in Open and Distance Learning, Fred Lockwood and Anne Gooley
Key Terms and Issues in Open and Distance Learning, Barbara Hodgson
The Knowledge Web: Learning and Collaborating on the Net, Marc Eisenstadt and Tom Vincent
Learning and Teaching in Distance Education, Otto Peters
Learning and Teaching with Technology, Som Naidu
Making Materials-Based Learning Work, Derek Rowntree
Managing Open Systems, Richard Freedman
Mega-Universities and Knowledge Media, John S Daniel
Objectives, Competencies and Learning Outcomes, Reginald F Melton
The Open Classroom: Distance Learning In and Out of Schools, Edited by Jo Bradley
Open and Distance Learning: Case Studies from Education, Industry and Commerce, Stephen Brown
Open and Flexible Learning in Vocational Education and Training, Judith Calder and Ann McCollum
Planning and Management in Distance Education, Santosh Panda
Preparing Materials for Open, Distance and Flexible Learning, Derek Rowntree
Programme Evaluation and Quality, Judith Calder
Reforming Open and Distance Learning, Terry Evans and Daryl Nation
Reusing Online Resources, Allison Littlejohn
Student Retention in Online, Open and Distance Learning, Ormond Simpson
Supporting Students in Open and Distance Learning, Ormond Simpson
Teaching with Audio in Open and Distance Learning, Derek Rowntree
Teaching Through Projects, Jane Henry
Towards More Effective Open and Distance Learning, Perc Marland
Understanding Learners in Open and Distance Education, Terry Evans
Using Communications Media in Open and Flexible Learning, Robin Mason
The Virtual University, Steve Ryan, Bernard Scott, Howard Freeman and Daxa Patel

Integrated E-learning

Implications for Pedagogy, Technology and Organization

Edited by
Wim Jochems,
Jeroen van Merriënboer
and
Rob Koper

RoutledgeFalmer
Taylor & Francis Group

LONDON AND NEW YORK

First published 2004 by RoutledgeFalmer
2 Park Square, Milton Park, Abingdon, Oxon OX14 4RN

Simultaneously published in the USA and Canada
by RoutledgeFalmer
270 Madison Ave, New York, NY 10016

Reprinted 2004, 2005

Transferred to Digital Printing 2006

RoutledgeFalmer is an imprint of the Taylor & Francis Group, an informa business

Typeset in Great Britain by JS Typesetting Ltd, Wellingborough, Northants
Printed and bound in Great Britain by TJI Digital, Padstow, Cornwall

British Library Cataloguing in Publication Data
A catalogue record for this book is available from the British Library.

Library of Congress Cataloging in Publication Data
Integrated e-learning : implications for pedagogy, technology and
organization / edited
    by Wim Jochems, Jeroen van Merriënboer, and Rob Koper
    p. cm.
    Includes bibliographical references and index.
    ISBN 0-415-33502-7 (hard) -- ISBN 0-415-33503-5 (pb) 1. Internet
in higher education. 2. Employees--Trainingof--Computer-assisted
instruction. 3. Instructional systems--Design. 4. Education, Higher--
Effect of technological innovations on. I. Jochems, Wim, 1947- II.
Merriënboer, Jeroen J. G. van, 1959- III. Koper, Rob, 1957-
LB1044.87.1547 2003
378.1'7344678--dc21
                                        2003013860

ISBN 10: 0-415-33502-7 (cased)
ISBN 10: 0-415-33503-5 (limp)

ISBN 13: 978-0-415-33502-7 (cased)
ISBN 13: 978-0-415-33503-4 (limp)

Contents

Notes on the editors — *vii*

Series editor's foreword — *ix*

Preface — *xi*

An introduction to integrated e-learning — **1**
Wim Jochems, Jeroen van Merriënboer and Rob Koper

1. **Instructional design for integrated e-learning** — **13**
   Jeroen van Merriënboer, Theo Bastiaens and Albert Hoogveld

2. **Designing integrated collaborative e-learning** — **24**
   Paul Kirschner, Jan-Willem Strijbos and Karel Kreijns

3. **Performance assessment in integrated e-learning** — **39**
   Dominique Sluijsmans and Rob Martens

4. **Virtual business e-learning: an approach to integrating learning and working** — **51**
   Darco Jansen, Marc van Laeken and Wessel Slot

5. **Learning technologies in e-learning: an integrated domain model** — **64**
   Rob Koper

6. **Educational Modelling Language**   80
    Henry Hermans, Jocelyn Manderveld and Hubert Vogten

7. **Interface design for digital courses**   100
    Huib Tabbers, Liesbeth Kester, Hans Hummel and Rob Nadolski

8. **Usability evaluation of integrated e-learning**   112
    Fred Paas and Olga Firssova

9. **Work processes for the development of integrated
    e-learning courses**   126
    Kathleen Schlusmans, Rob Koper and Wil Giesbertz

10. **Learning objects: are they the answer to the knowledge
    economy's predicament?**   139
    Peter Sloep

11. **Management and organization of integrated e-learning**   151
    Marcel van der Klink and Wim Jochems

12. **Coaching and training in integrated electronic learning
    environments (IELEs)**   164
    Henny Boshuizen and Paul Kirschner

13. **Implementing integrated e-learning: lessons learnt from the
    OUNL case**   176
    Wim Westera

14. **Evaluating integrated e-learning**   187
    Theo Bastiaens, Jo Boon and Rob Martens

15. **Epilogue**   199
    Wim Jochems, Jeroen van Merriënboer and Rob Koper

    Index   *207*

Notes on the editors

Wim Jochems, Jeroen van Merriënboer and Rob Koper are currently full professors in the Educational Technology Expertise Centre (ETEC) of the Open University of the Netherlands (OUNL).

Wim M G Jochems holds a Master's degree in psychology of learning and methodology from Utrecht University, the Netherlands, and a doctor's degree in technical sciences from Delft University of Technology (DUT), the Netherlands. He was a full professor of educational development and the dean of the faculty of Humanities at DUT. Since 1998, he has been a full professor of educational technology and general director of ETEC at the OUNL. His focus is now on the transformation of higher education institutes in relation to the use of educational technology, especially with respect to e-learning.
E-mail: wim.jochems@ou.nl

Jeroen J G van Merriënboer holds a Master's degree in experimental and cognitive psychology from the Free University of Amsterdam and a doctor's degree in instructional technology, with honours, from the University of Twente. He was associate professor of educational psychology at the University of Maastricht and since 1998 he has been a full professor of educational technology at the OUNL. His main research topics include instructional design for complex learning, intelligent performance support for instructional design, and interactive computer-based learning environments for complex skills. He heads the research programme of ETEC (www.ou.nl/otecresearch).
E-mail: jeroen.vanmerrienboer@ou.nl

Rob Koper holds a Master's degree in educational psychology from Tilburg University, the Netherlands, and a doctor's degree in educational technology from the OUNL. He was director of a company for teacher training before he became the head of ICT application development (e-learning infrastructures and educational software development) at the OUNL. Since 1998 he has been a full professor of educational technology, specifically in e-learning technologies. He was programme manager for the development of Educational Modelling Languages. His research focuses on personalized instructional, Web-based learning environments. He heads the technology development programme of ETEC (www.learning networks.org).
E-mail: rob.koper@ou.nl

Series editor's foreword

We are all aware that the educational environment in which we are working is changing, and changing dramatically; it is an environment that is responding to increasing numbers of learners, mature and part-time, often within a shrinking resource allocation. It is an environment in which governments typically stress the importance of investing in people via education and training, note the power of the knowledge economy and expound the potential of the new technologies – particularly e-learning. The government push, combined with the pull from learners – the growing expectations of our learners to study at their own pace, where and when they want – is transforming conventional teaching institutions into flexible learning institutions. The massive growth in the number of distance learning courses available (see http://icdl.open.ac.uk), and online courses available (see http://www.dlcoursefinder.com) is not just occurring in educational institutions but is mirrored in industrial, commercial and public service contexts. In my own university, for example, every faculty learning and teaching plan has identified e-learning as a priority, with the projected growth in the number of staff involved in designing and delivering online components of courses set to triple over the next two years (see http://www.mmu.ac.uk/vitael). I suspect a similar picture exists in your institution.

There is no shortage of virtual learning environments, technical fixes and enthusiasts. Furthermore, there is no shortage of content available; content that is often dumped onto the WWW and which has been termed computer supported page turning. However, where is the advice and assistance, based on models and theories, research evidence and good practice, that will help you and me design, produce and present our courses so as to make the most effective use of existing media and to provide a high quality learning experience? The answer is simple –

the collection of chapters in this book, and the associated Web site (www.iel.nl). This book is noteworthy for several reasons. First, the editors explain how an integrated approach to e-learning can contribute to societal and technological changes: changes that are based on the most appropriate use of the different media used in teaching, not just those associated with communications and information technology. Second, the book seeks to balance the pedagogic, technical and organizational elements that must be in harmony if any course is to be successful. The three-part structure addresses the instructional design issues associated with e-learning, the role of learning technologies in the development of integrated e-learning, and its implementation and evaluation. Third, it presents accounts from almost 30 scholars who have come together to share their thinking with you.

Whether you regard yourself as a teacher or trainer, instructional designer or course developer, I believe the insights, models, arguments and examples this book provides, positioned firmly within a constructivist perspective, are likely to be invaluable to you and your learners. If we are to meet the challenge presented by the changes we face, we need more books like this one.

Fred Lockwood
Manchester, April 2003

Preface

Integrated e-learning refers not only to Web-based learning but also to using the Web for learning in such a way that it is effectively embedded in a well-designed educational system with pedagogical, technological and organizational features that contribute to achieving its goals. Integrated e-learning often reflects elements from face-to-face learning, distance education, and where appropriate forms of structured on-the-job training and practical work. Because of the deliberate mix of Web-based learning, classroom learning, self-study and learning on the job, integration is needed so that the various elements are combined in the best possible way in order to facilitate reaching the desired learning goals. The main issues discussed in this book are not about e-learning as a solitary mode of learning, but rather about how to arrive at a form of e-learning which has manifest added value with regard to effectiveness, efficiency and attractiveness when compared with more conventional ways of learning.

The most common approach to e-learning is characterized by adding new technology to conventional forms of education. The traditional pedagogical approaches to learning generally remain unchanged in spite of the fact that the introduction of the new medium typically demands new instructional methods. At the Open University of the Netherlands, more than five years of hands-on experience with Web-based distance learning has demonstrated that e-learning is not simply a matter of 'digitizing' traditional learning materials. Moreover, several research projects have revealed more effective approaches to incorporating e-learning into educational programmes. The results of our practical experience and of these research projects are reflected in this book. Our starting point is not e-learning as one specific educational method. Instead we set out from an analysis of integrated learning goals or complex professional skills, and ask which instructional processes can (and not 'must') be supported by a combination of e-learning and other educational methods in order to reach those goals.

The main reason for writing this book is that the Educational Technology Expertise Centre of the Open University of the Netherlands receives a large number of enquiries pertaining to the design, development and implementation of e-learning in the field of higher education, both from traditional, campus-based institutes and institutes for distance education. We felt that our hands-on experience with e-learning and the results of our research projects would be of interest to our colleagues in the field of post-secondary higher education, and business and industrial training. It was therefore decided to treat a number of important aspects of integrated e-learning in a more or less structured fashion, which is possible because most of the contributions result from an integrated research and technology development programme on instructional design and learning technologies conducted by the Educational Technology Expertise Centre.

This book is intended for instructional designers, developers of course materials, educational technologists, consultants, training department managers, faculty managers, course directors, teachers and trainers at the post-secondary level, and students in educational sciences who are interested in introducing e-learning and developing e-learning materials. Guidelines and dos and don'ts are presented in each chapter, and examples have been included where necessary. Extracts from e-learning materials are available on the accompanying Web site: www.iel.nl. However, it should be noted that purely technical and infrastructural issues concerning e-learning environments fall beyond the scope of this book.

We should like to thank all our colleagues who have contributed to this volume, not only by writing their articles, but also by providing valuable comments on successive drafts both of the individual chapters and of the work as a whole. In particular we should like to mention Marion Timmermans, who provided invaluable organizational support and kept an eagle eye on the timetable; Chris Sion for editing our English; and Rinnie Oey who assisted in finalizing the manuscript according to the editorial guidelines. We should also like to thank Jeroen Berkhout and Jeroen Storm for developing the Web site that accompanies this book. Finally, we should like to express our appreciation to Fred Lockwood who encouraged us to write this volume and, of course, to the Kogan Page staff for their continuous support.

An introduction to integrated e-learning

Wim Jochems, Jeroen van Merriënboer and Rob Koper

Introduction

Change is part and parcel of the field of higher education, and societal and techno-logical developments will no doubt play their part in effecting it. New visions and ideas are entering education. New educational methods are being introduced to support complex learning and the development of professional competencies. These also stress the collaborative construction of knowledge through active learning ('social constructivism') and the importance of higher-order skills such as problem solving, learning strategies and self-regulation. Moreover, flexibility is being increased by making education less dependent on time and place, for example 'just-in-time' learning (see Goodyear, 1998) and by making personalized learning routes available for individual students. This is known as 'just for me' education. Finally, there is an ongoing integration of learning and working in order to close the gap between formal education and professional practice and to improve the transfer of acquired skills, knowledge and attitudes from schools to the workplace.

At the same time, new technologies are being developed and are becoming increasingly popular in work settings, in daily life and in education. Particularly information and communication technology (ICT) in the sense of the Internet and Internet applications such as the World Wide Web, e-mail, teleconferencing, groupware for computer supported collaborative learning (CSCL) and learning management systems are rapidly gaining ground in the field of higher education. Many technological optimists have expressed the hopeful expectation that 'the availability of technology in education will automatically change teaching processes, learning processes, and learning outcomes. . . Based on technological optimism, there is a strong tendency to distribute as much as possible technological equipment in the educational system' (Elen, Lowyck and Van den Berg, 1999: 191). However, the authors of this book neither share this technological optimism nor advocate the need for a strong technology push. Unfortunately, there are no simple technological solutions for the complex changes indicated above. Along with Spector and Davidsen (2000: 243), we do not believe 'that one single and typically simple approach to using technology to support learning will succeed'. Instead, our starting point is not the technology *per se* but the educational process itself. To be more precise, we focus on educational issues or problems that might possibly be solved, at least partially, by the provision of learning arrangements that make deliberate, effective use of technology. It is our firm conviction that e-learning can play an important role in facilitating learning in the near future, but only under certain critical conditions that enable the technology to become a bearer of educational improvement and innovation.

The basic question that will be addressed in this introductory chapter is how an integrated approach to e-learning can cope with the societal and technological changes and move in the direction of complex learning, high flexibility, and integration of learning and working. Such an integrated approach has to fulfil three critical conditions for innovation. First, integrated e-learning always has to take pedagogical, technical, and organizational aspects into account in order to be successful. Second, it is critical to take a systems design perspective on education, meaning that it might be necessary to mix Web-based instruction with face-to-face instruction, written self-study materials or other media in order to maximize the effectiveness, efficiency and appeal of integrated e-learning. It cannot simply 'replace' other types of learning but should be seen as an integral part of the larger educational system. And third, integrated e-learning should always be student-centred in order to deal with a diverse, widely distributed set of learners who need to learn and transfer complex skills to an increasingly varied set of real-world contexts and settings.

The structure of this introductory chapter is as follows. First, we discuss societal and technological developments and related changes in the field of higher education and lifelong learning. In the second section, we investigate which conditions should be fulfilled to make integrated e-learning truly responsive to those changes. The result is an initial, global description of the concept of integrated e-learning. Next we discuss how an educational systems approach may help to realize integrated e-learning in the field of higher education and lifelong learning. Finally, we explain the scope and focus of this book and present a preview of the remaining chapters, each of which elaborates on another important aspect of integrated e-learning.

Changes in the field of higher education

In response to societal and technological developments, major changes are taking place in the field of higher education and lifelong learning (see Bates, 1995; Laurillard, 1993). Some of these changes are related to the fundamental educational questions of what to teach and how to teach it. The general idea is that the skills, knowledge and attitudes that are taught should better prepare students for today's world, and particularly for the networked society of tomorrow, and that new educational methods are needed for teaching them. Other changes are related to the questions of where to teach and when to teach. In order to cope with the growing individualization and internationalization of a 24-hour economy, there is a clear need for a higher degree of flexibility in higher education. The combination of these changes leads to an educational concept that can best be characterized as complex, flexible, dual learning.

Complex learning

The term complex learning (Van Merriënboer, Clark and De Croock, 2002) reflects the view that another type of skills, sometimes referred to as '21st century skills' (Bereiter, in press), is needed for the society of tomorrow. Key concepts in complex learning are the coordination of constituent skills; the integration of skills, knowledge and attitudes into professional competencies; and the differentiation of various types of competencies. Coordination indicates that the ability to solve new problems or to reason about complex domains is not the result of simply adding up a number of acquired skills, but of being able to flexibly coordinate those skills in new situations. Integration indicates that teaching should not be directed at discrete skills, knowledge elements and attitudes, but at a combination of them in integrated learning goals or competencies. And finally, differentiation stresses that the traditional focus on first-order skills and competencies is insufficient. General problem solving, critical thinking, and metacognitive skills such as learning to learn, self-regulation and self-assessment are becoming more and more important.

New educational methods are being introduced to support complex learning. These methods include problem-based learning, case-based learning, competency-oriented learning, project-based learning and so forth. The common element in these approaches is that they stress the use of rich, meaningful, realistic learning tasks as the driving force for learning (Merrill, 2002). These learning tasks should offer the opportunity to practise the coordination of skills, promote the integration of skills, knowledge and attitudes, and differentiate between first order and higher order skills. The three basic elements of education, presentation, practice and testing, receive another, broader meaning. In the case of presentation, the focus is now on learning mental models through the cooperative and collaborative construction of knowledge based on discussion and guided exploration, and on learning cognitive strategies through the observation of experts who demonstrate how to solve non-trivial problems and explain why they are doing what they are doing.

When it comes to practice, the focus is on experiential learning from rich learning tasks, and on student guidance and scaffolds to support their problem solving performance. As for tests, formative performance-based assessment is becoming increasingly important because this provides meaningful feedback that may help students to improve their learning processes.

Flexible learning

Flexibility is a fertile concept with many relevant aspects, but for flexible learning there are two prevailing perspectives: flexibility with regard to time and place, and flexibility with regard to student needs (Schellekens, Paas and Van Merriënboer, in press). The desire to make education less dependent on time and place is mainly related to the increasing number of people who combine study and work in order to stay well prepared for changes in job requirements, to improve career perspectives, and to realize personal growth. People sometimes want to learn in such a way that it does not interfere with their job: typically, outside office hours and not at a fixed place. But employees also want to learn for the benefit of their job, and preferably consult relevant instructional materials precisely when they are needed to improve their job performance. Goodyear (1998) refers to this phenomenon as 'just-in-time learning'.

The second important aspect of flexibility is related to mass customization, that is the idea that products and services are more and more produced 'on demand', according to the specifications of an individual client. For instance, if someone buys a new car it is built especially for him or her, taking numerous options and specifications into account. In the field of education we can observe the same movement from supply-oriented, 'same for all' education, towards demand-oriented 'just for me' education. Student-centred instruction should provide individual students with personalized learning routes, taking competencies that have already been acquired into account, and should enable them to choose between different levels of guidance, different delivery modes and so forth.

Dual learning

Complex learning and flexible learning meet in the field of dual learning. On the one hand, dual learning stresses the importance of realistic learning tasks. Learning at the workplace is expected to promote the coordination and integration of skills, knowledge and attitudes (eg in professional and academic competencies) as well as the development of higher order skills (eg in social and career competencies). On the other hand, improved flexibility may help to close the gap between formal education and professional practice, and strengthen the transfer of acquired competencies from schools to the workplace. In higher education and lifelong learning the borders between learning and working are rapidly fading away. Higher education institutes could play an important role by offering special courses to alumni whose learner profiles are well known to the institute.

To sum up, current developments in the direction of complex, flexible and dual learning are propelling the innovation of higher education. The use of ICT is intricately connected with those developments, although the connection is far from straightforward. On the one hand, the changes cannot simply be anticipated with technological solutions, and ICT may even hinder particular innovations. For example, realistic and collaborative learning tasks are often easier to implement in a traditional face-to-face setting than in a highly distributed learning setting. On the other hand, ICT may simplify some innovations. Flexibility of delivery, for instance, can easily be accomplished by making instructional materials available on the Internet. Thus, ICT should at times be seen as a part of an innovation problem, and at other times as part of the solution to the same problem. To deal with these complexities, an integrated view of e-learning is necessary, as will be discussed in the next section.

Integrated e-learning

The term 'e-learning' is relatively new. Many comparable terms are in use also, such as technology-enhanced learning, Web-based learning and distributed learning, to mention only a few. This book follows the definition of Kirschner and Paas (2001: 350) that e-learning is learning (and thus the creation of learning and learning arrangements) where the Internet plays an important role in the delivery, support, administration and assessment of learning. However, we also need to consider integrated e-learning. We use this term to indicate that we need a variety of coherent measures at the pedagogical, organizational and technical levels for the successful implementation of e-learning in combination with more conventional methods. As stated above, our focus is on providing optimal learning arrangements by the use of a variety of methods, and e-learning is just one of the methods available. Integrated e-learning therefore typically tries to combine elements from face-to-face teaching, distance education and training on the job. Thus it is a media mix, that is to say, a mix of methods, each having certain characteristics in terms of costs, availability, effectiveness, efficiency, appeal and so forth on the one hand, but a coherent one in the sense that the specific combination of methods is the result of a systematic design procedure on the other.

One of the major problems in the successful application of an integrated strategy is that it demands collaboration between different disciplines during the analysis, design and implementation of the new facilities. Each of these disciplines follows another approach; each uses different concepts, tools and notation. Or, which is even more confusing, sometimes they use the same concepts, tools and notation but in a completely different way. In order to simplify the analysis, design and implementation of e-learning solutions, one often follows a less complex, but then ineffective approach by putting the lead solely in the hands of one of the disciplines.

A hazard of the first approach, technology in the lead, is arriving at solutions that are pedagogically poor and organizationally unmanageable, or simply too expensive. There are numerous examples of this approach. People buy and install various items of technological equipment and then ask themselves what to do with it. They frequently later conclude that they should have bought something else, or even nothing at all. Particularly most of the so-called 'learning management systems' introduced on to the market in recent years have to be categorized as systems that are all too often designed in ignorance of pedagogical insight and organizational processes in educational systems.

The second approach, pedagogy in the lead, risks delivering solutions that are technologically and organizationally poor, that is to say good ideas that cannot be implemented in the current techniques. Or, putting it the other way around, there are better technical solutions to the problem. A regular phenomenon of these approaches is that the level of refinement in the pedagogical concepts used is not elaborated fully enough for implementation. Moreover, these projects often have problems in basic technological requirements such as stability, scalability, security, interoperability, sustainability, quality of the user interfaces and so forth. From the organizational perspective, it may be argued that these new pedagogical models increase the overall costs of the educational system (see Curran and Fox, 1996).

The third approach, organization in the lead, frequently leads to pedagogically and technologically poor solutions. There are several specific approaches here. First is that of using technology to increase the image of the institute in terms of innovativeness and competitiveness. One tends to buy the most expensive, latest, most innovative technologies without asking the question whether these are functional from a pedagogical or technological point of view. Further down in the organizational hierarchy one also sees approaches to automating the workflow in the educational organization, seen from the sole perspective of cost-effectiveness. One can buy or build a student administration system that is not able to store the data needed in teaching. One buys a new, automated testing system without asking what the effects on the educational process will be when viewed from a peda-gogical perspective.

Of course, this analysis is somewhat extreme. In practice most projects will consult experts from different disciplines and try to strike a balance between the three approaches. However, an additional factor comes into play here. The require-ments for educational systems are becoming more and more complex, increasing the need for a genuinely integrated approach.

The first additional requirement that should be mentioned is that a mix of different media and settings is always used in modern education. In addition, the number of media concurrently used in education is increasing. No single new medium has ever completely replaced the previous media preceding it. Most new media increase the existing possibilities, with only the intensity of use varying from time to time. The tendency in the e-learning field is often to think of a single mode solution, for example, put everything online. The keywords, however, are flexibility and richness. The users, both students and staff, should always be in command. Depending on the personal situation or preferences of a student, online media may be preferred at one time and printed media preferred at another.

A second additional requirement refers to the demand for flexibility in an educational setting. The formal distinction between residential, distance teaching and on-the-job training institutes is disappearing as a result of network-based technologies in education. Today we are dealing with the need for an optimal combination of learning opportunities that are available in the classroom, at home or at work, by use of the Web, books and video, such as the distributed learning systems introduced by Wagner (1999). There is a continuous search for an optimal mix from the points of view of the desired learning outcomes, the user demands and cost-effectiveness (eg decreasing the amount of expensive face-to-face education).

As a result of the increasing complexity of conflicting demands and the overall complexity of successfully implementing e-learning, this book is a plea for an integrated approach to these problems. The keyword is balance. We have to strike a balance between the various requirements resulting from the different points of view. The next section will discuss two conditions for the productive use of an integrated approach, namely thinking in terms of educational systems to identify optimal learning arrangements, and applying learning technologies to bridge the gap between disciplines.

Educational systems and learning technologies

Integration of the different viewpoints is best guaranteed by using a systems approach for educational change (see Banathy, 1996). The complete educational system should be considered, at least from the three viewpoints mentioned, if changes are made to it. From this point of view the introduction of e-learning is not considered merely as an addition to instruction, but as an innovation, an integral part of the educational system. Accordingly, a redesign of the educational system is needed in order to arrive at added 'learning value', for instance in terms of higher order learning outcomes. Thus organizational, pedagogical and technological aspects have to be managed in harmony in order to solve an educational problem adequately (see Figure 0.1). For example, the implementation of an instructional approach will be much more powerful if it is also anchored in both the organization and the technological instrumentation. For the same reason the introduction of e-learning will have far more impact on education if it is able to support the organizational and instructional concepts that courses are based on. This is why this book advocates a design perspective focusing on learning arrangements.

As we said above, in order to bridge the gaps between the different disciplines, tools and concepts should be available that can serve as mediators on the conceptual level in analysis and design, as well as in actual implementation. So-called 'learning technologies' play a critical role in this bridging function. They can be considered as a means of formalizing pedagogical and organizational thinking in such a way that it can be implemented in a technical solution. For instance the learning technology 'Educational Modelling Language' (EML) (see Chapter 6) can be used to formalize an instructional design in such a way that it can be interpreted automatically by any suitably designed e-learning platform or ICT system. Conversely, this language advances the technical requirements of abstraction,

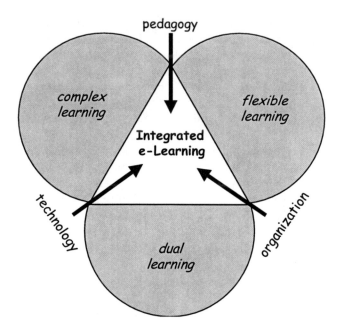

Figure 0.1 *An educational systems approach to integrated e-learning*

completeness and clarity in such a way that it will help instructional designers to find errors or ambiguities in their pedagogical designs. The development and use of learning technologies increase the possibilities of using advanced pedagogical designs, the technical interoperability, and the efficiency in an organization by maximizing the reuse possibilities (Littlejohn, 2003).

This book addresses a number of elaborations of the issues stated above, in addition to several other issues that are of importance in integrated e-learning. We believe that such an approach is of vital importance because there is a substantial need to make education available through e-learning in a way that is effective, efficient and attractive.

About this book

The preceding sections of this chapter discuss a number of important societal and technological developments, along with related changes in the field of higher education and lifelong learning. We argued that integrated e-learning might fruitfully anticipate these changes, if it is positioned at the intersection of complex, flexible, dual learning and takes an educational systems approach to combining pedagogical, technological and organizational demands. The following chapters elaborate on different features of integrated e-learning, following the line of design, development, implementation and evaluation of course materials. The book is meant for educationalists, educational designers and developers of educational materials. It is also directed at teachers at post-secondary level, and students of educational sciences who are interested in introducing e-learning and designing e-learning materials. Guidelines and dos and don'ts are presented for each of the topics discussed. Examples are added in text boxes, and larger pieces of illustrative e-materials are available on the Web site (www.iel.nl) that accompanies this book.

The scope of the book can be summarized as follows. First, it focuses on higher education, lifelong learning and postgraduate education. It might be expected that the boundaries between regular higher education on the one hand, and other forms of lifelong learning and continuous education on the other, will gradually fade away. Second, the book focuses on complex learning situations that aim at integrated learning goals, such as courses and programmes that are meant for the development of professional and academic competencies. Little or no attention is paid to e-learning systems that merely present job-related, factual information, or only provide drill and practice for particular procedural skills, or mainly fulfil the role of an encyclopaedia. Third, all the chapters start from a constructivist viewpoint on learning, stressing the use of activating educational methods in which the focus is on student learning. And finally, the key element in all the contributions is the use of ICT in education, particularly in terms of integrated e-learning. The use of the Internet in facilitating learning processes and improving learning technologies is discussed throughout the book, in a manner that bears out that the use of the Internet has a clearly specified added value to traditional instructional systems.

It should be clear that this book is not about ICT behind e-learning. Technical and infrastructural issues with respect to e-learning environments fall outside its scope. Nor is it about general issues with respect to instructional design, such as the development and production of instructional materials, or the implementation and evaluation of such materials. These issues are only discussed when they are specific to integrated e-learning and need an approach that is significantly different from conventional approaches to learning design. Third, it is not about policies or strategies relating to e-learning that institutes for higher education may need in order to cope with the new developments in education.

The structure of the book is as follows. Chapters 1 to 4 focus on instructional design issues for integrated e-learning. Chapter 1 discusses a general design model for complex learning and its implications for the design of e-learning. The chapter focuses on the design of learning tasks, but also discusses three subordinate blueprint components, namely supportive information, just-in-time information, and part-task practice. Each component defines its own requirements for educational methods as well as media. Chapter 2 focuses on one particularly important design aspect in e-learning, namely computer supported collaborative learning (CSCL). It discusses the design of conditions that facilitate cooperation and collaboration between students in terms of technological, social and educational affordances. Chapter 3 discusses the design of performance assessment for e-learning. While performance assessment is one of the driving forces for complex learning, it is typically neglected in current e-learning environments. Finally, Chapter 4 describes the virtual company concept, which is one concrete instance of integrated e-learning that seamlessly integrates our design guidelines for learning tasks, CSCL and performance assessment.

Chapters 5 to 9 focus on the role that learning technologies play in the development of integrated e-learning. Learning technologies bridge the gap in e-learning between educational, organizational and technical requirements. They formalize and describe instructional approaches in such a way that they can be processed automatically in ICT environments, and within a variety of organizational contexts. This formalization process is referred to as 'educational modelling', and the outcomes are models, specifications and standards.

Chapter 5 provides a general, state-of-the-art conceptual domain model for integrated e-learning. It defines the field and its basic structure, vocabulary and issues. The chapter identifies four major areas where e-learning systems have to be improved in future: the development of units of learning; the facilities to share and reuse components within and between organizations; the facilities for differentiated, personalized delivery of education; and assessment within e-learning environments. Chapter 6 presents a new model and specification language developed to formalize units of learning to enable processing within e-learning environments. It provides a semantic descriptive framework for instructional design approaches, which allows for reuse of learning objects and the combination of learning objects into purposeful units of learning. The model and the language are called Educational Modelling Language (EML). Chapter 7 provides concrete guidelines for graphical user interfaces and for the presentation of multimedia content, which are firmly based on both the human–computer interaction and the educational psychology literature. Chapter 8 presents guidelines for usability evaluation of integrated e-learning. It is argued that usability evaluation, as a fundamental method of evaluating and improving products and systems, can play an important role in the development of effective e-learning. However, the application of these methods in the field is still rare. The authors present borrowed methods, techniques, and standards from other fields, such as human–computer interaction, and propose their application in integrated e-learning. Chapter 9 focuses on the issue of effective, changed work processes in integrated e-learning. It is argued that the demands of creating high quality e-learning materials are too high for an individual tutor to meet, and that a more industrialized, teamwork approach is necessary. The approach that has been developed is presented and discussed.

Finally, Chapters 10 to 15 discuss implementation and evaluation issues for integrated e-learning. Chapter 10 focuses on learning objects, reusable bits of learning content. Although higher education would like to deliver personalized learning materials to students, more personalization implies increased costs per student. It is argued that reusable learning objects might provide at least the beginning of a solution to this dilemma. Chapter 11 concentrates on the topic of integrated e-learning from a managerial point of view, especially from the perspective of faculty management. The focus is on innovation in educational practice where technological, strategic, pedagogical and organizational issues of the implementation are perceived, managed and organized coherently. Chapter 12 focuses on coaching and training in integrated e-learning. It is argued that complex, flexible, dual learning implies a change in the roles of the teachers as skills training and coaching become more important. Attention is paid to different forms of electronic coaching and training. Chapter 13 discusses some relevant implementation issues using the Open University of the Netherlands as an illustrative case. Lessons that have been learnt with respect to vision on innovation, organizational change strategy and staff involvement are presented. Chapter 14 identifies important questions with respect to the evaluation of integrated e-learning. Specific elements to be evaluated are described, and a framework for evaluation is introduced and elaborated in an example. Finally, Chapter 15 provides some critical reflections on integrated e-learning, and refers to some of the limitations, problems and questions on the pedagogical, technological and organizational levels that have to be dealt with in the near future.

References

Banathy, B H (1996) Systems inquiry and its application in education, in *Handbook of Research for Educational Communications and Technology*, ed D H Jonassen, pp 74–92, Macmillan, New York

Bates, A W (1995) *Technology, Open Learning, and Distance Education*, Routledge, London

Bereiter, C (in press) 21st Century skills – challenge or fallacy?, in *Unravelling Basic Components and Dimensions of Powerful Learning Environments*, ed E de Corte *et al*, Elsevier Science, Oxford

Curran, C and Fox, S (1996) *Telematics and Open and Distance Learning*, National Distance Education Centre, Dublin, Eire

Elen, J, Lowyck, J and Van den Berg, B (1999) Virtual university: will learning benefit?, in *Socio-Economics of Virtual Universities: Experiences from open and distance education in Europe*, ed G E Ortner and F Nickolman, pp 29–51, Deutscher Studien Verlag, Weinheim, Germany

Goodyear, P (1998) *New Technology in Higher Education: Understanding the innovation process*, invited keynote paper presented at the International Conference on Integrating Information and Communication Technology in Higher Education (BITE), March 1998, Maastricht, Netherlands

Kirschner, P A and Paas, F G W C (2001) Web-enhanced higher education: a Tower of Babel, *Computers in Human Behavior*, **17**, pp 347–53

Laurillard, D (1993) *Rethinking University Teaching: A Framework for the effective use of educational technology*, Routledge, London

Littlejohn, A (2003) (ed) *Reusing Online Resources: A sustainable approach to e-learning*, Kogan Page, London

Merrill, M D (2002) First principles of instruction, *Educational Technology, Research and Development*, **50** (3), pp 43–59

Schellekens, A, Paas, F and Van Merriënboer, J J G (in press) Flexibility in higher professional education: a survey in business administration programmes in the Netherlands, *Higher Education*

Spector, J M and Davidsen, P I (2000) Designing technology-enhanced learning environments, in *Instructional and Cognitive Impacts of Web-based Education*, ed B Abbey, pp 241–61, Idea Publishing Group, London

Van Merriënboer, J J G, Clark, R E and De Croock, M B M (2002) Blueprints for complex learning: the 4C/ID-model, *Educational Technology, Research and Development*, **50** (2), pp 39–64

Wagner, E D (1999) Beyond distance education: distributed learning systems, in *Handbook of Human Performance Technology*, ed H D Stolovich and E J Keeps, pp 626–48, Jossey-Bass Pfeiffer, San Francisco, CA

Chapter 1

Instructional design for integrated e-learning

Jeroen van Merriënboer, Theo Bastiaens and Albert Hoogveld

Introduction

E-learning is characterized by its independence of place and time, its integrated presentation and communication facilities, and its opportunities for reuse of instructional materials in the form of learning objects (Khan, 2001). Many authors who claim that e-learning yields a 'technology push' that will increase the quality of education put these arguments forward. However, it remains an open question if media will ever influence learning (Clark, 1994). A viewpoint that can easily be defended is that it is only instructional methods, and not the media employed, that can improve the quality of education. Thus, one should rephrase the question and ask if the current technical and technological developments in the field of e-learning do indeed enable the use of innovative instructional methods that are necessary to make learning more effective, efficient and appealing.

An educationalist with an open mind who studies the overwhelming amount of e-learning applications that are currently to be found on the Web will be forced to conclude that from a pedagogical perspective, e-learning is a step backward rather than a step forward. The central concept appears to be 'content'. So-called 'content providers' such as publishers, universities and knowledge institutes 'deliver' this content to their students via the Internet. Pedagogy is not an issue. Instead, the most important questions typically relate to the costs, the necessary technical infrastructure, and the learning platform to use. A direct consequence of this approach is that many e-learning applications take us back to the early days of computer-based education with its programmed tutorials and electronic books. Student activities are limited to reading from the screen, filling out boxes, and at best, chatting with peer students about the content. The designers of e-learning applications themselves sometimes acknowledge these shortcomings and refer to e-learning as CSPT (computer supported page turning) or 'Simon says' training, where the computer demonstrates something that must be imitated by the learner. Some authors have introduced the term 'straight e-learning' as synonymous with these overly simplified forms of teaching.

In short, there is a sharp contrast between most current forms of e-learning and the social-constructivist ideas about learning that emerged in the late 1980s and 1990s. Forms of e-learning that stress the active engagement of learners in rich learning tasks and the active, social construction of knowledge and acquisition of skills are rare. The goal of this chapter is to sketch a fruitful approach to the pedagogical design of e-learning. First, it describes a general design model for complex learning, called the four-component instructional design model. Second, we discuss the application of this model and each of its four components in the design of integrated e-learning. Third, we provide illustrations of well-designed integrated e-learning courses. The chapter concludes with a discussion of the limitations of the approach that has been presented, and stresses that powerful instructional design models are needed to meet the very high expectations of e-learning.

Instructional design for complex learning

Modern instructional design models typically assume that realistic, rich learning tasks are the driving force for learning (Clark and Estes, 1999; Van Merriënboer and Kirschner, 2001; Merrill, 2002; Reigeluth, 1999). Well-designed learning tasks must stimulate learners to integrate required skills, knowledge and attitudes, and to coordinate different aspects of behaviour in a process of complex learning. This is believed to result in a rich knowledge base that allows for transfer to daily life or future work settings. Integration and coordination pertain both to non-recurrent aspects of performance, which are variable constituent skills that differ from problem to problem situation (eg problem solving and reasoning), and to recurrent aspects of performance, which are consistent constituent skills that are identical from one problem situation to another (eg application of procedures and routines).

An example of an instructional design model that stresses integration, coordination and transfer of learning is the four-component instructional design model that is known for short as the 4C/ID model (Van Merriënboer, 1997; Van Merriënboer, Clark, and de Croock, 2002; Van Merriënboer and de Croock, 2002). The basic message of this model is that well-designed learning environments can always be described in terms of four interrelated blueprint components:

1. *Learning tasks:* concrete, authentic and meaningful 'whole-task experiences' that are provided for learners.
2. *Supportive information:* information that is supportive to the learning and performance of non-recurrent, problem solving and reasoning aspects of learning tasks. It builds a bridge between what learners already know and what may be helpful to know in order to work on the learning tasks productively.
3. *Just-in-time (JIT) information:* information that is prerequisite to the learning and performance of recurrent aspects of learning tasks. It is best organized in small information units and presented to learners precisely when they need it during their work on the learning tasks.
4. *Part task practice:* additional exercises for those recurrent aspects of learning tasks for which a very high level of automaticity is required after the instruction.

Figure 1.1 provides a schematic overview of the four components. The learning tasks are represented as circles, while a sequence of tasks serves as the backbone of the course or curriculum. The learning tasks are performed in a simulated or real

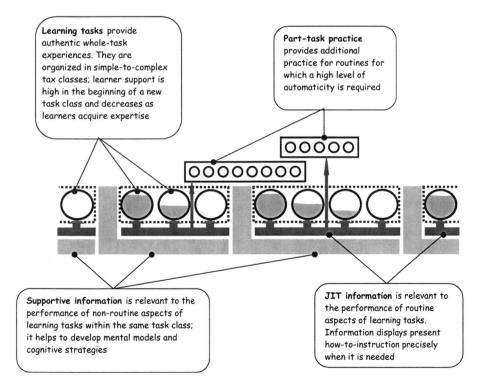

Figure 1.1 *A schematic overview of the four components: 1) learning tasks, organized in task classes and with scaffolding within each task class; 2) supportive information; 3) JIT information; and 4) part task practice*

task environment and provide 'whole task practice'. Ideally, they confront the learners with all aspects of a professional competency, both recurrent and non-recurrent, so that they can learn to coordinate and integrate those aspects. Equivalent learning tasks belong to the same task class. (See the dotted rectangles around the set of learning tasks in Figure 1.1.) They are equivalent to each other in the sense that they can be performed on the basis of the same body of knowledge, although they differ on the dimensions that also vary in the real world, that is to say they show high variability. Each new task class is more difficult than the previous task classes. Students receive a great deal of guidance and support for their work on the first learning tasks in a class. In Figure 1.1, this is indicated by the way the circles are filled in. However, guidance gradually decreases in a process of 'scaffolding' as learners acquire more expertise (Van Merriënboer, Kirschner and Kester, 2003). Students work without any support on the final learning tasks in a task class. These tasks can also be used as test tasks for the assessment of students' performance.

The supportive information for each subsequent task class is an addition to or an embellishment of the information previously presented, allowing learners to do things they could not do before. (See the L-shaped, light grey shapes in Figure 1.1.) It is the information that teachers typically call 'the theory', and consists of three parts. First, it describes mental models of how a learning domain is organized, answering questions such as 'what is this?' (conceptual models), 'how is this constructed?' (structural models) and 'how does this work?' (causal models). These models are typically illustrated with concrete examples or case studies. Second, supportive information describes cognitive strategies of how to approach problems in a learning domain. They describe the successive phases in a problem solving process and the rules of thumb that may be helpful to successfully complete each of the phases. They may be exemplified by showing an expert who is performing a non-trivial task and simultaneously explaining why he or she is doing what he or she is doing. Third, supportive information also pertains to cognitive feedback that is given on the quality of task performance. This will often invite students to compare their own solutions critically with expert solutions or with those of their peers.

The JIT information is represented in Figure 1.1 by dark grey rectangles, with upward pointing arrows indicating that information units are explicitly coupled to separate learning tasks. This information is preferably presented exactly when learners need it to perform particular recurrent aspects of learning tasks. This removes the need for memorization beforehand. JIT information primarily consists of procedural steps and rules, which algorithmically prescribe the correct performance of the recurrent aspects of learning tasks. If learners start to master the recurrent aspects, the presentation of the JIT information quickly fades away. This principle is called 'fading' (Kester et al, 2001). Demonstrations may be needed for difficult procedural steps or rules, and are preferably given in the context of the whole, meaningful task. Finally, corrective feedback may be given on the quality of performance of routine aspects. Such feedback indicates that there is an error, explains why there is an error, and gives hints that may help the learner to get back on the right track.

Part task practice is indicated in Figure 1.1 by the small series of circles representing practice items. Part task practice for a selected recurrent aspect is only necessary if the learning tasks do not provide enough repetition to reach the required level of automation, and never starts before this aspect has been introduced in a learning task. Thus, there should be an appropriate cognitive context. For instance, the model might specify that musicians only start practising a particular musical scale after this scale has been introduced in an actual musical piece, or primary school children only start practising a particular multiplication table after this table has been introduced in a meaningful arithmetical task. Part task practice is preferably combined with learning tasks so that the practice of the routines is distributed or spaced.

The four components in integrated e-learning

The 4C/ID model can certainly be used for the design of integrated e-learning, provided of course that the computer and the Internet are suitable media for a specific design enterprise. Many factors determine the selection of media in educational design (Romiszowski, 1988), making specific media selection models indispensable to reach an ultimate 'media mix'. The first category of factors pertains to constraints, such as available resources (eg personnel, equipment, time and money) and the necessity of delivering instruction independently of both time and/or place. The second category pertains to task requirements, such as media attributes that are necessary for performing the learning tasks and required response options for the learners. A third important category is target group characteristics such as the size of the group, computer literacy and handicaps. It is beyond the scope of this chapter to discuss this complicated process of media selection. We will rather focus on the relationship between the four blueprint components and the use of media.

The first component of the model presented contains the learning tasks. They form the backbone of the instruction. The primary medium must allow learners to work on these tasks, and takes the form of a simulated or real task environment. Examples would be a project room, a simulated office, a physical simulator or an internship in a real company. In the case of e-learning, the heart of the learning environment will consist of a computer simulated task environment. This may frequently be a low or very low fidelity simulation, which only represents those aspects of the real environment that are necessary to perform the task, and in which there is little or no physical correspondence with the real environment. However, particularly for more advanced learners, it may be necessary to use high fidelity simulation. For instance, students in medicine can first practise their diagnostic skills on the basis of simple textual descriptions of patients (low fidelity cases), while more advanced students also need to practise on simulated patients (high fidelity) and, possibly even real patients (internships). This example clearly shows the limitations of e-learning. For many competencies such as pleading a case in court, conducting psychological experiments, or troubleshooting in a chemical factory, current Web technology does not offer the possibilities that are needed for high fidelity simulation because of such factors as inadequate input–output facilities or lack of simulation models that can run in the background. Virtual reality (VR), broadband technology and new input and output devices such as VR helmets and data gloves promise improved opportunities in the near future. However, at the moment the technology necessary to implement optimal instructional methods is not always available.

Secondary media need to be selected for the other three components of the model. Traditional media for supportive information are textbooks, teachers and realia. Textbooks contain a description of the theory, that is, the mental models that characterize a learning domain, and regrettably, often to a lesser degree the systematic approaches and rules of thumb that may help to solve problems in the domain. Teachers typically discuss the highlights in the theory (lectures), demonstrate or provide expert models of problem solving approaches, and provide cognitive feedback on learners' performance. Realia or descriptions of real entities (cases) are used to illustrate the theory. Multimedia and hypertext systems may take over these functions in part or in full. They may present theoretical models and concrete cases that illustrate those models in a highly interactive way, and they may explain problem solving approaches and illustrate those approaches by showing, for example, expert models on video. As mentioned above, it is critical for students to elaborate and process this information in depth. Multimedia are not always helpful in reaching this goal. Salomon (1998) discusses the so-called 'butterfly defect' in multimedia and Web-based learning, saying, 'touch, but don't touch, and just move on to make something out of it'. Multimedia systems are termed 'hot' because they are fun and can even offer a means of relaxing. By contrast, textbooks are 'cool' in the sense that they are associated with hard work, and invite learners to process information in depth. If multimedia are used, it is thus more important than ever to provoke deep processing through asking questions, stimulating reflection and promoting discussion.

The traditional media for JIT information are the teacher and all kinds of job and learning aids. The teacher's role is to move around the laboratory or workplace and watch over the learners' shoulders. It is worth noting that the teacher's name is ALOYS (the assistant looking over your shoulder). The teacher should also give directions for performing the recurrent aspects of learning tasks (eg 'No, you should hold that instrument like this. . .', 'Watch carefully, you should now select this option. . .'). Job aids may be the posters with frequently used software commands that are displayed on the wall of a computer class, quick reference guides next to a piece of machinery, or booklets with safety instructions for trainees in industry. In e-learning environments, these functions are mainly taken over by electronic job aids, online help systems, electronic performance support systems (EPSS), wizards and 'intelligent agents' (Bastiaens et al, 1997). Such systems provide JIT information for the learner on request (eg online help) or on their own initiative (eg intelligent agents), preferably precisely when the students need it for their work on the learning tasks.

Particularly in the case of the last component, part task practice, the computer has proved its value in recent decades. Drill and practice computer programs are without doubt the most successful educational software. The computer is sometimes abused for its use of drills, but most critics seem to miss the point. They contrast drill and practice computer programs with educational software that focuses on rich, authentic learning tasks. However, in our approach drill and practice will never replace meaningful whole task practice. It merely complements the work on rich learning tasks, and is applied only when the learning tasks themselves cannot provide enough practice to reach the desired level of automaticity for selected recurrent aspects. If such part task practice is necessary, the computer is probably the most suitable medium because it can make drills effective and appealing by giving procedural support; compressing simulated time so that more exercises can be done than in real time; giving knowledge of results (KR); providing immediate feedback on errors; and using multiple representations, elements of games, sound effects and so forth.

Well-designed integrated e-learning applications should combine the four components in one coherent environment. It is certainly not necessary for all communication and presentation facilities to be computer-supported, but the Internet does need to be the primary medium allowing students to work on the learning tasks. If it is not, it makes little sense to call it e-learning. Furthermore, it is important to realize that the 4C/ID model is a design model, and not a pedagogical model *per se* (Ip and Naidu, 2001; De Boer and Collis, 2002). Depending on the context, the target group, the learning goals and various other factors, the 4C/ID model may yield very different pedagogical models. Two models that are consistent with the presented design methodology are discussed in the next section.

Two illustrative pedagogical models

The common denominator of pedagogical models that may result from the presented design methodology is that a sequence of learning tasks is the backbone of the course or curriculum. Other educational elements are always subordinate to, although carefully interconnected with, this backbone. The term 'learning task' is used here in a generic sense. For instance it may refer to a case study, an individual task, a group project or a practical problem. In this section, case-based teaching and project-centred learning will be described as two models that are consistent with the design methodology presented.

In case-based teaching, cases fulfil the role of learning tasks. A case is a complex real event, reported from the viewpoint of a professional, in which typical aspects or instances of professional problem solving can be observed. A case may be considered as 'frozen experience'. Students can observe, study and analyze real problems in their natural context but without time constraints. They may take alternative decisions or make mistakes and then learn from these mistakes. There are no dangerous consequences of being in error, while at the same time the authenticity of the situation remains intact. Good case designs support the solving

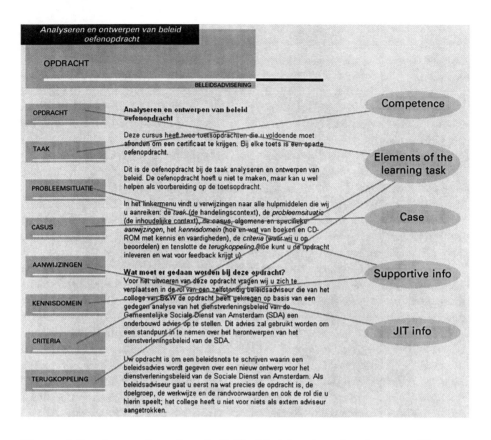

Figure 1.2 *A screen dump from the Public Administration e-learning course (Korsten et al, 1999). The three compulsory elements of the 4C/ID model, that is, case or learning task, supportive information and JIT information, are indicated in the figure. The course does not contain part task practice.*

of the problem by providing the students with resources for supportive information, that is, cognitive strategies and mental models used by professionals. Both before and during their work on the cases they may consult those resources (such as books, Web sites and experts) and discuss them with their peers (either synchronously or asynchronously). In addition, help systems or learning tools can be made available with JIT information that helps students to analyze the case, use necessary tools, gather data and so on.

An example of an integrated e-learning course that uses case-based teaching is the Open University of the Netherlands' Public Administration Course (see Figure 1.2). The backbone of this course for senior public administrators consists of a series of cases with which students learn professional systematic approaches for the design of policy documents and for solving problems of policy making (Korsten *et al*, 1999). The development of 12 professional competencies, such as analysis and preparation of policy decisions, and collecting documentation in anticipation of expected policy decisions, is supported by the set of cases. Students work individually or in small groups. The course Web site presents the cases, provides links to relevant resources with supportive information (methods and theoretical principles), and presents easily accessible help systems and EPSS with JIT information (eg definitions of concepts used in the case or tips to organize the problem approach). A tutor, who also provides feedback on task performance by e-mail and by participating in the discussion group, monitors student activities. In the learning task presented in Figure 1.2, the students must imagine themselves as senior policy advisors who have to make a recommendation to the Amsterdam City Administration about the redesign of the Social Services Department.

In project-centred learning, projects fulfil the role of learning tasks. Students work relatively independently as a group on a project, which is defined as 'an unfamiliar problem that has to be solved'. Projects are more or less authentic, offer the project members a reasonable degree of freedom in their way of working, and integrate several subjects in a curriculum. Project-centred learning approaches typically distinguish a number of logical steps or phases in a project. At certain moments, students have to complete a phase and make decisions that have an impact on the following phases and the continuation of the whole project. It is frequently important to pay special attention to control indicators such as time (spent and still available), budget, quality of intermediate processes and products, new information, communication and organization. The teacher or tutor monitors the learning process as a coach. Every phase is completed after either a formal or informal assessment of the process and/or the relevant, possibly intermediate, product or products that resulted from that phase. Project-centred learning in education is closely related to project-based working methods in business and industry.

In conclusion, it should be clear that case-based teaching and project-centred learning, as well as many other approaches that focus on rich learning tasks (eg competency-based learning, dual learning and problem-based learning), can easily be combined and yet still be consistent with the design model presented. For instance, the 4C/ID model suggests starting a new task class with learning tasks that provide the learners with a high level of support, and then ending with learning tasks in which guidance is not provided. This type of scaffolding could be realized by starting with case-based teaching, continuing with project-centred learning where the projects are carried out with ample guidance and support (eg with process worksheets that guide the students through the project), and finally working on complex projects with a high measure of independence.

Discussion

This chapter started with the assertion that many e-learning applications are of low pedagogical quality. We then tried to sketch a more fruitful approach to the design of e-learning. First, we presented a general model for complex learning. This model states that well-designed instruction aimed at integration of knowledge, skills and attitudes, coordination of recurrent and non-recurrent constituent skills, and transfer of learning always consists of four components, namely learning tasks, supportive information, JIT information and part task practice. This model was elaborated and illustrated for the design of integrated e-learning environments. Such applications are typically built around a simulated task environment and are seamlessly coupled to relevant multimedia systems, electronic performance support systems, and if necessary, drill and practice computer programs.

The framework presented has several limitations. First, it is limited to peda-gogical models where the Internet is the primary medium. This does not exclude the use of other media. On the contrary, secondary media other than the computer will typically be required to design a powerful environment for integrated e-learning. For instance, a tutor may provide guidance for the work on the learning tasks; textbooks may be consulted to learn supportive information; stand-alone skill training programs may help students to practise recurrent parts of the learning tasks; and many other media may be used. But it does exclude learning arrangements that are primarily based on face-to-face teaching and merely use the Internet as a secondary medium to present supportive information, offer additional communi-cation facilities, provide part task practice and so forth. These forms of 'blended learning' may pose other or additional design requirements than the ones discussed in this chapter. Second, positioned in the ADDIE model (analysis, design, develop-ment, implementation and evaluation) for instructional systems design, this chapter has focused on the second phase, the design of blueprints for integrated e-learning. We have paid little or no attention to the analysis of the target group, learning goals and context. Nor has the chapter dealt with the development of course materials, interfaces and navigation structures, the implementation of the system, and the assessment of learners and other evaluation issues. These are discussed in other chapters of this book.

It can be concluded that compared with traditional classroom teaching, inte-grated e-learning can offer major advantages with regard to its flexibility, presenta-tion and communication facilities, reuse of materials and interoperability between instructional systems. In addition, current technology already supports many of the instructional methods that are necessary for complex learning and transfer to occur, and further technological developments will rapidly increase these opportunities in the near future. Nevertheless, a major obstacle to reaching effective, efficient and appealing integrated e-learning environments is the lack of proven pedagogical models. From a teaching perspective, e-learning is still in its infancy. There is considerable demand for easy-to-use instructional design models that facilitate the realization in practice of the high expectations we have about e-learning.

References

Bastiaens, T, Nijhof, W J, Streumer, J N and Abma, H J (1997) Working and learning with electronic performance support systems: an effectiveness study, *Training for Quality*, **5** (1), pp 10–18

Clark, R E (1994) Media will never influence learning, *Educational Technology, Research and Development*, **42** (3), pp 39–47

Clark, R E, and Estes, F (1999) The development of authentic educational technologies, *Educational Technology*, **39** (2), pp 5–16

De Boer,W and Collis, B (2002) A changing pedagogy in e-learning: from acquisition to contribution, *Journal of Computing in Higher Education*, **13** (2), pp 87–101

Ip, A and Naidu, S (2001) Experience-based pedagogical design for e-learning, *Educational Technology*, **41** (5), pp 53–58

Kester, L, Kirschner, P A, van Merriënboer, J J G and Baumer, A (2001) Just-in-time information presentation and the acquisition of complex cognitive skills, *Computers in Human Behavior*, **17**, pp 373–91

Khan, B H (2001) *Web-Based Training*, Educational Technology Publications, Englewood Cliffs, NJ

Korsten, A F A, Crijns, M, Arendsen, G P, van Zanten, W P C, Hoogveld, A W M and Schlusmans, K H L A (1999) *Elektronisch Cursusmateriaal Beleidskunde* (Electronic Course Materials Public Administration), Open University of the Netherlands, Heerlen

Merrill, M D (2002) First principles of instruction, *Educational Technology, Research and Development*, **50** (3), pp 43–59

Reigeluth, C M (1999) (ed) *Instructional-Design Theories and Models: A new paradigm of instructional theory (Vol 2)*, Lawrence Erlbaum, Mahwah, NJ

Romiszowski, A J (1988) *The Selection and Use of Instructional Media*, Nichols Publishing, New York

Salomon, G (1998) Novel constructivist learning environments and novel technologies: some issues to be concerned with, *Research Dialogue in Learning and Instruction*, **1** (1), pp 3–12

Van Merriënboer, J J G (1997) *Training Complex Cognitive Skills*, Educational Technology Publications, Englewood Cliffs, NJ

Van Merriënboer, J J G and de Croock, M B M (2002) Performance based ISD: ten steps to complex learning, *Performance Improvement Journal*, **41** (7), pp 33–38

Van Merriënboer, J J G and Kirschner, P A (2001) Three worlds of instructional design: state of the art and future directions, *Instructional Science*, **29**, pp 429–41

Van Merriënboer, J J G, Clark, R E and de Croock, M B M (2002) Blueprints for complex learning: the 4C/ID*-model, *Educational Technology, Research and Development*, **50** (2), pp 39–64

Van Merriënboer, J J G, Kirschner, P A and Kester, L (2003) Taking the load off a learner's mind: instructional design for complex learning, *Educational Psychologist*, **38** (1), pp 5–13

Further reading

Anderson, J R and Lebière, C (1998) *The Atomic Components of Thought*, Lawrence Erlbaum, Mahwah, NJ

Perkins, D N and Salomon, G (1989) Are cognitive skills context-bound?, *Educational Researcher*, **18**, pp 16–25

Chapter 2

Designing integrated collaborative e-learning

Paul Kirschner, Jan-Willem Strijbos and Karel Kreijns

Introduction

Current research and design of integrated electronic collaborative learning environments (IECLEs), which are often referred to as computer supported collaborative learning (CSCL) environments, tend to focus on surface level characteristics. There is a myriad of educational researchers and designers who are busy, for example, with determining optimal group size for problem-based education as opposed to project-centred learning. To determine the optimal group size, students' collaborative efforts and the results of these efforts are compared for groups of varying sizes in the different educational settings. This approach resembles comparative research on the use of different media in education which was strongly, and we had hoped definitively, criticized by Clark (1983). He eloquently argued that researchers tend to focus on the media used and surface characteristics of the education they provide. As a consequence, comparative research tends to be inconclusive and the learning materials developed tend to be at best unreliable and at worst 'mathemathantic'. This word is derived from the Greek, *mathema* (learning) plus *thanatos* (death). This surface level approach disavows the fundamental differences between the real determinants of learning and behaviour in education.

A second problem is that educational institutions tend to take traditional classroom ideas and pedagogy and substitute them into non-contiguous collaborative learning environments. The assumption is that since these environments have features that admit the type of interaction we see in the classroom such as messaging, real-time meetings and shared applications, traditional pedagogy can be used. The immediate result is students and instructors who are often disgruntled or disappointed, motivation that is quickly extinguished, poorly used environments, wasted time and money, and showcase environments that are often not much more than computer assisted page turning. The final result is the same as in the case of the first problem: the death of learning.

The solution is as simple as it is elegant, dealing not only with technology, but also with the so-called educational and social 'affordances' for collaboration. This chapter provides a framework for designing IECLEs based upon three types of affordances: technological, social and educational. It then goes into somewhat greater depth with respect to three non-surface level factors central to collaboration, task ownership, task character and task control.

Affording collaboration

Classical instructional design focuses on individual learning outcomes, and attempts to control instructional variables to create a learning environment that supports the acquisition of a specific skill (ie person A will acquire skill B through learning method C). This is complicated by the use of groups in the case of collaboration. A multitude of individual and group-level variables affect the collaborative learning process, making it practically impossible to predefine the conditions of learning or instruction for a group setting so that interaction and competency development are controlled.

Instead of a classical causal view, the design of collaborative settings requires a more probabilistic approach to design, as shown in Figure 2.1 (Strijbos, Martens and Jochems, in press). This distinction corresponds with the one made by Van Merriënboer and Kirschner (2001) between the 'world of knowledge' (the outcomes) and the 'world of learning' (the processes). In the world of knowledge, designers construct methods by which given learning goals in a specific subject matter domain can be attained by the learner. In the world of learning, designers focus on methods supporting learning processes rather than on the attainment of predefined goals.

This probabilistic view implies that more attention should be paid to learning and interaction processes. Because of the interaction between learners, each member of a group may acquire a given skill by means of the chosen method, but may be equally likely to acquire only a part of the skill, or the skill together with other unforeseen elements. It might even be the case that the chosen method is abandoned by the group and replaced by another more idiosyncratic method for that group. The question is not what specific educational techniques and collaborative work forms cause. It is rather what they actually *afford*, which are often referred to as the *affordances* of a learning environment.

Causal design view:
World of knowledge

Probabilistic design view:
World of learning

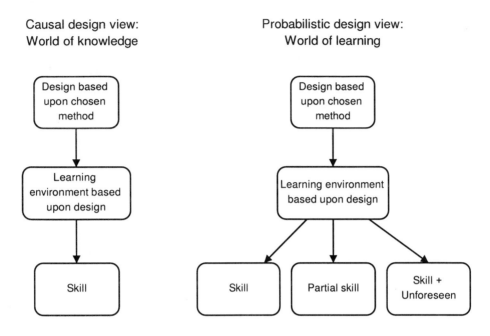

Figure 2.1 *Two views of instructional design*

Putting it in a nutshell, the notion of an affordance refers to the 'perceived and actual fundamental properties of a thing that determine how the thing could possibly be used' (Norman, 1988: 9). Affordances are most clearly visible in everyday life. Some door handles, for example, look like they should be pulled. Their shape leads our brains to believe that is the best way to use them. Other handles look like they should be pushed, a feature often indicated by a bar spanning the width of the door or even a flat plate on the side. Gibson (1977) originally proposed the concept of affordances in order to refer to the relationship between an object's physical properties and the characteristics of an actor or user that enables particular interactions between actor and object. 'The affordance of anything is a specific combination of the properties of its substance and its surfaces with reference to an animal' (Gibson, 1977: 67). These properties or artefacts interact with potential users and may provide strong clues as to their operation. In our view, the concept of affordances offers an alternative framework for designing and evaluating IECLEs if appropriated into the educational context.

The context of IECL is a unique combination of the technological, social and educational contexts. Figures 2.2a and 2.2b both represent learning situations, but the contexts are different. The educational contexts are competitive (rather than collaborative); the social contexts are individual (as opposed to group); and the technological, that is to say the physical, contexts are individual workspaces with a minimal assortment of materials vs group workspaces with a rich assortment of materials.

a

b

Figure 2.2   *Two learning environments that differ on three dimensions*

IECL represents yet another learning situation. The educational context is collaborative, the social context is the group, and the technological context is computer-mediated. The Open University of the Netherlands, for example, uses a computer mediated communication environment (technological) for competence-based learning grounded in social constructivism (educational) with minimal direct contact, maximal guided individual study, and primarily asynchronous, text-based contact between students (social).

When technology mediates the social and educational contexts we speak of 'technology affording learning and education'. This means that we must take the technological, social and educational affordances into account.

Technological affordances

Norman relates perceived affordances to the design aspects of an object suggesting how it should be used when he writes, 'Design is about [real and perceived affordances], but the perceived affordances are what determine usability' (1998: 23). Norman links affordances to an object's usability, and thus these affordances are designated technological or technology affordances (Gaver, 1991). 'Usability' is a well-known objective in industrial or product design dealing with physical objects ranging from video recorders to teapots. So it is in human–computer interaction (HCI), where usability deals predominantly with 'graphical user interfaces' composed of interface objects such as buttons and scrollbars. It is concerned with whether a system allows for the accomplishment of a set of tasks in an efficient, effective manner that satisfies the user (Preece *et al*, 1994). Usability is not a single dimension, but deals with ease of learning, efficiency of use, memorability, error frequency and severity, and subjective satisfaction (Shneiderman, 1998). When creating IECLEs it is, therefore, important to consider these aspects. Failing to do so risks creating IECLEs that contain all the needed educational and social functionality, which Norman terms 'usefulness', but which cannot be handled by their users (that is, the learners) because they are difficult to learn, access, and/or control in the same way video recorders are (Preece *et al,* 1994: 11–13).

Social affordances

Kreijns, Kirschner and Jochems define social affordances by analogy with techno-logical affordances as the 'properties of a CSCL environment [IECLE] that act as social-contextual facilitators relevant for the learner's social interaction' (2002: 13). Objects that are part of the environment can realize these properties and are accordingly designated as 'social affordance' devices. When social affordances are perceptible, they invite learners to engage in activities that are in accordance with them; that is, there is social interaction.

In the physical world, affordances abound for casual and inadvertent interactions. In the virtual world, social affordances must be planned and must encompass two relationships. First, there must be a reciprocal relationship between group members and the IECLE. The environment must fulfil the social intentions of members as soon as these intentions arise, while the social affordances must be meaningful and should support or anticipate these social intentions. Second, there must be so-called 'perception–action coupling'. Once a group member becomes salient (perception), the social affordances will not only invite, but will also guide another member to initiate a communication episode (action) with the salient member. Salience depends upon factors such as expectations, focus of attention, and/or the current context of the fellow member.

Educational affordances

Kirschner (2002) defines educational affordances as those characteristics of an artefact that determine if and how a particular learning behaviour could possibly be enacted within a given context. In other words, the chosen educational paradigm (the artefact) is instrumental in determining if and how individual and team learning can take place. Educational affordances can be defined by analogy with social affordances as the relationships between the properties of an educational intervention and the characteristics of the learners (in the case of IECL the learners and the learning groups) that enable particular kinds of learning by them and in IECL for the other members of the group.

Educational affordances in distributed learning groups encompass the same two relationships as social affordances. The IECLE must fulfil the learning intentions of the member as soon as these intentions arise, while the affordances must be meaningful and must support or anticipate the learning intentions of the group member. Moreover, once a learning need becomes salient (perception), the educational affordances will not only invite but will also guide him or her to make use of a learning intervention to satisfy that need (action). The salience of the learning intervention may depend upon factors such as expectations, prior experience, and/or the focus of attention. In the next section we go on to discuss how these ideas can be incorporated into the design process.

Design guidelines

We agree with Don Norman (1992: 65) when he says that the major problem with most new technological devices and programs 'is that they are badly conceived [and are] developed solely with the goal of using technology. They ignore completely the human side, the needs and the abilities of people who will presumably use the devices.' In our opinion, this also applies to their use in education. Good use implies both usability and usefulness, and requires a design process grounded in user-centred instructional design research.

General design level: six stages

We should like to propose a six-stage model for the design of IECLEs on a general level, as shown in Figure 2.3.

In this model, the designer must:

1. *Determine what learners actually do:* Watch students interact, observe collaborating groups interacting to solve problems, observe users interacting with software, and do this before designing and developing.
2. *Determine what can be done to support those learners:* Determine based on stage 1, what actually needs to be supported or afforded, and then proceed.
3. *Determine the constraints of the learner, learning situation and learning environment and the conventions that already exist:* Look further than the technological constraints and conventions, and take into account the educational and social constraints and conventions that play a role in IECLEs. Learners are products of their educational experience, and as such, are used to certain types of education and

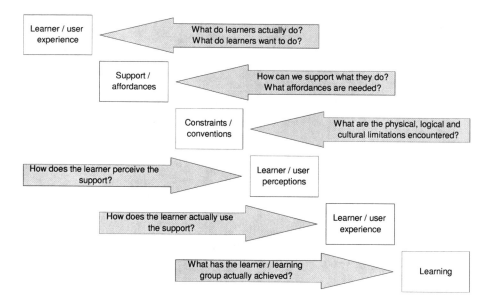

Figure 2.3 *A heuristic for the general design of IECLEs*

have been socialized to study, learn and act in specific ways. Denying or neglecting this will guarantee failure, both of the IECLE and the learning.

4. *Determine how learners perceive and experience the support provided*: There is a world of difference between intentions, or good intentions, and user perceptions of them. Research and design must be carried out as iterative, interacting processes. New 'products' must be tried out with intended users at various stages in their development where physical and conceptual changes can still be made. In this way the usefulness and the usability are both guaranteed.

5. *Determine how the learner actually uses the support provided*: By analogy with stage 1, and following up the more formative evaluations carried out in stage 4, determine if the learner actually does what is hoped or expected.

6. *Determine what has been learnt*: The goal of education is learning. There are three standards to determine the success of any instructional design: its effectiveness, its efficiency and the degree of satisfaction for both the learner and the teacher. An increase in one or more of the standards without a concomitant decrease in any of the others means success. We might be tempted to say that this is 'the proof of the pudding'.

Specific design level: six steps

These six stages provide a general approach to instructional design of IECLEs. However, this design needs also to ensure that the type of social interaction thought to be supportive for competency development does genuinely occur.

Thus, complementary to the six-stage model, a more specific, process-oriented design methodology is needed which supplies the designer with those questions that must be answered in order to actually develop an IECLE. Strijbos, Martens and Jochems (in press) propose just such a methodology. It consists of six steps:

1. Determining the competencies to be developed.
2. Determining the expected interaction and changes in it.
3. Selecting the task type.
4. Determining whether and how much pre-structuring support is needed.
5. Determining the group size that will ensure that the type of social interaction needed for competency development does itself develop.
6. Determining how computer support can be best applied.

Since this book has its design roots in the 4C/ID model, which centres around the design, development and implementation of learning tasks (see Chapter 1), we only discuss the educational affordances with respect to those tasks. We regard task ownership, task character and task control as defining factors in the educational affording of IECLEs, which will be illustrated through specific prototypical design questions related to these factors. In this discussion we make use of those specific questions pertaining to the third stage of the general model, in that they can be used to determine the constraints of the learning environment.

Task ownership

Until recently, education emphasized individual acquisition of knowledge and skills (Johnson, Johnson and Johnson-Holubec, 1992; Slavin, 1997). This end of the spectrum deals with IECLEs where the emphasis is on knowledge and skills that each group member must individually attain (eg those skills that are relatively fixed, the so-called 'closed' skills). This idea, however, is anathema to competency-based collaborative learning. Thus, at the other end of the spectrum there are competency-based IECLEs where it is not the individual acquisition and application of knowledge and skills that are the most important, but rather the performance of each individual in and with the rest of the group (eg those skills that thrive on interaction such as negotiation and argumentation, which are also called 'open skills'). In this respect the key question is, who owns the task?

Ownership in a group is influenced by two pedagogical principles, individual accountability and positive independence. The importance of 'individual accountability' (Slavin, 1980) was introduced to counter the 'free-rider' or 'hitchhiking' effect in which some students put little or no effort into the group performance. By stressing individual accountability, what the group does as a whole becomes less important. It is perfectly valid that in a group environment each group member is individually accountable for his or her own work. In many problem-based learning environments the students' sense of individual ownership is increased through grading them on their individual effort, irrespective of the group's performance. 'Positive interdependence' (Johnson, 1981) reflects the level to which group members are dependent upon each other for effective group performance (enhanced intra-group interaction). Positive interdependence holds that each individual can be held individually accountable for the work of the group, and the group as a whole is responsible for the learning of each of the individual group members. A crucial aspect of this is social cohesion and a heightened sense of 'belonging' to a group. Positive interdependence is evident when group members in a project-centred learning environment carry out different tasks within a group project when all of these tasks are needed for the final product. Interdependence can be stimulated through the tasks, resources, goals, rewards, roles or the environment itself (Brush, 1998).

Positive interdependence in turn provides the context within which 'promotive interaction' takes place. According to Johnson and Johnson (1996: 1028), promotive interaction 'exists when individuals encourage and facilitate each other's efforts to complete tasks in order to reach the group's goals'. In other words, individual accountability, positive interdependence and promotive interaction counter the tendency towards hiding and anonymity. There are a number of instructional decisions regarding ownership (individual versus group) and the type of competency development that can be afforded:

- What type of skills will be taught:
  - open skills: argumentation, negotiation, discussion of multiple alternatives?
  - closed skills: acquisition of basic skills, basic procedures (eg long division), concept learning?
- Are all students required to learn the same skill(s)?
- Must all students individually display mastery of the learning objectives?
- How will the students be graded: individual test scores; one group score for the group's performance; individual score for each member's participation and contribution; or a combination of these?

Task character

The character of a task for collaborative learning can be depicted along several dimensions: constructed versus authentic; well defined versus ill defined (wicked); individual versus group; and divergent versus convergent. Traditional school tasks are highly constructed and oriented towards the individual. They are well structured, short in length, well defined, and designed to match the content rather than reality. An archetypical problem is 'Two trains travelling in opposite directions. . .'. As such, these tasks are eminently suitable for acquiring individual skills, but not for achieving transfer or for acquiring complex skills and competencies. Spiro *et al* (1988) determined that many learning failures, including the inability to transfer knowledge and apply it to new cases, resulted from cognitive oversimplification.

The solutions to these archetypical school problems were usually too obvious to the students, while many students could not solve 'real life' problems involving sets of complex factors.

By way of contrast, authentic 'real life' problems are almost always ill structured (Mitroff, Mason and Bonoma, 1976) and/or wicked (Rittel and Webber, 1984; Conklin and Weil, 1997). They are often so complex and multifaceted that they can only be solved by multidisciplinary groups working together, with the group members assuaging cognitive conflict, elaborating on each other's contributions, and jointly constructing shared representations and meaning. Examples of such wicked problems are the building of a new type automobile and the legalization of marijuana. Below are some of the instructional decisions for task character (focusing on one possible distinction of well-structured versus ill-structured tasks) and the type of competency development that can be afforded.

- Which task type is best suited to acquisition of the selected skills:
  - open skills: ill-structured task with no clear solution, multiple alternatives, outcomes, opinions or procedures?
  - closed skills: well-structured task with a restricted number of possible solutions, outcomes or procedures?
- Are all students required to study the same material?
- Will they have to solve a complex and ambiguous problem with no clear solution?
- Will the chosen learning objectives and task type require communication?
- Will the chosen learning objectives and task type require coordination?

However, the character of a task is itself variable. It is, for example, not always clear for whom and to what extent an authentic task really is authentic. Is a task authentic when students have to play a role with which they have no immediate affinity, for example a bank manager? Is the problem that needs to be solved really 'our' problem rather than 'yours, his or theirs'? To what extent is a situation authentic for 'novices' if they are not familiar with actual practice?

Whatever the case, complex ill-structured problems require a different educational approach from simple, well-defined ones. In educating people to be able to solve these types of problems we need to opt for a whole task approach since, after all, real life tasks are not neat segments of some idealized whole. For a discussion of the whole task approach, see Chapter 1. Whole tasks need to be divisible into non-trivial, authentic part tasks, which aim at achieving 'epistemic fluency'. Morrison and Collins (1996: 109) define epistemic fluency as 'the ability to identify and use different ways of knowing, to understand their different forms of expression and evaluation, and to take the perspective of others who are operating within a different epistemic framework'. Ohlsson (1996) enumerates seven epistemic tasks that can be used as guiding principles for the design of collaborative environments, since they indicate the 'discourse-bound' activities that learners will have to fulfil during collaborative learning and working:

- *Describing:* to fashion a discourse referring to an object or event, such that a person who partakes of that discourse acquires an accurate conception of that object or event.
- *Explaining:* to fashion a discourse such that a person who partakes of that discourse understands why that event happened.
- *Predicting:* to fashion a discourse such that a person who partakes of that discourse becomes convinced that such and such an event will happen.
- *Arguing:* to state reasons for (or against) a particular position on some issue, thereby increasing (or decreasing) the recipient's confidence that the position is right.
- *Critiquing (evaluating):* to fashion a discourse such that a person who partakes of that discourse becomes aware of the good and bad points of that product.
- *Explicating:* to fashion a discourse such that a person who partakes of that discourse acquires a clearer understanding of its meaning.
- *Defining:* to define a term so as to propose a usage for that term.

Task control

'Task control' is closely related to 'learner control', which has had a somewhat fluid and eclectic history. In its broadest sense, learner control is the degree to which a learner can direct his or her own learning experience (Shyu and Brown, 1992). More specifically, learner control is the degree to which individuals control the path, pace and/or contingencies of instruction (Hannafin, 1984).

New learning paradigms and new technologies have expanded this concept, since they make it possible to provide learners with control over depth of study, range of content, number and type of delivery media, and time spent on learning. Using these options, learners can tailor the learning experience to meet their specific needs and interests. For this reason, learner control is not 'a unitary construct, but rather a collection of strategies that function in different ways depending upon what is being controlled by whom' (Ross and Morrison, 1989: 29). Indeed, learner control may be a continuum of instructional strategies in which the learner is provided with the option of controlling one or more of the parameters of the learning environment (Parsons, 1991). This control can be related to such aspects as context, content, sequencing, pacing, feedback, reinforcement and possibly even learning or presentation style. However, Reeves (1993) points out that researching learner control centres on the question of what learning control really is. It could be the pace of learning, or the sequencing, content or speed of a program, to mention only a few of the possibilities.

Task control in IECLEs relates to a number of interacting aspects of the total environment that deal with determining the relevant set of actions that students can, should or must perform, as well as what an adequate, applicable or best solution or solution path is. It relates to the roles of the teacher/coach (see Chapter 12) versus those of the learners with respect to selecting the relevant activities and learning approach. An underlying assumption here is that learners are self-sufficient enough to be given control over their own learning activities and collaboration methods. Below are some questions relating to design decisions on task control in terms of the 'pre-structuring' needed and the type of competence development that can be afforded.

- Determine in advance to what extent the group interaction processes will be pre-structured:
  - High level of pre-structuring: student interaction is prescribed by the teacher (giving or receiving feedback, suggestions or help). Content focused (content-based roles and resource interdependence).
  - Low level of pre-structuring: 'students shape their groups', interaction processes with little or no teacher involvement (knowledge building, case-based discussion of multiple alternative solutions and problem-based learning).
- Are students each assigned a portion of the material?
- Are students each assigned individual responsibilities for interaction and group performance?
- Are students dependent on each other during the whole course or only a part of the course?

Conclusions

We have outlined a theoretical framework for the design of IECLEs. The concept of affordances is central to this design, specifically in those cases where the learning environment centres on collaboration. With respect to the design of IECLEs, it is not of primary importance to establish what exactly is caused by different elements of the learning environment. Learning is no longer causal or deterministic, but has become probabilistic. A more important point is whether the elements of a learning environment afford the type of competency development that was targeted. With respect to collaboration, the question is whether the elements of the environment afford the emergence of that type of social interaction that is supportive of the acquisition of the targeted skill.

These questions cannot be answered easily. We, as designers, often think we know what our designs and products will do, and how the people for whom our designs and products are intended will use them. Unfortunately, this is not always the case. Each of the phases in the design process needs to be studied with respect to the specific choices that can and must be made. Some research is fundamental, such as research on how IECLE interface design, or the way information is presented, affects cognitive load and learning (Kester, Kirschner and Van Merriën-boer, in press). Other research is more application oriented, such as research on how group awareness widgets affect the perception of sociability, social space and social presence (Kreijns and Kirschner, 2002). And, finally, yet other research is applied, for instance how specific learners or learner groups perceive a specific IECLE. The research agenda is displayed in Figure 2.4.

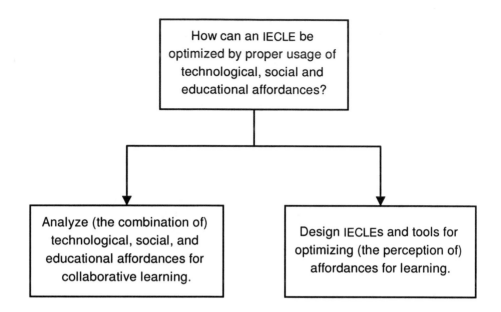

Figure 2.4   *A research agenda for IECLEs*

The design of IECLEs needs to be carried out at two levels: a generic and a specific level. The impacts of both levels have been illustrated with respect to task owner-ship, task character and task control. Clearly the design of an IECLE requires that both levels be taken into account, with the specific level being a detailed depiction of the third stage of the general model, in that it is used to determine the con-straints of the learning environment. Although teachers and designers may prefer a clear set of design rules (such as, first do A, then do B if you want to achieve C), a deterministic checklist with a limited number of categories is one step too far. We have, however, provided a number of specific design questions to stimulate teachers and designers to think more deeply about their instructional decisions and not simply rely on their traditional approach that 'has always worked so well'.

References

Brush, T A (1998) Embedding co-operative learning into the design of integrated learning systems: rationale and guidelines, *Educational Technology, Research and Development*, **46** (3), pp 5–18

Clark, R E (1983) Reconsidering research on learning from media, *Review of Educational Research*, **53** (4), pp 445–59

Conklin, E J and Weil, W (1997) *Wicked Problems: Naming the pain in organizations* [Online] www.touchstone.com/tr/wp/wicked.html (accessed 16 January 2003)

Gaver, W (1991) Technology affordances, *Proceedings of CHI (the Computer–Human Interaction Conference) 1991*, New Orleans, pp 79–84

Gibson, J J (1977) The theory of affordances, in *Perceiving, Acting and Knowing*, ed R Shaw and J Bransford, pp 67–82, Erlbaum, Hillsdale, NJ

Hannafin, M J (1984) Guidelines for using locus of instructional control in the design of computer-assisted instruction, *Journal of Instructional Development*, **7** (3), pp 6–10

Johnson, D W (1981) Student–student interaction: the neglected variable in education, *Educational Research*, **10**, pp 5–10

Johnson, D W and Johnson, R T (1996) Co-operation and the use of technology, in *Handbook of Research for Educational Communications and Technology*, ed D H Jonassen, pp 1017–44, Simon and Schuster/Macmillan, New York

Johnson, D W, Johnson, R T and Johnson-Holubec, E (1992) *Advanced Co-operative Learning*, Interaction, Edina, MN

Kester, L, Kirschner, P A and Van Merriënboer, J J G (in press) The optimal timing of information presentation during mastering a complex skill in science, *International Journal of Science Education*

Kirschner, P (2002) Can we support CSCL? Educational, social and technological affordances for learning, in *Three Worlds of CSCL: Can we support CSCL*, ed P Kirschner, Open University of the Netherlands, Heerlen

Kreijns, K and Kirschner, P A (2002) Group awareness widgets for enhancing social interaction in computer-supported collaborative learning environments: design and implementation, in *Proceedings of The 32nd ASEE/IEEE Frontiers in Education Conference*, ed D Budny and G Bjedov, pp 436–42, IEEE, Piscataway, NJ [Online] fie.engrng.pitt.edu/fie2002/index.htm (accessed 15 February 2003)

Kreijns, K, Kirschner, P A and Jochems, W (2002) The sociability of computer-supported collaborative learning environments, *Educational Technology & Society*, **5** (1), pp 8–25

Mitroff, I I, Mason, R O and Bonoma, T V (1976) Psychological assumptions, experimentation and real world problems, *Evaluation Quarterly*, **2** (4), pp 639–62

Morrison, D and Collins, A (1996) Epistemic fluency and constructivist learning environments, in *Constructivist Learning Environments*, ed B Wilson, pp 107–19, Educational Technology, Englewood Cliffs, NJ

Norman, D A (1988) T*he Psychology of Everyday Things*, Basic Books, New York

Norman, D A (1992) *Turn Signals are the Facial Expressions of Automobiles*, Perseus, Cambridge, MA

Norman, D A (1998) *The Invisible Computer*, MIT Press, Cambridge, MA

Ohlsson, S (1996) Learning to do and learning to understand, in *Learning in Humans and Machines*, ed P Reimann and H Spada, pp 37–62, Elsevier, Oxford, UK

Parsons, J A (1991) *A Meta-Analysis of Learner Control in Computer-based Learning Environments*, Unpublished doctoral dissertation, Nova University, Fort Lauderdale, FL

Preece, J, Rogers, Y, Sharp, H, Benyon, D, Holland, S and Carey, T (1994) *Human–Computer Interaction*, Addison-Wesley, Wokingham, UK

Reeves, T C (1993) Pseudoscience in computer-based instruction: the case of learner control research, *Journal of Computer-Based Instruction*, **20** (2), pp 39–46

Rittel, H W J and Webber, M M (1984) Planning problems are wicked problems, in *Developments in Design Methodology*, ed N Cross, pp 135–44, Wiley, Chichester (originally published as part of Dilemmas in a general theory of planning, *Policy Sciences*, **4** (1973), pp 155–69)

Ross, S M and Morrison, G R (1989) In search of a happy medium in instructional technology research: issues concerning external validity, media replications and learner control, *Educational Technology, Research and Development*, **37** (1), pp 19–33

Shneiderman, B (1998) *Designing The User Interface: Strategies for effective human–computer interaction*, 3rd edn, Addison Wesley Longman, Reading, MA

Shyu, H Y and Brown, S W (1992) Learner control versus program control in interactive videodisc instruction: what are the effects in procedural learning?, *International Journal of Instructional Media*, **19** (2), pp 85–95

Slavin, R E (1980) Co-operative learning in teams: state of the art, *Educational Psychologist*, **15**, pp 93–111

Slavin, R E (1997) *Educational Psychology: Theory and practice*, 5th edn, Allyn and Bacon, Needham Heights, MA

Spiro, R J, Coulson, Feltovich and Anderson (1988) *Cognitive Flexibility Theory: Advanced knowledge acquisition in ill-structured domains* (Tech. rep. no 441), University of Illinois, Center for the Study of Reading, Champaign, IL

Strijbos, J W, Martens, R L and Jochems, W M G (in press) Designing for inter-action: six steps to design computer supported group based learning, *Computers and Education*

Van Merriënboer, J J G and Kirschner, P A (2001) Three worlds of instructional design: state of the art and future directions, *Instructional Science*, **29**, pp 429–41

Further reading

Gaver, W (1996) Affordances for interaction: the social is material for design, *Ecological Psychology*, **8** (2), pp 111–29

Norman, D A (1999) Affordance, conventions, and design, *Interactions*, **6** (3), pp 38–44

Chapter 3

Performance assessment in integrated e-learning

Dominique Sluijsmans and Rob Martens

Introduction

Assessment is the weak link in e-learning systems. E-learning designers have relied predominantly on tools that are directed at the construction of test items. The disadvantage of such items is that they tend to focus on the measurement of low-level retention of isolated facts, rather than on the application of knowledge to solve ill-structured problems (Baker and Mayer, 1999; Reeves, 2000). Appropriate performance assessment turns out to be difficult to develop. As a consequence, assessment is often a process of gathering data and returning results, instead of a process of providing opportunities for learning. Literature on assessment in e-learning focuses mainly on tools that are item-based and on tools that are directed at test-based assessment. Zhang *et al* (2001), for example, reviewed 10 Web-based assessment tools that were all based on item-type assessments. One well-known application of these item-based tools in e-learning is computerized adaptive testing (CAT). In CAT, the computer continuously re-evaluates the ability of the student, resulting in a test that is tailored to each individual student. This fine tuning is achieved by statistically tailoring the test to the achievement level of each student, while avoiding questions which are either very easy or very difficult (Herb, 1992). Although Zhang *et al* (2001) conclude that independence of time and place are the main advantages of these Web tools, they also acknowledge that none of the tools uses performance assessments. Internet tests are still nowhere near providing assessments that support relevant professional performance and student learning. In current e-learning environments the emphasis is far more on testing than on assessment, and the integration of test tasks with learning tasks is often overlooked.

This contribution focuses solely on performance assessment in e-learning and the implications of integrating performance assessment with e-learning. Assessment that is fully embedded in instructional practice in general, and in e-learning in particular, is still in its infancy, so that it lacks structured frameworks that guide teachers in the design of performance assessments. This chapter presents a framework that specifically supports the implementation of performance assessments in e-learning. First, we briefly discuss the importance of performance assessment. Second, we go on to outline how performance assessments can be designed in e-learning. Third, we present an integrated framework for the design of performance assessment in e-learning. Finally, we address the role of students in performance assessment. At the end of the chapter we cast a critical glance at the role that performance assessment can have in e-learning.

The importance of performance assessment

While from the learner's perspective, assessment is usually the element of greatest importance, in practice assessment is often the neglected child of innovation. First, the influence of tests on what is taught is potentially quite considerable. Frederiksen (1984) refers in this respect to the 'real test bias'. There is evidence that tests do influence teacher and student performance, and that, for example, multiple choice tests tend not to stimulate the development of complex cognitive abilities. It is suggested that other formats such as performance assessment encourage the teaching of higher level cognitive skills and provide practice with feedback.

Second, there is a distinction between 'what is meant to happen', that is the curriculum stated officially by the educational system or institution, and what teachers and learners actually do and experience 'on the ground', a kind of *de facto* curriculum. Snyder (1973) labels this the 'hidden curriculum'. In a laboratory researchers can ask students to read texts, but in real life the students have their own curriculum, 'adopting ploys and strategies to survive in the system' (Lockwood, 1995: 197). Based on this, it is important to stimulate students to work on assessment tasks that are to some extent authentic, and that are closely related to the learning tasks.

A shift is occurring from a test culture to an assessment culture. This shift strongly emphasizes integration of instruction, learning and assessment. The compatibility between learning, instruction and assessment, which represents the core issue of this chapter, is described within the theory of constructive alignment (Biggs, 1996). When there is alignment between what teachers want to teach, how they teach and how they assess, teaching is likely to be more effective. To pursue the theory of constructive alignment, it is worth investing in the design of performance assessments. Performance assessment can be based on multiple products or processes, for example essays, reflection papers, oral assessments, process analyses, group products and work samples. The term 'performance' is used because the assessment task is described in terms of a certain performance, which is perceived as worthwhile and relevant to the student (Wiggins, 1989). Performance assessment focuses on the ability to use combinations of acquired skills and knowledge, and therefore fits in well with the theory of constructive alignment and powerful learning environments (Linn, Baker and Dunbar, 1991).

Performance assessment in e-learning

In e-learning, we see that simulations of hands-on tasks are found useful for performance assessment on a large scale (Shavelson, 1991). In the area of aviation, for example, simulators have been developed for certifying pilot competencies (Bennett, 1999). Recent research projects focus on the assessment of problem solving skills (eg Mayer, 2002; O'Neil, 2002). The computer keeps a record of every move made by the student in solving a task, to provide a detailed profile of his or her performance for assessment. Video recordings are also a realistic option for performance assessment. The video recordings can be applied to educational activities such as analysis of the observation, peer review or other assignments.

Information and communications technology (ICT) is often used today to simulate the context of professional practice (Bastiaens and Martens, 2000). Modern distance learning courses are often set up as realistic 'games' or simulations. ICT here presents 'virtual' reality as an authentic problem, and serves as a provider for competency-based learning.

Performance assessments should preferably be integrated with the instructional process to provide additional learning experiences for students. Stiggins (1987) provides some guidelines for designing sound, integrated performance assessments:

- *Define the purpose of the assessment:* List the skills and knowledge you wish to have the students learn as a result of completing a task.
- *Define performance assessment tasks:* Design a performance task that requires the students to demonstrate the skills and knowledge.
- *Define performance criteria:* Develop explicit performance criteria, which measure the extent to which students have mastered the skills and knowledge.
- *Create performance rubrics:* Use one scoring system or performance rubric for each performance task. The performance criteria consist of a set of score points, which define the range of student performance in explicit terms.

First, the purpose of the performance assessment has to be defined. Several important questions are, in order (see Herman, Aschbacher and Winters, 1992):

- What cognitive skills or attributes do I want my students to develop? (For example, do I want them to be able to communicate effectively in writing; to analyze issues using primary source and reference materials; or to use algebra to solve everyday problems?)

- What social and affective skills or attributes do I want my students to develop? (Should they be able to work independently; to work cooperatively with others; to have confidence in their own abilities; and to be conscientious?)
- What metacognitive skills do I want my students to develop (for instance to reflect on the writing process; evaluate the effectiveness of research strategies; or review progress over time)?
- What types of problem do I want my students to be able to solve (for example to undertake research; to understand the types of practical problems that geometry will help to solve; or to solve problems that have no single correct answer)?
- What concepts and principles do I want my students to be able to apply? (Is it necessary for them to understand cause and effect relationships or to apply principles of ecology and conservation in everyday life?)

This first step can result in a skill decomposition in which the relevant skills are hierarchically ordered (Van Merriënboer, 1997; see also Chapter 1). When the purpose of the assessment has been defined, decisions are made concerning the performance assessment task. Relevant questions are (Herman, Aschbacher and Winters, 1992):

- How much time will it take students to develop or acquire the skill or accomplishment?
- How does the desired skill or accomplishment relate to other complex cognitive, social and affective skills?
- How does the desired skill or accomplishment relate to long-term school and curricular goals?
- How does the desired skill relate to the school improvement plan?
- What is the intrinsic importance of the desired skills or accomplishments?
- Are the desired skills and accomplishments teachable and attainable?

The performance assessment task may be a product, behaviour or extended written response to a question that requires the student to apply critical thinking skills. Some examples of performance assessment tasks include compositions, presentations and research projects. It is important that the performance assessment task can be performed in an electronic learning environment if you want students to take the task from their computer.

After the assessment task has been determined, we need to define which elements of the task determine the measure of success of the student's performance. These can sometimes be found in so-called 'job profiles'. Although these resources may prove to be very useful, they often include lists of criteria with too many skills or concepts, or they may not be entirely appropriate. Most of the time teachers must develop their own criteria. The teacher has to analyze skills or products to identify performance criteria on which to judge achievement. It is worth using expert products or first-rate examples to define the appropriate criteria. Communicating information about performance criteria provides a basis for the improvement of that performance. Quellmalz (1991) offers a set of specific guidelines for the development of quality performance criteria. Criteria should be significant, specifying key performance components, and should represent standards that would apply naturally to determine the quality of performance when it typically occurs. The criteria must be clear and understandable to all persons involved.

The final step is the creation of 'performance rubrics'. As opposed to most traditional forms of testing, performance assessments in which the students are confronted with ill-defined problems do not provide clear-cut right or wrong answers. The performance is evaluated in a way that allows for informative scoring on multiple criteria. This is accomplished by creating assessment forms or performance rubrics. The different levels of proficiency for each criterion can be defined in the performance rubric. Using the information on the assessment form, the students are given feedback on their performance in the form of either a narrative report or a grade. A criterion-referenced qualitative approach, by means of which the assessment is made with reference to the previously specified performance criteria, is desirable. An analytic or holistic judgement is then given on the basis of the standard the student has achieved on each of the criteria. An example of a performance-scoring rubric is demonstrated in Table 3.1.

The purpose of a performance scoring rubric is to design performance assessment tasks that represent the type of learning that is aimed at. The five major criteria for judging the quality of performance assessments are reliability, validity, feasibility, utility and security. Reliability emphasizes the question whether an assessment score can be repeated. If a performance assessment task leads to a certain score for a particular student, this student should get the same result if he or she were to undergo the assessment task for a second time. Validity raises the question whether a test measures what it should measure. In a competence-based curriculum where many subjects and aspects are combined in performing authentic tasks, in which the students require all kinds of skills and are asked to collaborate, a paper and pencil question that only requires factual knowledge is not a valid measurement. Feasibility means the extent to which assessment can be conducted efficiently. Utility concerns the extent to which assessment discriminates between those who possess desired knowledge, skills and attitudes, and those who do not. Security involves the extent to which the assessment process is protected against cheating or other unauthorized access. Regarding this last point, it is important to design performance tasks that require individual contributions and not always straightforward right or wrong answers.

When a teacher has completed the design procedure for performance assessments keeping the quality criteria in mind, learning tasks can be designed in which students are prepared for the performance assessment. These learning tasks are directly related to the performance assessment task at the end of a study unit. To design these learning tasks, the four component instructional design (4C/ID) model works well with our approach for designing performance assessments. In the next section, we introduce the relevant aspects of this model in line with our view on performance assessment.

Table 3.1 *Part of a performance-scoring rubric for writing a report on sustainable development (SD)*

Criteria	Above standard	Standard	Below standard	Points earned
Sustainable development is made operational	10–9 Students give a definition used in their report and give practical tools to measure their solutions on these points	8–6 Students give a definition used in their report but do not give practical tools to measure their solutions on these points or vice versa	5–0 Students do not give a definition used in their report and do not give practical tools to measure their solutions to these points	/10
The different aspects of SD are used in coherence	5 The ecological, social and economic aspects of sustainable development are used and are coherent and balanced. Arguments relating to priority are advanced	4–3 Not all aspects of sustainable development are used, but the ones that are used, are balanced and coherent	2–0 The different aspects of sustainable development are neither coherent nor balanced	/5
Relation problem definition–analysis–solution	10–9 Scientific quality of report and logical conclusions and recommendations. All the questions asked at the beginning are answered	8–6 Scientific quality of report and logical conclusions and recommendations. Not all the questions asked at the beginning are answered	5–0 Low scientific quality of report and conclusions and recommendations do not come from the chapters in the report. Not all the questions asked at the beginning are answered	/10
... Summary	... A two to three page summary is added, containing background research, recommendations, target group and possible implementation route. The summary is critical and provocative	... Summary omits one of the four points mentioned or leaves room for interpretation	... Summary omits two or more of the four points mentioned and leaves room for interpretation, or no summary is added at all	... /10

Instructional design for performance assessment: an integrated framework

According to the 4C/ID model, the backbone of a unit of study consists of a series of learning tasks that confront students with all the important aspects of the complex skills that need to be acquired. Learning tasks that can be solved on the basis of the same body of knowledge are organized in 'task classes', and each new task class is more difficult than the previous one. Students receive a great deal of guidance and support for their work on the first learning task in a task class, but this gradually diminishes so that the final tasks are independently performed without any guidance or support. In addition to the learning tasks, the 4C/ID model distinguishes three other components: supportive information, part task practice, and just-in-time information.

Figure 3.1 depicts a framework for performance assessment that is intertwined with the four components. In general, different assessment methods are appropriate

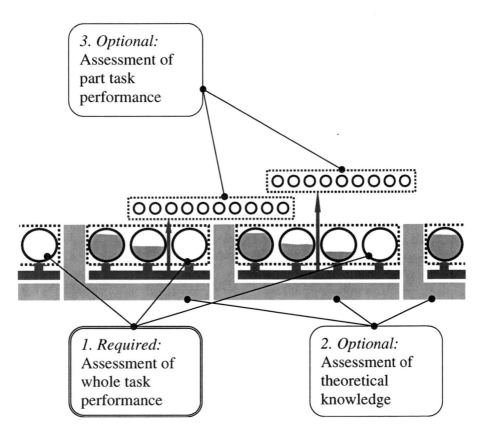

Figure 3.1   *A framework for designing performance assessment in integrated e-learning*

for each of the components (Van Merriënboer, 1997). However, the model strongly suggests directing assessment at the first component, that is, the learning tasks. The most obvious approach is to use the last, unguided, unsupported learning task(s) in a task class (the empty circles in the diagram) for the assessment of whole task performance. On the level of complexity that is characteristic of this particular task class, students working on the assessment task have to show their progress on both the recurrent aspects of performance, which are routines that are consistent from one problem situation to another, and the non-recurrent aspects of performance, which involve problem solving or reasoning, and vary between situations. As part of the instructional design process, both the recurrent and non-recurrent aspects are described as constituent skills with associated performance objectives, including conditions for performance as well as standards and criteria for acceptable performance. These standards and criteria provide the basis for the development of a performance-scoring rubric (as demonstrated in Table 3.1) which enables the teacher and/or the students to rate performance on relevant aspects. For formative assessment, the performance-scoring rubric can be a valuable tool for providing the students with feedback. For summative assessment, the performance-scoring rubric helps the teacher to achieve balanced grading and reach a final decision. It is up to the teacher or designer to decide if each 'empty circle' is used for summative assessment or, for example, only the empty circle at the end of the most complex task class.

From a theoretical viewpoint, assessment of whole task performance is the only form of assessment that is unconditionally required in integrated e-learning or any other educational setting for complex learning. The 4C/ID model states that students cannot satisfactorily perform such whole assessment tasks if they do not possess the mental models and cognitive strategies (that is, the theoretical knowledge) that help them to perform the non-recurrent aspects of the task, and the procedures or rules that govern the performance of the recurrent aspects of the task. Nonetheless, additional assessment of theoretical knowledge may be applied for a number of reasons. First of all, it may help to diagnose students' conceptual problems or misconceptions, and yield the necessary information to give them formative feedback for overcoming these problems. Furthermore, it may be used to corroborate the findings from the assessment of whole task performance, making the whole assessment more reliable.

Like the assessment of theoretical knowledge, the assessment of part task performance or single recurrent skills may also be considered as an additional element in the whole assessment system. The same tools that are used for part task practice should also preferably be used for the assessment of the recurrent skill under consideration. Most drill and practice computer programs (such as those for using grammatical rules in second language learning, applying safety procedures in industry, or operating particular software packages in business) do assess students on their accuracy and speed. They use this information to diagnose errors, to indicate to students that there is an error, and to provide hints that may help students get back on the right track.

In conclusion, we should like to argue that one should always try to focus on performance assessment of whole tasks. The definition of those assessment tasks early in the design process may also be helpful to the development of appropriate learning tasks that guide students towards the assessment task(s) at the end of a task class. Moreover, one may consider including additional assessments for theoretical knowledge, and for recurrent skills that have been practised separately.

The role of students in the integrated framework: peer assessment

In the outline of the integrated framework, the point that peers can play a valuable part in performance assessment has already been briefly addressed. This can be for educational reasons or for more practical reasons, such as saving teacher time. Peer assessment implies that students evaluate the performance of peers and provide constructive feedback (Sluijsmans, 2002). It is advisable to embed peer assessment activities in learning tasks in which students are expected to criticize each other or comment on their content-related performances.

Three arguments support the case for the implementation of peer assessment in integrated e-learning. First, integrating peer assessment supports students in their development into competent professionals who reflect continuously on their behaviour and learning. There are several ways in which students can be involved in assessment: for example they can have a role in the choice of performance assessment tasks and in discussing assessment criteria (Mehrens, Popham and Ryan, 1998). Second, peer assessment promotes the integration of assessment and instruction by viewing the student as an active person who shares responsibility, reflects, collaborates and conducts a continuous dialogue with the teacher. Third, peer assessment can decrease the teacher's workload.

Peer assessment represents a way in which the students can collaborate (see also Chapter 2). For effective collaborative learning in peer assessment activities, at least three issues are important: social interaction, individual accountability and positive interdependency (Slavin, 1990). We can specify these principles for assessment in e-learning. First of all, students can negotiate about performance criteria in peer assessment tasks. To establish sound criteria, interaction with others in which multiple perspectives on reality can be made more explicit is desirable. Second, for the group to be successful as a whole, members need to understand that they are each individually accountable for at least one aspect of the task at hand. When students are made individually responsible for an active contribution to group discussions, and are assessed on these contributions, they become aware of their personal responsibility in a group task. Individual accountability shows that students learn better cooperatively. When students are accountable for a different aspect in each learning task, they gradually come to understand the whole task. Third, when the group's task is to ensure that every group member has learnt something, in our case to conduct a peer assessment, it is in the interest of every group member to spend some time explaining concepts to his or her peers. Positive interdependence is successfully structured when the group members perceive that they are linked with each other in such a way that no one member can succeed unless everyone succeeds. It is the 'glue' that holds the members together.

Role interdependence, in which the specific roles of assessor and assessed are assigned to the students, plays a key part in peer assessment. The interdependence occurs when one student receives feedback from a peer, and this student is in turn responsible for giving feedback to another peer. In this situation a win–win situation can be established. If a student fails to give feedback, the student to be assessed will be the one who suffers. Thus the way to ensure that positive interdependence occurs is by promoting interaction between group members so that the students have to report their feedback to their peers in the group.

Implementing performance assessment in integrated e-learning: is it worth the effort?

The implementation of performance assessments in e-learning contains a number of advantages as well as risk factors (Surgue, 2002). The advantages are related to the integration of assessment and instruction, the possibilities for adequate feedback, the involvement of students, and the authenticity of performance assessments. When looking at its implementation in e-learning, Baker and Mayer (1999) state that computers can have a threefold value in Web-based performance assessment. First, computers have the ability to record process differences. It is possible to trace indicators that provide information about which thinking processes contributed back to a particular performance. Second, computers allow teachers to make complex processes visible. And third, online scoring and feedback can be provided, based either on fixed moments or on a student model.

The advantages that are often mentioned, such as ease of distribution, timeliness, immediate feedback, variety of delivery modes, tracking, long-term cost savings and convenience, are mostly true of item-based tests. They are less applicable to performance assessments, where the benefits are predominantly based on educational grounds. Item-based tests can be valuable for assessment of theoretical knowledge and part task practice, but they are not very useful for whole task assessment, which remains the central element in performance assessment.

A risk factor in integrated performance assessment is that the design of these assessments places heavy demands on teachers and developers (eg Beijaard *et al*, 2000; Sluijsmans *et al*, 2001). Introducing e-learning in combination with performance assessment requires new teacher roles. Teachers have to collaborate with an increasing number of stakeholders, which may be difficult and time-consuming.

Nevertheless, it is our belief that performance assessment is a crucial factor in educational innovation, which to date has all too often failed. When students are genuinely motivated to perform, study, learn and collaborate in a new way, and if learning goals and learning processes are more closely in tune with each other, educational problems such as low motivation, early drop-out, and poor test behaviour may be reduced significantly.

References

Baker, E L and Mayer, R E (1999) Computer-based assessment of problem solving, *Computers in Human Behavior*, **15**, pp 269–82

Bastiaens, T and Martens, R (2000) Conditions for Web-based learning with real events, in *Instructional and Cognitive Impacts of Web-based Education*, ed B Abbey, pp 1–32, Idea Group, Hershey/London

Beijaard, D, Verloop, N, Wubbels, T and Feiman-Nemser, S (2000) The professional development of teachers, in *New Learning*, ed R J Simons, J van der Linden and T Duffy, pp 261–74, Kluwer Academic, Dordrecht, Netherlands

Bennett, R E (1999) Using new technology to improve assessment, *Educational Measurement: Issues and practice*, **18** (3), pp 5–12

Biggs, J (1996) Enhancing teaching through constructive alignment, *Higher Education*, **32**, pp 347–64

Frederiksen, N (1984) The real test bias: influences of testing on teaching and learning, *American Psychologist*, **3**, pp 193–202

Herb, A (1992) Computer adaptive testing, *Advance*, 17 February

Herman, J L, Aschbacher, P R and Winters, L (1992) *A Practical Guide to Alternative Assessment*, Association for Supervision and Curriculum Development, Alexandria, VA

Linn, R L, Baker, E L and Dunbar, S B (1991) Complex, performance-based assessment: expectations and validation criteria, *Educational Researcher*, **20** (8), pp 15–21

Lockwood, F (1995) Students' perception of, and response to, formative and summative assessment material, in *Open and Distance Learning Today*, ed F Lockwood, pp 197–207, Routledge, London

Mayer, R E (2002) A taxonomy for computer-based assessment of problem solving, *Computers in Human Behavior*, **18**, pp 623–32

Mehrens, W A, Popham, W J and Ryan, J M (1998) How to prepare students for performance assessments, *Educational Measurement: Issues and practice*, **17** (1), pp 18–22

O'Neil, H F (2002) Perspectives on computer-based performance assessment of problem solving, *Computers in Human Behavior*, **15**, pp 255–68

Quellmalz, E (1991) Developing criteria for performance assessments: the missing link, *Applied Measurement in Education*, **4**, pp 319–32

Reeves, T C (2000) Alternative assessment approaches for online learning environments in higher education, *Journal of Educational Computing Research*, **23**, pp 101–11

Shavelson, R J (1991) Performance assessment in science, *Applied Measurement in Education*, **4**, pp 34–62

Slavin, R E (1990) *Co-Operative Learning: Theory, research and practice*, Prentice Hall, Hillsdale, NJ

Sluijsmans, D M A (2002) Student involvement in assessment. The training of peer assessment skills, unpublished doctoral dissertation, Open University of the Netherlands, Heerlen

Sluijsmans, D M A, Moerkerke, G, Dochy, F and van Merriënboer, J J G (2001) Peer assessment in problem based learning, *Studies in Educational Evaluation*, **27** (2), pp 153–73

Snyder, B (1973) *The Hidden Curriculum*, MIT Press, Cambridge, MA

Stiggins, R (1987) Design and development of performance assessment, *Educational Measurement: Issues and practice*, **6**, pp 33–42

Surgue, B (2002) Performance-based instructional design for e-learning, *Performance Improvement*, **41** (7), pp 45–50

Van Merriënboer, J J G (1997) *Training Complex Cognitive Skills*, Educational Technology, Englewood Cliffs, NJ

Wiggins, G (1989) A true test: toward a more authentic and equitable assessment, *Phi Delta Kappan*, **70**, pp 703–13

Zhang, J, Khan, B H, Gibbons, A S and Ni, Y (2001) Review of Web-based assessment tools, in *Web-Based Training*, ed B H Khan, pp 287–95, Educational Technology, Englewood Cliffs, NJ

Chapter 4

Virtual business e-learning: an approach to integrating learning and working

Darco Jansen, Marc van Laeken and Wessel Slot

Introduction

Learning is not restricted to formal education, and can take place anywhere and at any time. Only a small amount of professional knowledge and skills is acquired through formal education, for example secondary and higher professional training, university programmes or post-university courses (Baskett and Marsick, 1992). The bulk of knowledge and experience is acquired 'on the job'. This process of informal learning takes place largely unconsciously (Coffield, 2000) and is intertwined with and embedded in work and daily routines (Marsick and Watkins, 2001).

It is almost a commonplace that formal education has to adapt to this situation and should move towards further integration of learning and working. Concurrent learning while working is highly relevant in augmenting professional competencies for innovative business behaviour. This kind of learning, focusing on the development of clusters of interrelated complex skills and know-how, can best be enhanced by intentionally embedding it in an authentic business setting or in contexts that closely resemble real company life.

The integration of learning and working has been approached from at least two different perspectives, formal education and human resource development (HRD).

The integration of working and learning has progressed along separate paths in both camps, often motivated by different interests and conditions of organizational or personal development. In formal education integration is exemplified by the introduction of work-like elements into learning programmes. Project-oriented learning and the use of authentic problem situations help improve the practical value of the learning process. Although much attention has been paid to learning in groups (collaborative learning) and learning in an organizational setting (for instance using role plays), the main focus of these educational approaches is on individual development.

From an HRD point of view, learning arrangements must in the first place serve the overall productivity of a firm, and should help to attune individual performance to overall business performance. Nowadays, corporations tend to invest substantially in e-learning, in the hope that this will accelerate the pace of learning and improve its cost-effectiveness. In line with the vital role of learning and knowledge productivity, there is a tendency to connect e-learning and HRD to knowledge management initiatives. It is thus hoped that e-learning will boost the stimulation of tacit knowledge, enhance competence growth, and instil knowledge management and organizational learning practices.

We feel there is much to be gained from merging the formal education and HRD viewpoints. The primary challenge is to bridge the gap between the domains of learning and working, with a view to their being strengthened reciprocally. We also expect e-learning to play an important role in this merger, particularly in the form of 'virtual business e-learning' (VBeL). This chapter begins by introducing the concept of VBeL as a specific means of integrating learning and working. It discusses this concept in regard to other related educational settings, then goes on to focus on two major issues specific to VBeL: its continuous development in interaction with its participants, and the way the teachers or designers need to set conditions rather than provide information and assignments. The final section gives a summary and a short discussion of the potential of the VBeL approach.

Characteristics of virtual business e-learning

The VBeL concept situates learning in a business environment. Students in a VBeL environment have roles as starting professionals. They work in distributed project teams for real customers. In addition, they perform duties and have responsibilities for the development of the VBeL organization as a whole. In doing so they work explicitly on their personal development. Arranging the work is to a large extent the responsibility of the students themselves. Key components of a VBeL environment are:

- a real business setting;
- complex, non-routine, ill-structured tasks;
- explicit facilitation of active construction of knowledge, new ideas and working methods;

● assessments according to professional practice and its performance standards;
● a supporting infrastructure of information and communications technology (ICT), allowing distributed teamwork.

To give an indication of the activities that a student has to perform, Table 4.1 shows the schedule of a student who is working in a VBeL environment called 'InCompany'. As indicated in the table, some activities are related to personal development (left-hand column) while others are related to the work in the project team (right-hand column). A VBeL environment is an educational setting with its own specific aspects compared with other methods of active learning. In order to illustrate some of the characteristics of VBeL, it will be contrasted with simulation, gaming, project-oriented problem-based learning (PBL) and work placement.

Simulation is an educational setting by which reality is imitated. The operating processes by which the part of reality chosen 'works' are simulated. The visual or dramatic resemblance to reality can be more or less accurate (the 'fidelity' of the simulation), with more or less involvement of and interaction with the student-spectator. The essential characteristic of all simulations is exhaustive control over the parameter settings, and consequently the simulated process. When the simulation is repeated with the same parameter settings the outcomes are identical. What is trained is basically the understanding of the cause–effect relationships, which are mostly combined with rapid effective intervention based on algorithmic handling schemes (such as decision trees). As with simulation, VBeL simulates the general working processes in a company. However, unlike simulation, VBeL does not control the parameters to secure safe, comparable results exhaustively. Simulations can be repeated, but VBeL activities can only be done once in the same form, as they are in a continuous state of development.

Simulation becomes gaming by building an element of competition into the role play. Both are crucial to the idea and the perception of a game. One can win a game, but one cannot win a play or drama. This additional factor (competition) can strongly motivate people, to the extent that they become completely immersed in the gaming environment. The element of role play brings us closer to the VBeL approach. Complex training games ask people to take roles in order to obtain an inside understanding of the multiplicity of viewpoints and contradictory interests that go along with them. VBeL uses the strength of taking a role, both on the level of a student becoming an employee, and on the level of the intra-group task differentiation, for example students taking different roles by turns. In this sense VBeL includes group decision processes in the same way as classical management games. The crucial difference is that a management game has an algorithmic parameterization of the company's working processes built into it (intervention decisions on production, stocks, prices, personnel and so forth), whereas each VBeL project employs a unique chronology without a fixed parameterization.

The third educational method, project-oriented PBL, creates a rich educational setting by combining several strong pedagogical principles. The converging focus on a 'problem' structures the mobilization of cognitive resources, along with the dynamics of the group process. In VBeL the problem is a real problem formulated

Table 4.1   *Example of a student schedule*

The shaded rows represent planned face-to-face meetings.

Activities related to personal development	Date	Activities related to projects
Application for preferred roles and competencies	10 March	Application for preferred projects (internal and external)
First meeting in Heerlen	12 March	
Which roles and competencies? Who is my coach?	Initial agreement 14 March	Participation in which projects for which customer? In which team?
Draft personal development plan (PDP) to be sent to coach	24 March	Draft project plan to be sent to the InCompany management and customer
Feedback on PDP from coach		Feedback information on project plan by InCompany management and customer
Approval PDP	28 March	Approval of project plan
	'Work in progress' meeting in Maastricht 14 April	Presentation of preliminary results (face-to-face)
Feedback to peers on their competence development	25 April	
Mid-term reflection report Comments on mid-term reflection report by coach	6 May	Partial or preliminary results to InCompany management and customer
	13 May	Feedback on partial or preliminary results
	16 May	Review report to InCompany management
	23 May	Comments on review report by InCompany management
	6 June	Draft final results to InCompany management and customer
	17 June	Lessons learnt to InCompany management
	18 June	Feedback on draft by InCompany management and customer
	Final meeting in Eindhoven 20 June	Presentation of final results
Feedback to peers on their competence development	24 June	
Final reflection report	26 June	Final project results

by a real customer. With respect to this, VBeL stresses the importance of the irreplaceable surplus value of a real, urgent problem, compared with a problem that occurred in the past. The effective deadline, together with an effective commissioner waiting for an interesting solution or for advice as the outcome of the group work, are conditions that favour the shift from just 'role playing' towards an effective employee perception. This will strongly affect the depth at which competencies can effectively be trained. Another element in comparing VBeL with project-oriented PBL relates to the shifting contexts of discourse, essentially between learning and working. In project-oriented PBL the basic perspective is learning, while in VBeL it is working.

Finally, VBeL may be compared with work placement. Nothing can ever replace the actual experience of working in a real workplace, albeit as a trainee. Almost every curriculum acknowledges the value of *in situ* training, which can be found in traditional programmes with internship periods, dual learning programmes, and structured on-the-job training programmes in some professions. This should not blind us to some of the persisting remarks of students formulated after their work placement experience. Having a student-trainee status at the workplace, the student is often disappointed by only having limited responsibilities. Paradoxically, a student can more fully function as an actual employee in a VBeL than in a real workplace, where a trainee is often asked to do the 'odd jobs' that do not challenge the competencies of a starting professional. Moreover, most work placements are single events where a student works for a number of months in a company or organization. The tasks that have to be performed are rarely based on a group responsibility process. In VBeL, on the contrary, the group responsibility for the problem solving is the starting point. Thus effective training can be given in the social competencies that are necessary in an actual work environment.

Designing and developing a VBeL environment

The way a VBeL environment is developed differs in several respects from common educational development and educational innovation projects. In discussing some of the important issues, it is useful to refer to the ADDIE cycle (see Dick and Carey, 1996). This cycle distinguishes:

- analysis of needs (setting goals);
- design of a blueprint for the (improved) environment;
- development and implementation of the (next) educational environment;
- evaluation to set the new goals (analysis) for the next development cycle.

Continuous development of a VBeL environment

In the development of, for example, a course for distance education the ADDIE cycle is passed through once, and the course material will be in use for about five years with only marginal adaptation within fixed frameworks. By contrast, the development of a VBeL environment is an ongoing process as a result of its own dynamics. In particular, development is achieved during working and learning by the employees, who are mostly students! Their active participation may even result in a complete redesign of the business processes. Therefore a VBeL environment should be an 'organization for learning' as well as a learning organization. The innovative and collective learning of the team and the organization are pursued and supported in parallel with the effective development of the individual professional.

The development of a VBeL environment ideally occurs as a natural consequence of working in the environment itself. However, this continuous development may be difficult to achieve in practice, as will be illustrated with a concrete example of a VBeL environment called 'InCompany', which is a non-profit environmental consulting agency. Participating in its activities serves as the final compulsory project for students graduating in Environmental Sciences. InCompany started as a pilot project in 1998. Since then, the company has been operating discontinuously because this form of education has only been offered at intervals, namely Spring 1998, Autumn 2000, Spring 2002 and Spring 2003. Accordingly, it has been improved incrementally in four runs, roughly following the ADDIE cycle, as part of the regular educational development process at the Open University of the Netherlands. The distinct development phases are shown in the quadrants in Figure 4.1.

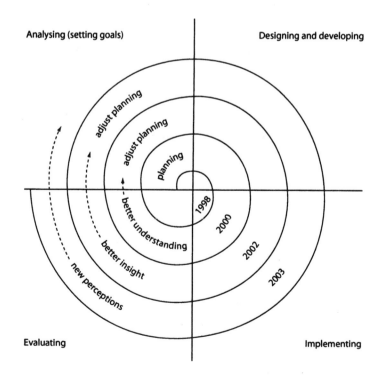

Figure 4.1   *The InCompany development cycle*

In each run the tutors had a short-term perspective on improving the business and learning processes, and therefore restricted themselves to palliatives such as organizing an ICT helpdesk and giving *ad hoc* explanations on working methods and procedures. Because InCompany was offered in the same way as a normal course (with a beginning and an end), the tutors were able to improve the processes, or sometimes even redesign the environment in between two course periods. However, students were not involved in these improvements.

In the near future InCompany will operate continuously, as more educational institutes are becoming involved, so students can start new projects throughout the year. Tutors will no longer have the opportunity to adjust and redesign the company at interim periods. A second change is the increased involvement of students in the development processes. Since 2002 students became partly responsible for setting the business objectives and the further development of InCompany. They were assigned roles relating to communication and knowledge management, and other employees could even consult them as internal experts.

From initiating to implementing a VBeL environment

Special attention is needed to initiate VBeL in an existing curriculum. Since it radically changes education (for example, bringing about new roles for tutors or teachers, and more responsibilities for students), it should be handled as an educational innovation project. A great deal of attention should be paid to the initiating and analyzing stages, including measures to gain support and commitment from faculty members.

It is tempting to analyze all the specific needs and to propose detailed solutions after the initial stage, but in practice this will be very difficult, if not impossible. Among other things, this is because of the widely differing expectations and interpretations of what a VBeL environment might look like. It is therefore important to present a simple but convincing prototype environment as early in the process as possible. Ongoing adaptation of this prototype in continuous interaction with the users (tutors and students) will promote its acceptance. The prototype will help demonstrate the consequences of earlier design decisions. Possible expectations can be adjusted, or lead to new aims and plans. This also redirects the elements of a VBeL environment one wishes to incorporate in the first release, and the opportunities that must remain open for further development in the VBeL environment itself. This might gradually lead to more confidence in its chances of success, and in increasing the level of ambition for the next prototype.

The investment in the initial design (that is, for the first release) should be limited. The VBeL organization, its culture and its working methods will be determined to a large extent by the 'employees' themselves, and not by instructional designers from behind their desks. Thus it is of the utmost importance that the initial design sufficiently facilitates the continuous further development of the VBeL environment by all its employees.

The initial VBeL environment may even be an almost empty shell. The first project teams could mainly consist of educational and professional experts who bring the VBeL organization into existence by working for real external clients, and on internal projects that focus on organizational development. When these teams have finished their projects they will have also created a rich company environment including new, consolidated knowledge, leading practices, working methods and techniques. Hence, the professional teams will have created the VBeL environment by doing what students will be expected to do. The next teams embellish these achievements, and thus get acquainted with the working methods and knowledge they need to apply. These are the rudiments for competent working and learning that can subsequently grow in scope and quality. Gradually, more and more starting professionals (that is, students) will take the place of the experts.

Use of ICT

As has been said above, because of common expectations and acceptance it is important to realize a prototype environment as early in the development process as possible. However, the ICT infrastructure of this environment does not need to be extremely advanced or high tech. Although new working and learning methods may require new ICT tools or components, the primary consideration is that the users in a VBeL environment feel comfortable, as this favours receptiveness to new methods for learning and work. The ICT tooling should merely enable the major virtual communications and actions required. Moreover, the group processes in a VBeL environment can be sustained by the utilization of a platform for computer-supported collaborative work up to a point. This is partly because blended scenarios (an intelligent mix of face-to-face meetings, telephone conferencing and asynchronous communication such as e-mail and groupware) prove to be the strongest ones. A hybrid communication infrastructure is optimal as long as non-mediated communication maintains an important role.

For example, ICT mediation for InCompany primarily focuses on both learning and working, and acts as unobtrusively as possible. The InCompany learning environment consists of an intranet Web environment grafted on to existing facilities that the Open University of the Netherlands uses for its whole educational programme (see Chapter 13). All the organizational and working information resides within the InCompany environment. For collaborative work, existing groupware platforms have been tailored to fit InCompany's needs. At first, BSCW (basic support for collaborative work) was used to sustain collaborative work, but in the second cycle (as shown in Figure 4.1), a shift was made to a highly flexible groupware platform called 'eRoom'.

Developing by setting conditions

Developing a VBeL environment is about creating an open, complex business environment. It is about setting the conditions for learning and working, rather than about giving information, assignments and feedback. A VBeL environment uses the same control and steering mechanism as professional practice. The conditions for work processes comprise a system of quality control in such a way that the products and services meet professional standards and satisfy customers' needs, while supporting individual learning at the same time. In designing a VBeL environment the business process (rendering products and services) and the educational process (training students to be starting professionals) should be fully integrated. We will illustrate these issues by first discussing the quality cycle of project work (see Figure 4.2) and then the quality cycle of personal development (see Figure 4.3).

Quality control and project work

There are many methods for project management, but in general we can distinguish three stages: preparation, operation and closing. During the first two stages, the project team specifies the needs, performs activities, stores results (and draft results) in a project file, organizes review sessions, and formulates follow-up actions (see Figure 4.2).

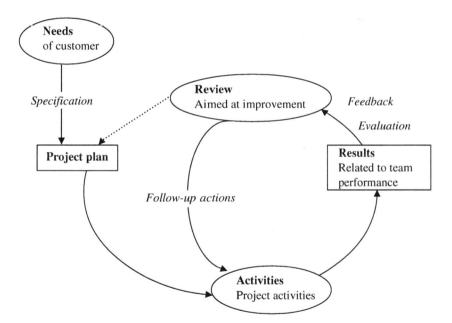

Figure 4.2 *The quality cycle for project work*

A project team is responsible for choosing and justifying its own quality standards, including the criteria for intermediate and final products, and team performance. These criteria are usually set out in a project plan, together with the specified needs of the external client in relation to what the VBeL organization has to offer. The results, both the products for the client and the process results (such as reports and reflections on team performance) are stored in a project file. The quality of processes and products is assessed regularly. Review sessions are generally used for this purpose (start-up review, intermediate process and product reviews), but sometimes tests (such as acceptance tests for software) or inspections (such as walk-through sessions) may be more appropriate. Reviews include process criteria such as activities that the team undertakes to meet professional standards, and the efficiency of cooperation in the team, and between team members and other stakeholders. The outcome of the review is set down in a list of follow-up actions, but could also lead to adjustments in the contract and/or the project plan.

Quality control and personal development

The VBeL organization is not just an environment in which students can use information at their own discretion, but a structured workplace that facilitates learning via intake assessments, matching individual learning objectives with challenging roles and tasks, regular feedback and coaching. The VBeL infrastructure includes just-in-time help for learning, a knowledge base with background information, and external experts who may be consulted as required.

Duties and responsibilities for project work (for the client as well as for the VBeL organization itself) are attributed to individual students according to their learning needs. At times changes are negotiated to match the project to available skills, time and expertise, as tasks and duties have to be rich and challenging enough to enable the students' competence to develop as envisaged.

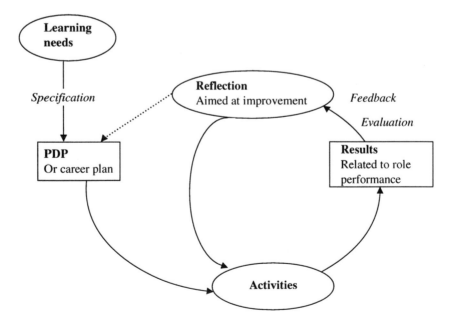

Figure 4.3 *The quality cycle for personal development*

Providing specific support also stimulates the personal development in a VBeL organization. In that respect, it is useful to distinguish between organizational support for role performance (eg portfolio, coaching, 360 degree assessment) and support for the knowledge organization.

The personal development plan (PDP) or career plan is an agreement between the student and the VBeL organization about which competencies receive priority, which roles the student will perform, and the performance criteria that will be applied. These performance criteria are not fixed in advance, but are open to negotiation. The more complex the skill or competency to be acquired, the more complex it is to determine the criteria (Sluijsmans, 2002). Thus the professional in a VBeL environment, whether starting or experienced, must have a fair degree of influence on setting these role performance criteria.

The individual also needs to reflect on his or her actions and activities, as shown in Figure 4.3. The reflection may possibly lead to an adjustment of the learning objectives, the performance criteria, or the duties and responsibilities agreed on during a performance interview. The quality of the individual learning process is largely determined by closing the quality cycle for personal development (see Figure 4.3). Indeed the differences between an experienced and a starting professional lie partly in the capacity to reflect and thus to learn from experience, that is, to define follow-up actions (see Schön, 1987). Other people's support is frequently necessary for this reflection to be successful. This support could come, for example, from colleagues (that is, peer students), managers, clients or external experts who give informative feedback.

Experience with InCompany show that in practice, students tend to give priority to finishing their project and business work. As a consequence activities such as documenting their own achievements in a portfolio, processing feedback from others, or reflecting on personal processes and products may be somewhat neglected (Ivens and Sloep, 2001). In the near future InCompany will try to integrate these activities more closely with team and organizational duties. This will be done first by demanding that personal development goals from the PDP are sufficiently related to project work, and second by making the students partly responsible for the assessment criteria (that is, for role and team performance as well as for intermediate and final products).

Conclusion and discussion

This chapter first clarified the educational position of VBeL by comparing it with four related educational settings. The key achievement of the VBeL concept is that working and learning are seamlessly integrated into one activity, which addresses professional development, team learning and organizational development at the same time. In a VBeL environment individual learning (defined as increasing one's capacity to take effective action) is coupled with team learning and organizational learning (defined as increasing an organization's capacity to take effective action) (Kim, 1993). For example, role performance is explicitly linked to business performance. This guarantees that learning occurs as a natural consequence of work itself. The cycles of quality control illustrate that VBeL should essentially be seen as a form of 'double-loop learning' (see Argyris and Schön, 1996; Senge, 1990). Learning at all levels implies analyzing and questioning the influence of given conditions.

On the basis of our experiences with InCompany and a few other VBeL environments, it may be concluded that introducing the VBeL concept in an educational institute does not always run perfectly smoothly, as it touches the very foundations of education. The design of a VBeL environment must go hand in hand with change management. This does not mean that there should be a large initiating innovation project concentrating on the complete design of an ideal VBeL organization. On the contrary, the development should be continuous, and should be directed at a constantly increasing level of ambition. In addition, we have argued that the student-employees should have a major role in this continuous improvement of the VBeL environment.

The necessity that both students and teachers perceive the VBeL environment as a real company is related to this view. Students should not have the feeling that they are 'just playing' or that the teacher is actually controlling the learning and working experience. The justification of all choices, including methods of assessment, is part of the responsibility of the starting professionals or the project team. Reaching high-quality personal development as well as high-quality performance of the project team and the VBeL organization as a whole is largely achieved by formulating specific demands on working methods and the standards involved.

This chapter only discussed the InCompany example, which had a strong focus on personal professional development. However, a VBeL environment may vary according to the learning and performance objectives that are envisaged. Other VBeL examples, which are mostly used in companies, have a stronger focus on improving collective task performance and organizational knowledge processes (see Bitter-Rijpkema, Sloep and Jansen, 2003). VBeL is an example of integrated e-learning (as defined in the Introduction) enabled by the many possibilities offered by ICT. It is also consistent with the design guidelines for integrated e-learning that were discussed in Chapter 1.

A VBeL setting can be confronted with several problems and dilemmas, most of which have been mentioned only briefly in this chapter. They include among other things the changing role of teachers within a VBeL environment; the tension between the logic and discourse of work versus the logic and discourse of learning; the breakdown of real problems in order to fit in with the growth of competence according to the role-taking of student-employees in the group; and the timing of real-life deadlines to harmonize with course schedules. Moreover, VBeL encounters the same problems as virtual organizations and learning organizations.

The continuous improvement of the VBeL concept and its implementation require considerable effort from both educational institutes and companies. Neither educational designers nor HRD managers can achieve the desired integration of learning and working on their own. Such integration requires the cooperation of all actors and stakeholders involved, which can thus give further meaning to a continuously growing VBeL community.

References

Argyris, C and Schön, D A (1996) *Organisational Learning II: Theory, method, and practice*, Addison Wesley, Reading, MA

Baskett, H K M and Marsick, V J (1992) Confronting new understandings about professional learning and change, in *Professionals' Ways of Knowing: New findings on how to improve professional education*, ed H K M Baskett and V J Marsick, Jossey Bass, San Francisco, CA

Bitter-Rijpkema, M, Sloep, P B and Jansen, D (2003) Learning to change: the virtual business learning approach to professional workplace learning, *Educational Technology and Society*, 6 (**1**), pp 18–25

Coffield, F (2000) The structure below the surface: re-assessing the significance of informal learning, in *The Necessity of Informal Learning*, ed F Coffield, Polity Press, Bristol, UK

Dick, W and Carey, L (1996) *The Systematic Design of Instruction*, 4th edn, Scott Foresman, Glenview, IL

Ivens, W P M F and Sloep, P B (2001) Changing environmental sciences education needs: how can we meet them? Experiments with constructivist learning within environmental sciences curricula, *Proceedings auDes-conference Bridging Minds & Markets*, 5–7 April 2001, Venice, Italy

Kim, D H (1993) The link between individual and organizational learning, *Sloan Management Review*, **3**, pp 37–50

Marsick, V and Watkins, K (2001) Informal and incidental learning, in *New Directions for Adult and Continuing Education*, ed S Merriam, pp 24–34, Jossey-Bass, San Francisco, CA

Schön, D A (1987) *Educating the Reflective Practitioner: Toward a new design for teaching and learning in the professions*, Jossey-Bass, San Francisco, CA

Senge, P (1990) *The Fifth Discipline: The art and practice of the learning organization*, Currency Doubleday, New York

Sluijsmans, D M A (2002) Student involvement in assessment: the training of peer assessment skills, unpublished doctoral dissertation, Open University of the Netherlands, Heerlen

Chapter 5

Learning technologies in e-learning: an integrated domain model

Rob Koper

Introduction

In the modern world, e-learning has become a fact of life. No one disputes whether e-learning should be applied or not. The only questions are how and when it should be applied. Most of the basic technologies are available, and the pedagogical principles have been worked out to a certain extent. There are different business models available for e-learning, and the content can be transformed to be delivered electronically. Although this sounds rather promising, in fact there is little knowledge in the field of how to integrate all these different approaches and technologies in order to create the best possible e-learning solution for the many different needs and situations. There is a lack of integration and harmonization in the e-learning field, and even very basic theories and models about e-learning are in short supply, leading to a great deal of conceptual confusion which hinders implementation and the further development of the field.

In this chapter we try to unite the different dimensions by introducing an integrated conceptual framework that enables researchers, developers, implementers, managers and others to understand, organize, classify, plan and approach the issues in e-learning. The framework is presented as a domain model. It defines the field of e-learning and its basic structure, vocabulary and issues.

Integrated e-learning systems

In integrated e-learning, the system under consideration is not restricted to computer systems, but concerns the entire organization of the educational system. An 'integrated e-learning system' (IEL) is defined here as an educational system that uses network-based learning technologies to support its primary educational functions. Figure 5.1 provides a basic model of an IEL.

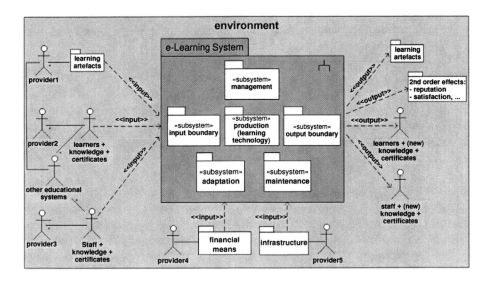

Figure 5.1   *The organizational structure of an integrated e-learning system*

The primary input of an IEL is the learners with their entry characteristics. The primary output is the 'transformed' learners with additional knowledge (declarative and procedural at a certain level of competency) along with evidence of that knowledge (such as certificates). Another input–output factor is the staff members (such as teachers). Staff members bring their knowledge into the learning process, and this knowledge changes during their work. The characteristics of learners and staff members that are changed by the system are called the 'properties' of learners and staff.

The system also operates on 'learning artefacts', that is, all the physical products produced before, during or after learning, such as courses, programmes, learning designs, activity descriptions, books, reports, tests, remarks and comments. Most

IELs create added value for the learning artefacts that are provided on the input side. Courses can be constructed from lower-level artefacts.

As an IEL is an educational system of sorts, which is in turn a kind of organization, it inherits characteristics of organizations and educational systems: for example, its classification of subsystems (Daft, 2000). In e-learning systems we can distinguish the following subsystems:

- A *production* subsystem. This is responsible for the transformation process of the input to the output. In IELs the primary means of the production system are what are known as 'learning technologies', some of which are network-based. Learning technologies are the specific means of establishing the functionality of the IEL, that is, to analyze, design, develop, deliver and evaluate learning opportunities for learners in certain contexts and knowledge domains.
- An *adaptation* subsystem which is responsible for the innovation and change of the production system so that it more closely matches the environmental constraints and opportunities.
- A *maintenance* subsystem which is responsible for the *status quo* of the system, including the training and support of the staff.
- An *input boundary spanning* subsystem which communicates directly with the environment, for example to attract and enrol students, buy resources and communicate with the financial bodies.
- An *output boundary spanning* subsystem which communicates directly with the outside world to deliver products and services such as certificates.

The most significant difference between an IEL, and a regular educational system is that the IEL has a different kind of production subsystem. Instead of classrooms there are computer networks that connect learners, teachers and learning artefacts. This provides a completely new set of possibilities in the relationship with the outside world, for example freedom of place and time; scope for automating parts of the teaching–learning process; the possibility of simulating parts of the learning environment; and the possibility of radically renewing the pedagogical models (Koper, 2001a). In this chapter we want to focus on the production subsystem.

IEL can be studied at three different levels of analysis: individual, group and organizational. As a result of the inherent network organization characteristics of the ICT technologies used, we have opted for the organizational level. Each of these levels can be studied from a micro, meso or macro perspective. At the micro level one looks at the function of the smaller parts within the system. At the macro level one looks at the overall functionality of the system in its relationship with the environment. However, we prefer to focus on the meso level of analysis, which combines both perspectives by considering the macro phenomena as emergent behaviours that result from the activities of the subsystems at the micro level (Prietula, Carley and Gasser, 1998).

This position is elaborated in complexity theory (Waldrop, 1992; Kauffman, 1995); the study of emergence and self-organization (Johnson, 2001; Varela, Thompson and Rosch, 1991; Maturana and Varela, 1992); computational organization theory (Carley, 1995); pattern analysis (Gamma *et al*, 1995; Fowler, 1997; Larman, 2002); and technological approaches such as peer to peer systems (Barkai, 2002), multi-agent approaches (Axelrod, 1997; Ferber, 1998) and the GRID (Foster, Kesselman and Tuecke, 2001).

This brings us to an interesting notion in IEL. In establishing an IEL, one creates connections between people and resources that were not previously available. When designed properly, this can invoke a new kind of 'emergent' organization that introduces and supports completely new ways of learning, teaching and knowledge transfer. We tend to name this type of organization a 'learning network', and it forms the scope of our new research and technology programme into learning technologies (see www.learningnetworks.org).

Dimensions in the e-learning domain

In the previous section we introduced the structure of IELs. In this section I should like to focus on the different characteristics of IELs to facilitate their further understanding, comparison and design. Three interrelated dimensions can be distinguished:

- The *functional* dimension which deals with the pedagogical and knowledge issues. This dimension is closely connected to the production subsystem.
- The *organizational* dimension which deals with structural characteristics, contextual characteristics, the economic (or business) characteristics and legal issues.
- The *technical* dimension which deals with the architectural aspects, the interoperability protocols and standards, the network infrastructure, the servers and applications, and the user interfaces.

The functional dimension

We will now look into this production system more closely in order to identify its different subsystems (see Figure 5.2, modelled in UML; see also OMG; Booch, Rumbaugh and Jacobson, 1999; Warmer and Kleppe, 2001).

In the production subsystem we distinguish three core processes and two data stores:

- The *development* process in which learning artefacts are created and adapted. It retrieves existing learning artefacts from the repository. The process can be set and called from outside.
- The *repository* is a data store for learning artefacts. It can import and export learning artefacts from other systems.
- The *learning* process in which the actual learning and teaching take place. It can be set and called from outside. It retrieves existing learning artefacts from the

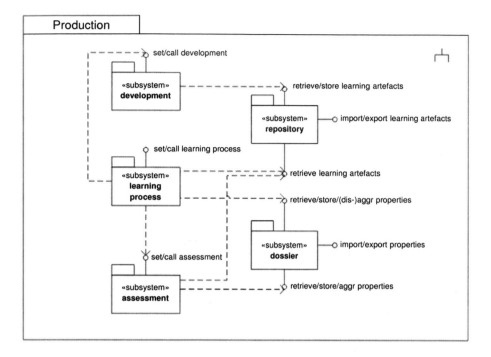

Figure 5.2   *The subsystems of the production system*

repository, and can set and call the development process during learning to create and store new learning artefacts. In addition to having access to the repository, the learning subprocess also has access to the dossier to retrieve and store properties.

● The *dossier* is a data store for the properties of individual users, groups and roles which are local or global in scope. The dossier can import properties from or export them to the outside.

● The *assessment* process which can be set and called from the learning subsystem at different moments, before, during and after learning. It uses properties from the dossier and learning artefacts from the repository. It stores new or aggregated properties in the dossier, representing the learner's position grades and so forth.

Different issues can be identified for each of these subsystems and combinations of them. These are again considered from the dimensions of functionality, organization and technology. More complex issues are related to the subsystems.

The organizational dimension

Any organization has both structural and contextual characteristics. These are summed up in Table 5.1 (Daft, 2000). The structural characteristics are the internal

Table 5.1 *Structural and contextual characteristics of an organization*

Structural characteristics	Contextual characteristics
1. Formalization	1. Targets and strategy
2. Specialization	2. Environment
3. Standardization of work process	3. Size
4. Hierarchy	4. Technology type (= education)
5. Complexity	5. Culture
6. Centralization	
7. Professionalism	
8. Personnel ratios	

characteristics that allow the measurement and comparison of different organizations. See the scale referred to by Marcic (Scale for the measurement of the dimensions of organizations, 1996; see Daft, 2000). The contextual characteristics describe the complete organization in its relationship with the environment.

In organization theory, several patterns have been derived from the comparison of the characteristics of organizations. For instance, certain contextual characteristics are correlated with certain other structural characteristics. Thus large size, routine technology and a stable environment are correlated with high formalization, standardization, specialization and centralization. How these characteristics are related to the organization of institutes delivering e-learning, what the optimal characteristics are for IELs, and how organizations can change, remain unknown in the field of e-learning.

The technical dimension

When it comes to the technical dimension, a large number of issues can be identified. Here is a selection of some of the more important ones:

● There is a great need for interoperable *reference architectures* in e-learning but there are too many architectures at the moment (see LTSC WG1; Sim, 2002; Livingston Vale and Long, 2003). They are incomplete, with a large number of underlying protocols and standards missing. By its very nature we cannot expect the architecture to be standardized in the near future. However, it is advisable at the moment to sketch and update the architecture to see how the lower level issues fit together.

● *Interoperability specifications* are crucial for the establishment of larger interconnected networks and collaborations such as learning networks and the GRID. There are several successful initiatives, which release specifications on a regular basis in the e-learning field. Examples are the AICC, IMS, IEEE LTSC and ISO SC36. The most important initiative to date is IMS, a consortium of e-learning vendors, universities and training departments. The current status, however, is that there are still many specifications unavailable in this field, and that many others also have to be harmonized.

● Having reference architectures is one thing; having the actual implementations in terms of *network facilities, servers and applications* is another. Most of this work, with the exception of several specific services and applications, is not powered by e-learning. There are more generic facilities for all types of application fields. The major problems in this domain are the lack of standardization and the lack of valid, accepted ideas about e-learning requirements and specifications.

● Last but not least, *user interfaces* are of specific importance in e-learning. The requirements are different from those in most business applications, such as word processors, because these interfaces are the primary means for the realization of learning. This issue is addressed in Chapter 7.

Improvement of e-learning

Current e-learning systems have many shortcomings. In addition to implementation issues, one of the major aspects that causes problems is the restrictions of the current learning technologies used in the production subsystem. To further improve IELs it is imperative to improve at least the following learning technologies:

● The IELs *development* subsystem, that is, the facilities that allow providers, teachers and learners to develop learning artefacts in a more effective, efficient, attractive, accessible, adaptable way.

● The facilities to support the *sharing and reuse* of learning artefacts within and between organizations. This issue is related to the improvement of the repository.

● The facilities for *differentiated delivery and use* of learning artefacts by different groups and individuals. This issue is related to the improvement of the learning process subsystem and the dossier.

● Concerning the *assessment* possibilities of IELs, the facilities must support assessment in the most effective, efficient, attractive, accessible, adaptable way. This issue is related to the improvement of the assessment subsystem and the dossier.

Development issues

In IELs, one has to develop digital learning artefacts such as units of learning (courses or programmes) and learning objects. A major problem for organizations when introducing e-learning is the question of how to deal with this development process of digital learning artefacts. The development process is complex and expensive. Technology creates many new possibilities but there are also constraints, to say nothing of the major copyright and interoperability issues. Possibly the most challenging point is that in e-learning the expected quality of the units of learning cannot easily be provided by the one person who is traditionally responsible for this job, the teacher. Multidisciplinary teamwork is one approach to creating units of learning of acceptable quality. Issues such as interactivity, personalization, use of multimedia, granularization of the units, coding of content in standard formats (such as xhtml, jpeg, mathml and smile) have to be taken into account. The issue of the work processes in e-learning is elaborated in Chapter 9.

A further problem is the question of what to develop: not only what must be developed, but in what format and in how much detail in order to provide for a unit of learning (both usable and reusable) that can be delivered through a computer facility. An integrative model is needed to answer these questions. This model should describe the semantic components and the relationships between them. We have been working on such a model in recent years, and it has now been published as the 'Educational Modelling Language' (EML) (see Chapter 6; Koper *et al*, 2000). EML has provided the basis for the IMS Learning Design specification (IMSLD, 2002). This model provides an abstract, generic description of the semantic structure of a unit of learning. It is based on a pedagogical metamodel, or better still, an abstraction of instructional design theories and models (Koper, 2001b).

This abstraction can be summarized as follows: in a designed learning situation, learners and staff members are engaged in one or more activities that are dynamically related in a learning design method. Every activity is performed in an environment that consists of a collection of one or more learning objects and services. Specific learning design (instructional design) models, like the 4C/ID model discussed in Chapter 1, are specializations of this abstract model. The specific models prescribe the preferred type of activities, the preferred method and the preferred environment (Duffy and Cunningham, 1996: 171). One specific unit of learning uses one instance of such a specialized model. A summary of the abstract model is presented in Figure 5.3. In addition to the relationship discussed above, it states that a unit of learning contains a 'learning design' which organizes physical resources in a semantic instructional framework. The learning design method connects the learners and staff members to various activities and environments.

This model can be used in a variety of ways. It defines the semantic components and the relationships between them which have to be developed in the development process. It serves as a framework to identify the validity of a unit of learning in terms of its structure and completeness. It can be used to compare specific instructional design approaches in research settings. Moreover, the model can be used to create XML bindings to design and express concrete courses and programmes in a format that can be interpreted by a computer program. Some applications of this model are EML and the IMS Learning Design.

The final problem to be discussed here raises the issue of the tools needed to support the development process. In a complete development process one needs tools to design, edit, search, store, manage and test the units of learning and the underlying resources. In e-learning there are still a great deal of practical problems with the development tools. Putting it bluntly, genuinely interoperable tools have yet to be developed. All the current solutions are suboptimal.

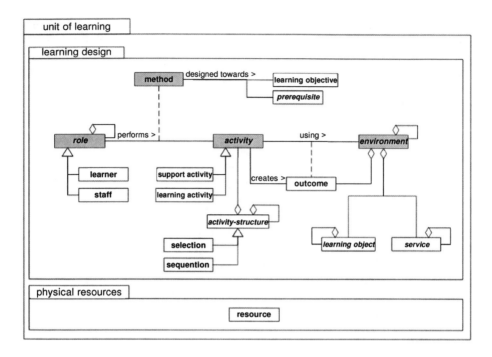

Figure 5.3 *The abstract structure of a unit of learning, expressed as an UML class diagram*

Sharing and reuse issues

Perhaps the most promising advantage of e-learning, but also one of the most complex advantages, is that it provides the possibility of the sharing and reuse of learning artefacts. This increases the economic benefit of e-learning. However, several issues need to be resolved before sharing and reuse become feasible.

The first issue addresses the question *which* types of learning artefacts are reusable and which are not. The basic idea is that courses are the least reusable units, and that the smaller underlying non-purposed learning objects are the most reusable (Downes, 2000). In addition to the learning objects, we also expect that the learning activities, the environments and the learning designs can be reused in different units of learning.

The second issue concerns the *granularization* of learning artefacts (Wiley, 2002; Duncan, 2003). How small or how large must a learning artefact be to make it suitable for reuse? For what purpose and for which actors are the learning artefacts available? Are they for authors, teachers or learners? The smallest meaningful unit for learners is a learning activity that includes the necessary environment and the connected support activities. Developers can also easily build new units of learning from these activities, by repurposing and sequencing them into an instructional method.

The third issue raises the question of *aggregation and repurposing*. How can lower-level resources and artefacts be aggregated to activities and units of learning? Are there rules and principles that can support the automation of this process so that the task is made easier?

The fourth issue is that of *disaggregation* of existing course materials. In most institutes there is a large quantity of existing materials that have not been prepared for, and are not at all suitable for, e-learning. Nor can they be reused. How should we deal with these materials? From an economic point of view it is not appropriate to replace everything with the attributes of e-learning.

The final issue is the problem of finding and sharing learning artefacts for reuse. We start from the assumption that there is a large, shared, distributed repository where users can search for learning artefacts, obtain them, adapt them, store new ones, and where legal and economic principles are supported in a workable manner. Such a repository functions in the context of what is called a 'learning object economy'. The principles for such an economy to succeed have not yet been established. Campbell (2003) identifies the following issues in a learning object economy: the granularity, interoperability, resource description and discovery, incentives, quality control and peer review, intellectual property rights and digital rights management, pedagogical frameworks and cultural barriers. Some sharing initiatives have already been put into practice, for example Ariadne (Forte *et al*, 1997), Cuber (Krämer, 2000) and Merlot (see merlot.org) but overall evaluation data relating to the success and failure factors of the approaches are not yet available.

Differentiated delivery issues

One of the possible advantages of e-learning is the ability to provide for differentiation or personalization in the delivery and use of learning artefacts. Usage can be varied according to factors such as:

- characteristics and preferences of learners (pre-knowledge, learning style, needs, personal circumstances and disabilities);
- context characteristics (integrated into the work environment, classroom teaching and distance teaching);
- delivery medium (eg Web, print or DVD);
- the quantity and quality of the educational services offered (amount of tutoring and assessment services).

Although e-learning does promise smooth differentiation, this has not yet been achieved. The basic mechanisms are available, but the integrated models, tools and guidelines for use have not yet been developed. The cost–benefit balance is also unknown. Does differentiated use and delivery increase the effectiveness and efficiency of the educational system? Does it attract new target groups? Does it make education more accessible to certain groups?

The following questions reflect some further complications in differentiation. Who should control the differentiation and under which conditions? Should it be the learner, the teacher, an intelligent agent, the developer or a mixture of these?

There is a need for a strong integration of development and delivery mechanisms. Students should be able to use the development environment to add to or adapt learning artefacts or to create personalized learning routes. Designers must also be able to adapt learning artefacts, and it must be possible to integrate easily the learning artefacts that are created in 'run time' (for example, during collaborative learning) into new units of learning.

Differentiation has several implications which are not very well known yet. It implies, for instance, the availability of 'global dossiers' for learners, where the preferences and characteristics are stored independently of the units of learning. These dossiers must be accessible from a variety of different implementations. The IMS Learner Information Package (IMSLIP, 2002) in combination with the IMS Learning Design property mechanisms provides the first mechanisms for this, although they have not been completely integrated or tested yet. This also implies the problem of the positioning of learners in a kind of global competency grid.

Differentiation seems to be an important improvement, but further technology development is needed before it can be put into real practice.

Assessment issues

Assessment in IEL has the same purposes as in regular education, namely feedback, monitoring, tracking, quality rating and overall evaluation of the effectiveness of the educational system. In e-learning there are still many problems in this area, mostly because of the repositioning of the function of assessment in modern education. The field is evolving rapidly. New, alternative assessment methods are being developed and applied (Hambleton, 1996; Sluijsmans, 2002). Moreover, new problems are also occurring in e-learning environments, specifically the problem of learner positioning in learning networks. This raises the following question: what is the current state of knowledge of the learner relative to the learning opportunities provided? The answer is needed to allow for differentiated delivery.

Traditional tests are implemented in most current e-learning systems. Newer ones are not. In addition, the only open specification available in the assessment field, the IMS QTI, restricts itself to traditional tests. It specifies the interoperability format at a rather technical level, but does not connect this to the functional use of a test within the context of a unit of learning. What we need is an integrated model specifying what assessment method should be applied and under what conditions. This should be done very specifically but also semantically.

In order to provide such a model we have undertaken some preliminary work (Vermetten *et al*, in press). To begin with, we defined a matrix of assessment methods, considering five basic questions: what is assessed; how is it assessed; why is it assessed; when is it assessed; and who assesses it (Brown and Glasner, 1999; Van der Vleuten and Driessen, 2000). These questions can be applied to any assessment form in order to map all the components systematically. Second, we have started working towards the creation of a semantic domain model specifying all the types of interactions with the learners within the context of a unit of learning semantically (Hermans *et al*, 2002). Such integrative frameworks are needed to specify the assessment requirements for e-learning systems at a later stage, as shown in Figure 5.4 (overleaf).

Conclusion

In this chapter we have presented an integrative domain model for IEL. Basically it states that e-learning issues must be approached at the organizational level of analysis. IEL are approached as complex, dynamic, non-linear, evolving, adaptive systems. The model deals with two aspects of IELs: subsystems (adaptation, production, management, maintenance and boundary spanning) and dimensions (functional, organizational and technical). The most critical part for the effectiveness of an e-learning system is the production subsystem. This subsystem typically uses network-based learning technologies and contains five interrelated sub-subsystems (development, repository, learning process, dossier and evaluation). Several issues for future improvement have been addressed from the functional, organizational and technical perspectives for each of the sub-subsystems of the production subsystem.

The framework presented here provides the basic terminology, definitions and some of the models. It can be used in a variety of ways, for example:

● to identify future research and development questions in the field;
● to build better e-learning systems by integrating the requirements from the issues discussed in the model;
● to stimulate and plan effective implementation;
● to be able to identify the different issues in building e-learning courses and curricula.

As has been said above, the most interesting, but also the most complex issues deal with the coherence, connectivity and emergence of the different fragments of the model. In future, attention should be paid not only to the isolated issues of e-learning, but also particularly to the integrative relationships that are responsible for the overall effectiveness, efficiency, attractiveness, accessibility and adaptability of e-learning. The approach we plan to take is to consider these issues from the perspective of so-called 'learning networks', that is, self-organized, emergent, distributed systems created to facilitate learning and lifelong learning in some knowledge domains (see www.learningnetworks.org). These learning networks promise to change the way we learn in future quite fundamentally.

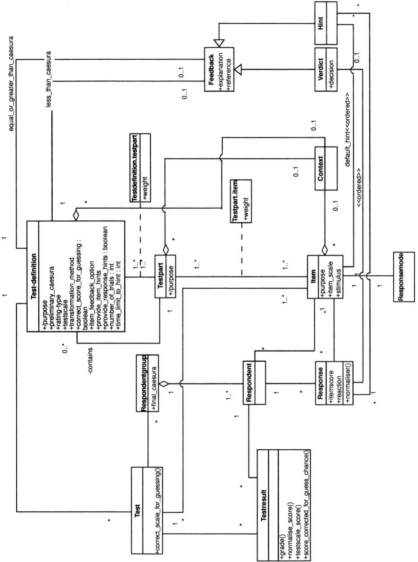

Figure 5.4 Part of the semantic domain model specifying types of interaction

Acknowledgement

This work is supported in part by a grant from the EU Fifth Framework RTD project eLearnTN. I should like to thank Eric Kluijfhout, Jan van Bruggen, Ellen Rusman, Slavi Stoyanov, Pierre Gorissen and René van Es for their fruitful participation in the discussions concerning the domain model.

References

Axelrod, R (1997) *The Complexity of Cooperation: Agent-based models of competition and collaboration*, Princeton Press, Princeton, NJ

Barkai, D (2002) *Peer-to-Peer Computing: Technologies for sharing and collaborating on the Net*, Intel Press, Santa Clara, CA

Booch, G, Rumbaugh, J and Jacobson, I (1999) *The Unified Modelling Language User Guide*, Addison-Wesley, Reading, MA

Brown, S and Glasner, A (1999) *Assessment Matters in Higher Education*, St Edmundsbury Press, Society for Research into Higher Education (SRHE) and Open University (UK), Suffolk

Campbell, L M (2003) Engaging with the learning object economy, in *Re-Using Online Resources: A sustainable approach to e-learning*, ed A Littlejohn, pp xx-xx, Kogan Page, London

Carley, K M (1995) Computational and mathematical organizational theory: perspective and directions, *Computational and Mathematical Organization Theory*, **1** (1), pp 39–56

Daft, R L (2000) *Organization Theory and Design*, 7th edn, South-Western College Publishing, Mason, OH

Downes, S (2000) *Learning Objects: Academic technologies for learning*, University of Alberta [Online] www.atl.ualberta.ca/downes/naweb/Learning_Objects.doc

Duffy, T M and Cunningham, D J (1996) Constructivism: implications for the design and delivery of instruction, in *Handbook of Research for Educational Communications and Technology*, ed D H Jonassen, pp 170–98, Macmillan, New York

Duncan, C (2003) Granularisation, in *Re-Using Online Resources: A sustainable approach to e-learning*, ed A Littlejohn, pp xx–xx, Kogan Page, London

Ferber, J (1998) *Multi-Agent Systems*, Addison-Wesley, Reading, MA

Forte, E, Wentland-Forte, M and Duval, E (1997) The ARIADNE project (part I and II): knowledge pools for computer based and telematics supported classical, open and distance education, *European Journal of Engineering Education*, **22** (1/2), pp 61–74 (part I), pp 153–66 (part II)

Foster, I, Kesselman, C and Tuecke, S (2001) The anatomy of the grid: enabling scalable virtual organizations, to be published in *International Journal of Supercomputer Applications* [Online] www.globus.org/research/papers/anatomy.pdf

Fowler, M (1997) *Analysis Patterns: Re-usable object models*, Addison-Wesley, Boston, MA

Gamma, E *et al* (1995) *Design Patterns: Elements of re-usable object-oriented software*, Addison-Wesley, Boston, MA

Hambleton, R K (1996) Advances in assessment models, methods and practices, in *Handbook of Educational Psychology*, ed D C Berliner and R C Calfee, pp 899–925, Macmillan, New York

Hermans, H *et al* (2002) *Modelling Test-Interactions*, research report, Open University of the Netherlands, Heerlen

IMSLD (2002) *IMS Learning Design: Information model, best practice and implementation guide, binding document, schemas* [Online] imsglobal.org

IMSLIP (2002) *IMS Learner Information Package: Information model, best practice and implementation guide, binding document, schemas* [Online] imsglobal.org

Johnson, S (2001) *Emergence*, Scribner, New York

Kauffman, S (1995) *At Home in the Universe*, Oxford University Press, Oxford

Koper, E J R (2001a) Van verandering naar vernieuwing (From change to renewal), in *Handboek Effectief Opleiden* (Handbook of effective training), 26, ed P Schramade, pp 45–86, Elsevier, Den Haag [Online] eml.ou.nl

Koper, E J R (2001b) *Modelling Units of Study from a Pedagogical Perspective: The pedagogical meta-model behind EML*, Open University of the Netherlands, Heerlen [Online] eml.ou.nl/introduction/docs/ped-metamodel.pdf

Koper, E J R *et al* (2000) *Educational Modelling Language Reference Manual*, Open University of the Netherlands, Heerlen [Online] eml.ou.nl

Krämer, B J (2000) Forming a federated virtual university through course broker middleware, Paper presented at LearnTech2000, Karlsruhe [Online] www.cuber.net/web/html/publications.html

Larman, C (2002) *Applying UML and Patterns*, 2nd edn, Prentice Hall, Upper Saddle River, NJ

Livingston Vale, K and Long, P D (2003) Models for open learning, in *Reusing Online Resources: A sustainable approach to e-learning*, ed A Littlejohn, pp 60–73, Kogan Page, London

LTSC WG1. *IEEE Architecture and Reference Model Working Group P1484.1* [Online] ltsc.ieee.org/wg1

Maturana, H and Varela, F J (1992) *The Tree of Knowledge: The biological roots of human understanding*, rev edn, Shambhala/New Science Press, Boston, MA

OMG (undated) *UML Specification, version 1.4* [Online] www.omg.org/technology/documents/formal/uml.htm

Prietula, M J, Carley, K M and Gasser, L (1998) A computational approach to organizations and organizing, in *Simulating Organizations*, pp 13–19, MIT Press, Cambridge, MA

Sim, S (2002) *e-learning Reference Architecture*, SUN, Nijmegen

Sluijsmans, D (2002) *Student Involvement in Assessment: The training of peer assessment skills*, Thesis, Open University of the Netherlands, Heerlen

Van der Vleuten, C M and Driessen, E W (2000) *Toetsen in Probleemgestuurd Onderwijs* (Assessment in problem-based education), Wolters Noordhoff, Groningen

Varela, F J, Thompson, E and Rosch, E (1991) *The Embodied Mind: Cognitive science and human experience*, MIT Press, Cambridge, MA

Vermetten, Y *et al* (in press) Justifiable choices for adequate assessment in higher education: analysis in terms of basic questions and quality criteria

Waldrop, M (1992) *Complexity: The emerging science at the edge of chaos,* Simon and Schuster, New York

Warmer, J and Kleppe, A (2001) *Praktisch UML* (Practical UML), Addison-Wesley, Amsterdam

Wiley, D (ed) (2002) *The Instructional Use of Learning Objects* [Online] www.re-usability.org/read

Further reading

Banathy, B H (1996) Systems inquiry and its application in education, in *Handbook of Research for Educational Communications and Technology,* ed D H Jonassen, pp 74–92, Macmillan, New York

Hoogveld, A W M *et al* (2001) The effects of a Web-based training in an instructional systems design approach on teachers' instructional design behavior, *Computers in Human Behavior,* **17**, pp 363–71

IMSQTI (2002) *IMS Question and Test Interoperability: Information model, best practice and implementation guide, binding document, schemas* [Online] imsglobal.org

Koper, E J R (2003) Combining re-usable learning resources and services to pedagogical purposeful units of learning, in *Reusing Online Resources: A sustainable approach to e-learning,* ed A Littlejohn, pp 46–59, Kogan Page, London

Liber, O, Olivier, B and Britain, S (2000) The TOOMOL Project: supporting a personalized and conversational approach to learning, *Computers and Education,* **34**, pp 327–33

Mayer, R E (1992) *Thinking, Problem Solving, Cognition,* 2nd edn, Freeman, New York

Sharp, H *et al* (1996–9) *Pedagogical Patterns: Successes in teaching object technology* [Online] www-lifia.info.unlp.edu.ar/ppp/public.htm

Shuell, T J (1988) The role of the student in learning from instruction, *Contemporary Educational Psychology,* **13**, pp 276–95

Shuell, T J (1993) Towards an integrated theory of teaching and learning, *Educational Psychologist,* **28**, pp 291–311

Stolovitch, H D and Keeps, E J (eds) (1999) *Handbook of Human Performance Technology,* Jossey-Bass, San Francisco, CA

Chapter 6

Educational Modelling Language

Henry Hermans, Jocelyn Manderveld and Hubert Vogten

Introduction

This chapter deals with an open learning technology specification called Educational Modelling Language (EML), which is the first implementation of a general set of notions as presented in the domain model for integrated e-learning (see Chapter 5). EML is defined as 'a semantic information model and binding, describing the content and process within a "unit of study" from a pedagogical perspective in order to support re-use and interoperability' (Rawlings *et al*, 2002). The development of this language should be seen in the broad perspective of working towards an instrumentation for the creation of effective, efficient, attractive integrated e-learning environments. The Introduction stresses that requirements for e-learning environments are becoming more complex, thereby increasing the need for an integrated approach. The challenge for the development of EML has been to adhere to these requirements.

In this chapter we provide a closer look at EML (version 1.0) and its background. First we discuss the general requirements that have led to its design and development. These requirements have led among other things to the construction of a pedagogical meta-model to meet the demands of supporting a variety of educational notions and settings. This meta-model is discussed, and we then go on to describe the conceptual structure of EML and the corresponding XML binding.

An important part of this chapter describes how EML can be used and what it looks like by presenting several examples. These examples follow a series of design steps needed to implement a pedagogical design in EML. Several screenshots of the so-called 'Edubox system' are provided to show how these examples can be interpreted. Edubox is an application that is able to process EML encoded files by publishing them on the World Wide Web. The chapter also contains an evaluation of EML in the light of the stated requirements, and in particular the intended pedagogical flexibility. We conclude with a word on the evolution EML is undergoing in a worldwide perspective.

Requirements

Koper (2001) summarized the 11 requirements that an educational modelling language should meet as follows:

- *Formalization:* EML must be able to describe pedagogical models formally, so that it is machine-readable and automatic processing is possible.
- *Pedagogical flexibility:* EML must be able to describe units of study that are based on different theories and models of learning and instruction.
- *Explicitly characterized learning objects:* EML must be able to express the semantic meaning of different learning objects within the context of a unit of study.
- *Completeness:* EML must be able to describe a unit of study completely, including all the characterized learning objects, the relationship between the objects, and the activities and the workflow of all students and staff members with the learning objects.
- *Reproducibility:* EML must describe the units of study so that repeated execution is possible.
- *Personalization:* EML must be able to describe aspects of personalization so that the learning materials and learning activities can be adapted based upon preferences, prior knowledge and educational needs.
- *Medium neutrality:* Wherever possible, the notation of units of study must be medium neutral, so that it can be used in different publication formats, such as the Web, paper, e-books or mobile phones.
- *Interoperability and sustainability:* The description standards and interpretation technique must be separated. In this way, investments in educational development will become resistant to technical changes and conversion problems.
- *Compatibility:* EML must match available standards and specifications.
- *Reusability:* EML must make it possible to identify, isolate, decontextualize and exchange useful learning objects, and reuse them in other contexts.
- *Life cycle:* EML must make it possible to produce, mutate, preserve, distribute and archive units of study and all of the learning objects they contain.

Three requirements will be elaborated in the following, as they have played an important role in the design and development of EML.

Formalization

This is arguably the most important requirement for an e-learning environment, as it is the guarantee that the resulting binding can be processed by computers. The requirement implies that EML should be a formal language, with its own alphabet, words and syntax. Note that processing does not mean that computers really understand the language. For the specification to become machine-understandable, the semantics expressed by the formal language could for example be interpreted by future means of artificial intelligence.

Pedagogical flexibility

An important requirement of EML is pedagogical flexibility. This requirement has been derived from the changing landscape of training and education. New paradigms of teaching and training such as competency-based learning (Schlusmans *et al*, 1999), collaborative learning (Dillenbourg and Schneider, 1995), and performance improvement approaches (Robinson and Robinson, 1995) have become widely accepted. Most of these new learning paradigms are based on constructivist principles (Brown, Collins and Duguid, 1989). They should be implemented in e-learning environments. In order to support these new paradigms, learning environments need to be rich, flexible and available at any time and in any place (Scott Grabinger, 1996; Manderveld and Koper, 1999). However, most e-learning environments do not support a variety of pedagogical models. Instead they provide their own didactic premises, implicit or otherwise, or present no didactics at all.

By defining the requirement of pedagogical flexibility, EML is safeguarded from a lack of supporting a variety of pedagogical models or no pedagogical model at all.

Interoperability

Educational institutions are increasingly faced with large investments in infrastructure and the problem of rapidly changing technology, particularly when course development and delivery are integrated into technology. Most e-learning environments develop and store courses and their contents in proprietary formats. As a result it becomes difficult or even impossible to export these courses and content to other formats (Koper, 2003). Cross-platform exchange of content is hardly possible at all. The only possible solution is often to convert the content manually, which can be time-consuming and expensive. Major software upgrades sometimes lack backward compatibility, which makes manual conversion necessary.

These problems cause a growing demand for interoperable solutions. Interoperability can be defined as 'the ability of a system or a product to work with other systems or products without special effort on the part of the customer' (see whatis.com). The key issue in this respect is to create and manage information in such a way that opportunities for exchange and reuse of information, either within or between institutions, are maximized (Miller, 2000). The above reasoning led to the definition of interoperability as an important requirement of EML.

Pedagogical meta-model

The requirement for pedagogical flexibility was described above as the demand that the language to be designed should be able to elaborate different theories and models of learning and instruction. In order to meet this demand a pedagogical meta-model has been designed which should be neutral to the different approaches to learning and instruction. The essence of such a model should be that it models other pedagogical models (Koper, 2001), which implies that it serves as an abstraction. Specific pedagogical models, such as problem-based learning or collaborative learning, could be described in terms of the meta-model that is based on research and literature on learning and instruction, and on instructional design theories (see Reigeluth, 1987, 1999; Stolovitch and Keeps, 1999).

The meta-model consists of four axioms (see Koper, 2001):

- People learn by performing activities in an environment in interaction with that environment. This is the most important axiom. When a person has learnt, he or she is able to perform new activities, or perform activities better or faster in similar environments, or is able to perform the same activities in different environments.
- An environment consists of a set of objects and/or human beings that are related in a particular way.
- A person can be encouraged to perform certain activities when:
  - this person, given the requirements in terms of prior knowledge, personal circumstances and the performance context, can perform the activities;
  - the required environment is made available;
  - the person is motivated to perform the activities.
- What has been stated here with respect to a single person, also applies to a group of persons.

It can be concluded from the axioms that instruction should consist of providing students with coherent series of activities, including specific learning environments, so that learning can actually take place. This pedagogical meta-model also supports the first requirement of integrated e-learning, described in the Introduction, which is known as flexibility of educational setting.

Educational Modelling Language

EML has been developed based upon the requirements and the pedagogical meta-model. EML will be described below from several different points of view.

Conceptual structure

The conceptual model of the structure of EML is based upon the pedagogical meta–model. The basic idea is shown in Figure 6.1. The smallest autonomous part in education is labelled a 'unit of study'. A unit of study can take any form (course, workshop, lesson or whatever), depending on its pedagogical function. Within the unit of study there are always one or more roles that can be defined, starting with the student role.

Students learn by doing things ('activities') in a specific context ('environment'). These activities are in fact the stimuli offered to the student to actuate learning. Examples of activities are attending a lesson, studying a chapter, solving a problem, preparing a presentation and so on. However, these activities are not performed in a vacuum but in a specific setting or environment. This environment consists of all kinds of objects such as books, readers, teachers, fellow students and libraries that make the actual learning possible. This model applies to any pedagogical approach. In this respect EML should be able to handle all pedagogical orientations.

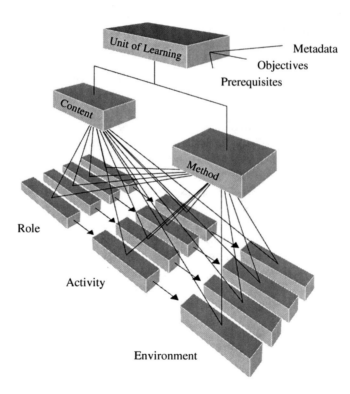

Figure 6.1   *Basic structure of EML*

The personalization requirement has been elaborated as follows. EML units of study contain all the components that can create personalized learning paths based on individual student characteristics. The decision on which characteristics are used and the way they influence the learning path is the choice of the educational designer. Show and hide conditions make it possible to provide the students with adapted units of study, which match their profiles. Parts of a unit of study that may be hidden or shown may vary from specific content parts (such as a text section) to complete activity structures. Students' profiles are created from a combination of variable student properties. These properties may be set by students themselves, by other actors in the learning environment or by the system. Examples of these properties are variables such as prior knowledge, learning style and preferences. These are set at run time. Within so-called 'conditions', the rules can be written down for hiding and showing components based on the properties.

XML binding

Requirements for formalization, medium neutrality and interoperability have led to the decision to implement EML as an XML application (Bray, Paoli and Sperberg-McQueen, 1998). XML (eXtensible Markup Language) is a generally accepted meta-language for the structured description of documents and data based on the ISO standard SGML (Standard Generalized Markup Language).

Figure 6.2 shows the way the conceptual ideas behind EML are translated into an XML document type definition (DTD). This DTD serves as a kind of format to which all EML files must conform. The basic structure of the EML DTD is shown here. Only a selection of the elements and relationships and none of the attributes are shown. All the elements and attributes of EML are described in the EML reference manual (Hermans *et al*, 2000). Both this manual and the complete DTD can be downloaded from eml.ou.nl.

The figure shows the hierarchy of the unit of study. According to this structure each EML file representing a unit of study should at least consist of metadata (general descriptive information), a role definition, and a method section. 'Content' covers activity descriptions and environment specifications, including all kinds of objects that can exist within an environment. Content need not be required. When the content is available elsewhere it can be included in the unit of study by using referring mechanisms in the method.

Designing within EML

The central starting point in creating a pedagogical design is the student who wants to learn. In order to attain the objectives of a unit of study students have to respond to the stimuli (that is, the activities) presented in the learning environment. The learning path and support environment reflect the pedagogical principles that have been advocated. In this way, EML is not pedagogically prescriptive but enables one to implement one's own pedagogical choices.

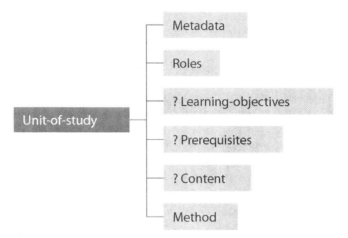

Figure 6.2   *Basic structure of EML binding*

This section describes the steps which have to be taken in order to implement a pedagogical design in EML. Several EML examples are shown. They are accompanied by screenshots taken from the Edubox EML player.

In order to publish, deliver and test EML a system ('Edubox') was designed and developed in which EML files can be imported, published and personalized in several media (see www.ou.nl/edubox). Edubox has currently been developed to the stage that it can import, publish and deliver EML files to the World Wide Web.

Roles

The first step in preparing a design for EML is to specify who plays a role in the instructional design. Student roles and staff roles (such as tutor, instructor or teacher) have been separated in this respect. The latter represent the educational organization or institute (see Figure 6.3). Which roles are present in the EML design depends on the pedagogical model that has been chosen.

EML example 6.1 shows a role declaration within EML. This example has been derived from a problem-based learning model and states that along with the role 'student' there is also a specific subrole 'chair', who has specific responsibilities within this model. In addition to these two student roles there is also a staff role, 'tutor'.

EML example 6.1 Role declaration

```
1.   <Roles>
2.       <Learner Id = "Student">
3.           <Role Id = "Chair"/>
```

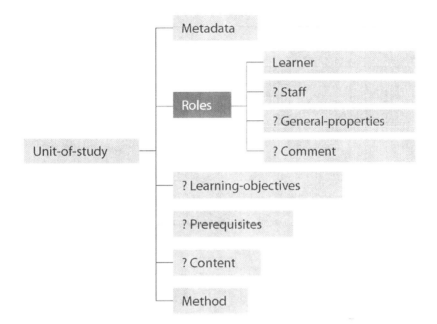

Figure 6.3   *Role specification within EML*

4.   </Learner>
5.   <Staff Id = "Tutor"/>
6.   </Roles>

Activities

The second step in the design is to specify what the people in these roles are expected to do. In EML this is referred to as 'activities' (see Figure 6.4). There are two types of activities: learning activities (to be performed by student roles) and support activities (to be conducted by either staff roles or student roles). For example, in the case of peer assessment these support activities are typically reserved for students. The EML design of the learning activities depends on the pedagogical model, and might take the form of analyzing problems, attending college, searching through literature, presenting findings or taking tests. Typical staff activities consist of assessing students, providing feedback, monitoring, answering questions and so forth.

In EML example 6.2, a learning activity has been briefly elaborated. Typical parts of a learning activity are the 'metadata', the 'learning objectives', the actual instruction, a description of how the activity is to be carried out, and the condition under which an activity is to be considered completed. In this particular case, the completion is set to 'User-choice' (line 23), meaning that users can decide for themselves (for example, by clicking a check box) when the activity has been

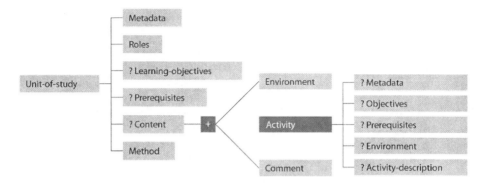

Figure 6.4   *Activity specification within EML*

completed. Completion rules play an essential part in workflow modelling. If explicit rules are stated, the workflow within a course or curriculum can be supported or fully managed by the EML player.

EML example 6.2 Activity specification

```
1.<Activity Id = 'a-conflict'>
2.        <Metadata>
3.                <Title>Identifying an intercultural conflict on the workplace.
                </Title>
4.        </Metadata>
5.        <Learning-objectives>
6.                <Learning-objective Id = 'LO-1'>
7.                        <Objective-description>
8.                                <P>After completing this activity you are
                                able to describe and
9.                                analyze a conflict situation.</P>
10.                        </Objective-description>
11.                        <Objective-type><Skill></Objective-type>
12.                </Learning-objective>
13.        </Learning-objectives>
14.        <Activity-description>
15.                <What>
16.                        <P>In order to have sufficient and realistic material
                        to analyze, you
17.                        will first need to. . .</P>
18.                </What>
19.                <How>
```

20.   <P>Describe the conflict at surface level, ie. . .</P>
21.   </How>
22.   </Activity–description>
23.   <Completed><User-choice/></Completed>
24.</Activity>

In example 6.2, lines 5 to 13 show there is only one learning objective present for this learning activity, which has been characterized as a skill. Instead of stating the learning objective in this position, reference could also have been made to one or more learning objectives stated elsewhere, for example, at course level.

Environment

As was stated above, a learning activity is not performed in a vacuum, but takes place in a specific setting or context. This setting or context is generally referred to as the environment of a learning activity (see Figure 6.5). Thus the next step is to indicate which sources, tools and services an environment may consist of in order to support the student and/or staff. Sources may consist of incorporated or

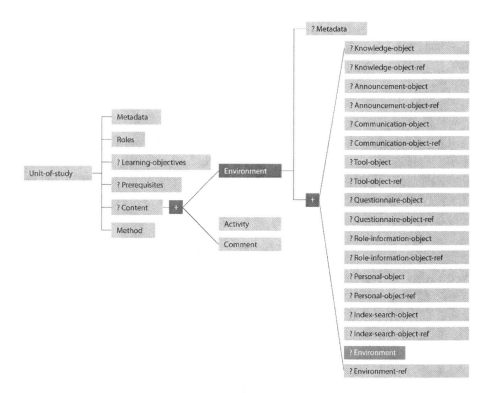

Figure 6.5   *Environment specification within EML*

external (and linked) learning material such as books, articles, cases or references. Tools and services cover objects such as search engines, glossaries, portfolios, notes, e-mail or computer conferences.

EML example 6.3 provides an environment specification. Note that environments can be recursive, meaning that one environment can occur in another. In this way 'environment trees' can be built and environment objects can be classified. The 'Environment-ref' element indicates that other environments are included. These environments and objects belonging to them may have been defined by others.

EML example 6.3 Environment specification in EML

```
1.<Environment Link-name = "support environment">
2.        <Environment-ref Id-ref = "env-curriculum-guide"/>
3.        <Environment Link-name = "module guide">
4.            <Knowledge-object Link-name = "about this module"/>
5.            <Knowledge-object Link-name = "method"/>
6.            <Knowledge-object Link-name = "timetable"/>
7.        </Environment>
8.        <Environment Link-name = "communication">
9.            <Communication-object Link-name = "FirstClass"/>
10.        </Environment>
11.        <Environment-ref Id-ref = "env-who-is-who"/>
12.        <Environment-ref Id-ref = "env-resources"/>
13.        <Environment Link-name = "dossier">
14.            <Role-information-object Link-name = "progress"/>
15.        </Environment>
16.</Environment>
```

A possible rendering of this environment specification by the Edubox system is shown in Figure 6.6. The area on the left provides several nodes representing the environment structure in EML. These nodes can be collapsed or expanded by the user by clicking on the triangle. The leaf nodes represent particular learning objects, tools or services.

Method

Specifying the roles, activities and environments provides the building blocks for creating one or more learning paths throughout a course or curriculum. The next step is to specify how activities, particularly learning activities, are related, what the learning path looks like, and how it can be influenced. The 'Method' section of EML was designed for these purposes (see Figure 6.7).

First, possible relations between activities can be defined within 'activity-structures'. Within these structures, activities can be grouped and put either in a fixed order ('sequence') or free order ('selection'). EML example 6.4 provides an activity structure with a fixed order, called 'Student tasks'. This structure contains

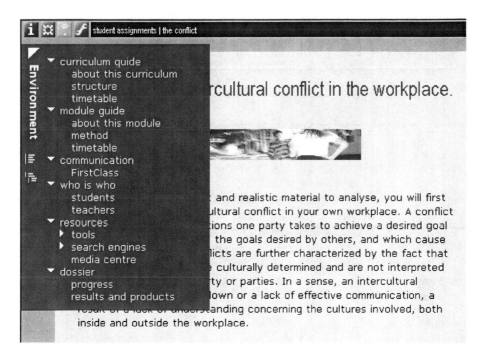

Figure 6.6   *Environment representation in Edubox*

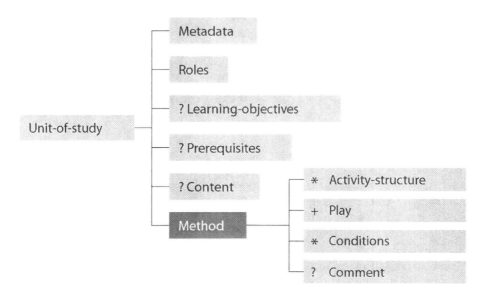

Figure 6.7   *Method specification within EML*

five learning activities (lines 5 to 10) which are to be performed sequentially. The representation of this example in Edubox is shown in Figure 6.8. Note that as a consequence of modelling a sequence, an activity only becomes accessible when the preceding activity has been completed. This is an example of how workflow can be modelled.

EML example 6.4 Sequencing example within EML

```
 1.<Method>
 2.        <Activity-structure Id = "AS-student">
 3.                <Activity-sequence Link-name = "Student tasks">
 4.                        <Environment-ref Id-ref = "Support-
                            environment"/>
 5.                        <Activity-ref Id-ref = "A-Introduction"/>
 6.                        <Activity-ref Id-ref = "A-Conflict"/>
 7.                        <Activity-ref Id-ref = "A-Theory"/>
 8.                        <Activity-ref Id-ref = "A-Analysis"/>
 9.                        <Activity-ref Id-ref = "A-Memo"/>
10.                </Activity-sequence>
11.        </Activity-structure>
12.</Method>
```

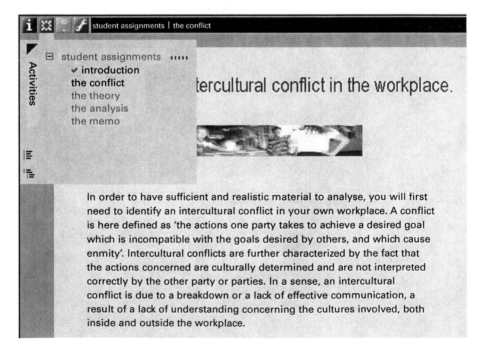

Figure 6.8   *Sequencing example in Edubox*

Second, the educational script or scenario throughout, a course or curriculum for example, should be specified in the 'Play' section of an EML file. In this section, activities, activity structures, or complete units of learning can be assigned to specified roles. EML example 6.5 provides a simple example in which two separate activity structures are assigned to two different roles (Student and Teacher). This means that teachers and students get their own set of activities in run time. Figure 6.9 provides the corresponding views in Edubox.

EML example 6.5 Play example within EML

```
1.<Method>
2.  <Play Id = "Default-play">
3.     <Role-ref Id-ref = "Student"/>
4.     <Activity-structure-ref Id-ref = "AS-student"/>
5.     <Role-ref Id-ref = "Teacher"/>
6.     <Activity-structure-ref Id-ref = "AS-teacher"/>
7.  </Play>
8.</Method>
```

The third part of the method section of an EML file ('Conditions') can be used to specify how the learning path, or parts of it, can be manipulated and adapted (in other words, personalized) to students' characteristics. EML example 6.6 is derived from a problem solving model in which there is a specific student role called 'Chair'. Persons in this role are expected to perform specific activities (line 8) while working in groups, and are provided with additional information within several learning objects, which has been characterized as 'only-for-chair' (line 7).

EML example 6.6 Conditions example within EML

```
 1.<Method>
 2.  <Conditions Id = "Chair-conditions">
 3.     <If>
 4.        <Is><Role-ref Id-ref = "Chair"/></Is>
 5.     </If>
 6.     <Then>
 7.        <Show><Content-type Type = "only-for-chair"/>
 8.        <Activity-structure-ref Id-ref="AS-chair"/></Show>
 9.     </Then>
10.     <Else>
11.        <Hide><Content-type Type = "only-for-chair"/>
12.        <Activity-structure-ref Id-ref="AS-chair"/></Hide>
13.     </Else>
14.  </Conditions>
15.</Method>
```

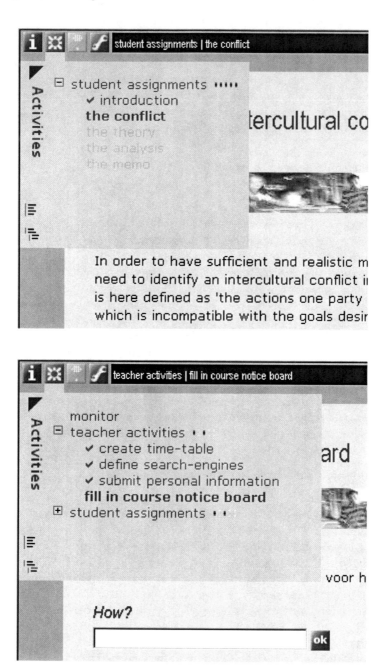

Figure 6.9 *Play example in Edubox*

Curricula

Previously in this chapter a unit of study was presented as the smallest building block in assembling curricula, courses and so forth. The way in which these units of study are connected is expressed as 'Method'.

EML example 6.7 Modelling a curriculum or programme within EML

```
1.<Unit-of-study Id = "sample-curriculum">
2.    <Metadata><Title><P>Sample curriculum</P></Title></Metadata>
3.    <Roles><Learner Id = "Student"/></Roles>
4.    < Method>
5.        <Activity-structure Id = "Course-structure">
6.            <Activity-selection Number-to-select = "3">
7.                <Unit-of-study-ref Worldwide-unique-id-ref = "UoS-Course-1"/>
8.                <Unit-of-study-ref Worldwide-unique-id-ref = "UoS-Course-2"/>
9.                <Unit-of-study-ref Worldwide-unique-id-ref = "UoS-Course-3"/>
10.           </Activity-selection>
11.       </Activity-structure>
12.       <Play>
13.           <Role-ref Id-ref = "Student"/>
14.           <Unit-of-study-ref Worldwide-unique-id-ref = "UoS-
              PostAssessment"/>
15.           <Continue><When-completed/></Continue>
16.           <Role-ref Id-ref = "Student"/>
17.           <Activity-structure-ref Id-ref = "Course-structure"/>
18.           <Continue><When-completed/></Continue>
19.           <Role-ref Id-ref = "Student"/>
20.           <Unit-of-study-ref Worldwide-unique-id-ref = "UoS-
              PostAssessment"/>
21.       </Play>
22.   </Method>
23.</Unit-of-study
```

Lines 13 to 20 of EML example 6.7 show the learning path throughout a simple curriculum. A student starts with some kind of pre-assessment. Having finished this assessment, he or she may continue by choosing one of three specific courses. These courses are wrapped in an 'Activity-structure'. Adding an 'Activity-selection' gives the student the freedom to choose which course to start. The 'Number-to-select' attribute in line 6 puts a completion constraint on this structure. The student must have completed all three courses before he or she can progress to the next part, in this case a post-assessment.

Evaluation

Of course, the proof of the pudding is in the eating. The requirements stated earlier in this chapter and the pedagogical meta-model have resulted in the EML version as described and illustrated above. We should now like to review how the major requirements have been met in this version of EML.

It should be clear from the examples that EML has succeeded in designing a formalized language (requirement 1) for expressing an educational design with a focus on semantics rather than on technical aspects (requirement 3). This statement is supported by the fact that Edubox is able to interpret various EML files and deliver the content in a personalized manner to users in concrete educational settings. Moreover, the choice to develop EML as an application of XML meets demands such as interoperability, compatibility and medium neutrality.

The extent to which EML appears to be suitable for expressing divergent pedagogical models (requirement 2) is of particular interest. After some laboratory tests were performed with EML, several implementations have been developed successfully in a variety of educational settings in the last two years.

One major implementation is situated within the area of higher vocational education. A translation of the pedagogical model of dual mode competency-based learning was made in EML for a hotel management college. Almost all the modules within this dual mode curriculum have been elaborated in EML, and they can be delivered to the students using the Edubox system. EML concepts such as 'activity' and 'environment' appeared to be strong, useful concepts for modelling tasks, and support tools and resources corresponding to the designers' intentions.

At university level, EML is being tested within our own institute, the Open University of the Netherlands (OUNL), as well as within the context of the Digital University (DU), a consortium of four universities and six institutes for higher vocational education. Institutes work together at the DU to create reusable learning materials. Most of these institutes have their 'own' e-learning environments. As a result there is a strong focus upon interoperability, reusability and use of open standards with respect to the learning material. EML appears to be well suited to these demands.

Within the OUNL itself, a number of pilot projects have been initiated within several faculties. The institute has adapted its pedagogical model to competency-based learning in an electronic learning environment (Koper, 2000). Several courses with different instructional designs have been implemented in EML. Another application area can be found within the field of in-company training. A renewed model for training the call centre employees at a major pension fund has been translated and elaborated using EML, which proved to be a powerful instrument in the innovation process.

Moreover, EML proved to be interoperable and sustainable as work on the EML specification evolved (see below). It was possible to design and implement automated translation routines, allowing the 'upgrade' of existing EML materials. A large number of the courses produced using EML are already being successfully converted, thus safeguarding all the investments made in producing the courses.

The way ahead

This chapter has provided a detailed description of EML and its requirements. A great deal of experience has been gained using EML in an increasing number of courses and settings. Although in principle this might satisfy the desire to have a specification that is pedagogically flexible and interoperable, the latter only holds for the scope of our institute, and for some of our partners who are closely involved in the development of EML.

Looking critically at the definition of interoperability (the ability of a system or product to work with other systems or products without special effort on the part of the customer), one can conclude that true interoperability can only be achieved if the following criteria are met:

● A specification should be publicly endorsed by the key players in the field, such as educational content providers (such as publishers), providers of e-learning environments, and the educational community in general. By endorsing this, all key players basically commit themselves to the specification.
● E-learning environment providers should have local support for the specification in their products, guaranteeing interoperability between the different e-learning environments.
● A specification should support standards and other specifications that are generally accepted.

There are a number of ways to achieve the criteria mentioned above. Some time ago it was decided that the best way to proceed with EML was to get the specification accepted by a group of key players (end users, vendors, purchasers and managers), thereby creating a *de facto* standard. Formal standardization would then be the secondary, long-term aim, which would also be the final one.

The great advantage of the approach that has been chosen, is that results can be achieved in a relatively short period of time. An important group of key players with sufficient influence have been organized into the IMS Global Learning Consortium. IMS has a working group dealing with the topic of learning design. In close cooperation with the other parties involved, EML was chosen as the basis for the IMS Learning Design specification. Using EML in this way did not imply that nothing would change. The major difference between EML and the IMS Learning Design specification is the integration of existing IMS specifications into the new specification. However, at the conceptual level there are no differences between EML and the Learning Design specification (IMSLD, 2002). The IMS Learning Design specification has now reached the status of a final specification and is available from imsglobal.org.

References

Bray, T, Paoli, J, and Sperberg-McQueen, C M (1998) *Extensible Markup Language (XML) 1.0*. World Wide Web Consortium (W3c). [Online] http://www.w3.org/TR/REC-xml (accessed 15 February 2003)

Brown, J S, Collins, A, and Duguid, P (1989) Situated cognition and the culture of learning, *Educational Researcher*, **18** (1), pp 32–42

Dillenbourg, P and Schneider, D (1995) Mediating the mechanisms which make collaborative learning sometimes effective, *International Journal of Educational Telecommunications*, **1**, pp 131–46

Hermans, H J H, Koper, E J R, Loeffen, A, Manderveld, J M and Rusman, E M (2000) *Reference Manual for Edubox-EML/XML binding 1.0/1.0* (Beta version), Open University of the Netherlands, Heerlen [Online] http://eml.ou.nl (accessed 15 February 2003)

IMSLD (2002) IMS Learning *Design: Information model, best practice and implementation guide, binding document, schemas* [Online] http://imsglobal.org (accessed 15 February 2003)

Koper, E J R (2000) *From Change to Renewal: Educational technology foundations of electronic learning environments* (inaugural address), Open University of the Netherlands, Heerlen

Koper, E J R (2001) *Modelling Units of Study from a Pedagogical Perspective: The pedagogical meta-model behind EML* [Online] http://eml.ou.nl/introduction/docs/ped-metamodel.pdf (accessed 15 February 2003)

Koper, E J R (2003) Combining reusable learning resources and services to pedagogical purposeful units of learning, in *Reusing Online Resources: A sustainable approach to e-learning*, ed A Littlejohn, pp 46–59, Kogan Page, London

Manderveld, J M and Koper, E J R (1999) Building a competence based electronic learning environment, in *Ed-Media 1999: World conference on educational multimedia, hypermedia and telecommunications*, ed B Collis and R Oliver, pp 1543–44, Association for the Advancement of Computing in Education (AACE), Charlottesville, VA

Miller, P (2000) Interoperability: what is it and why should I want it? *Ariadne*, 24 [Online] http://www.ariadne.ac.uk /issue24/interoperability/intro.html (accessed 15 February 2003)

Rawlings, A, van Rosmalen, P, Koper, E J R, Rodrigues-Artacho, M and Lefrere, P (2002) *Survey of Educational Modelling Languages*, Learning Technologies Workshop, CEN/ISSS Workshop on Learning Technology, Brussels

Reigeluth, C M (ed) (1987) *Instructional Theories in Action*, Lawrence Erlbaum, Hillsdale, NJ

Reigeluth, C M (ed) (1999) *Instructional-Design Theories and Models: A new paradigm of instructional theory*, Lawrence Erlbaum, Mahwah, NJ

Robinson, D G and Robinson, J C (1995) *Performance Consulting: Moving beyond training*, Berrett-Koehler, San Francisco, CA

Schlusmans, K, Slotman, R, Nagtegaal, C and Kinkhorst, G (eds) (1999) *Competentiegerichte leeromgevingen* (Competence based learning environments) Lemma, Utrecht, Netherlands

Scott Grabinger, R (1996) Rich environments for active learning, in *Handbook of research for educational communications and technology*, ed D H Jonassen, pp 665–92) Macmillan, New York

Stolovitch, H D and Keeps, E J (eds) (1999) *Handbook of Human Performance Technology*, Jossey-Bass, San Francisco, CA

Chapter 7

Interface design for digital courses

Huib Tabbers, Liesbeth Kester, Hans Hummel and Rob Nadolski

Introduction

The most important delivery medium in integrated e-learning is the computer interface, not only because it is very suitable for presenting rich environments in which students can work collaboratively, but also because its multimedia capabilities make it possible to present educational content in any modality imaginable. Therefore, it will not come as a surprise that instructional designers have greeted the opportunities presented by networked multimedia computers with open arms. One problem often overlooked in all the enthusiasm, however, is the lack of clear guidelines on what to put where on the screen, and it is often not known what the consequences are of certain choices for the learning processes of the student working with the computer (Park and Hannafin, 1994). Most existing ideas are based on a designer's intuition and common sense rather than theories about how people learn from a computer screen. This can lead to some very satisfactory screen designs, but can also produce designs that make students despair rather than motivate them to learn.

The importance of good interface design might be illustrated by the use of 'banners' on Web sites. No one likes a Web site that is filled with ads that are noisy and flashy and attract the attention away from what one is looking for. Now imagine that a student has to learn something in this overcrowded environment, but does not know where to look and what information is relevant. Moreover imagine what it is like when he or she is simultaneously listening to a narration that does not seem to have any relationship at all to what is presented on screen. Although this search process might be a learning goal in itself, it will not always be the aim of the instructional designer to discourage most of the students by mentally overloading them with information. Usually, the designer will strive for an environment in which students know their way and with which they can work effortlessly, so that all effort can be put to the task at hand, and not to the peculiarities of the specific environment or to the search for disparate pieces of information.

Of course, a lot of research has been done on the relation between interface design and learning, especially in the fields of human–computer interaction and educational psychology. Two important areas of interest are the layout of the graphical user interface and the way in which multimedia content is presented. Recent research has provided some promising results that can be translated into guidelines for interface design to help designers increase the effectiveness of integrated e-learning. In this chapter we will present these guidelines for the design of graphical user interfaces and for the presentation of multimedia content, which are firmly based on both the human-computer interaction and the educational psychology literature, and are illustrated with cases from our own experiences at the Open University of the Netherlands.

Graphical user interfaces

The graphical user interface (GUI) acts as an intermediary between a computer program and the user. In other words, a GUI is a collection of techniques and mechanisms that allow the user to interact with the computer program. The main interaction mechanism in a GUI is a pointing device equivalent to the human hand. With the pointing device in the GUI, the user interacts with the elements in the computer program (that is, objects) by pointing, selecting and manipulating them (Galitz, 1997). A good GUI distinguishes itself predominantly by 'invisibility'. The best GUI designs are the ones most users never notice (Lynch and Horton, 1999). The next sections will focus on principles of good GUI design, guidelines for GUI design in e-learning, and an example of GUI design in actual practice.

Designing GUIs

Before the design of a GUI is even started it must be made clear what are the characteristics of the future users, the task and the context. In a process of investigation and collaboration with the future users it has to be determined who the intended users are, what their characteristics are, what the intended task domain is and what its characteristics are, and finally, in which context the technology will be used (Johnson, 2000). Then a thorough analysis has to be made of the purpose, structure and function of the user interface. A conceptual model has to be created in which a list of objects and actions, a lexicon and task scenarios are set down. When the user, task and context characteristics are made clear and the conceptual model is ready, the actual design process can start. During and after the design process, tests are needed to find out whether a design is working or not. Usability tests (that is, GUI try-outs on future users; see Chapter 8) have to be carried out early in and throughout the development or prototyping phase, to inform the developer about aspects of the GUI that cause difficulty and need adjustment.

In the literature, a lot of guidelines for good GUI design are given but they often have a different level of abstraction and are overlapping or even contradictory (Galitz, 1997; Johnson, 2000; Shneiderman, 1992; Van der Harstt and Maijers, 1999). Moreover, the development of a GUI is always an optimization process in which more practical preconditions have to be met as well. In spite of the problems of overlap, contradiction and practical preconditions, a number of generic guidelines can be distinguished.

Guideline 1: do not complicate the user's task

The GUI should not make the task more difficult than necessary. A good GUI does not let the user perform unnatural acts, avoids computer jargon and visibility of the software's internal workings, finds an optimal balance between power, complexity and usability, makes common tasks easy by providing customization support and wizards, and finally, minimizes the need for deductive reasoning in operating the software. This will only distract users from their own tasks and goals (Johnson, 2000; Van der Harstt and Maijers, 1999).

Guideline 2: promote mastering the GUI

The user has to learn how the GUI works. The design of the GUI should facilitate this process. Therefore it is very important that a developer looks through the eyes of a lay person instead of through his or her own expert eyes while designing a GUI. Experts tend to think that users automatically perceive and understand all features of a GUI the way they have intended it. Needless to say, this is often not the case. Useless confusion at the user's side can be prevented by avoidance of textual, typographical and graphical ambiguity, consistency, and provision of a low-risk environment (Johnson, 2000; Van der Harstt and Maijers, 1999).

Guideline 3: deliver only relevant information

Instead of simply presenting all available information, relevant information should be displayed so that the user's attention is focused on only this information and not distracted from it. Careful display design, preferably by a professional, should facilitate this. Moreover, the software should not change (much) on its own initiative. A good GUI is based on direct manipulation of information by the user. Furthermore, the display changes that occur because of manipulations by the user should be minimal (Johnson, 2000).

Guideline 4: design for responsiveness

Responsiveness, the perceived speed of the software, is very important to users. To optimize the responsiveness it is important that software provides feedback on what it is doing, when it is busy and when not. Moreover, it should let the user know how much time a certain action will take. The software should enable the users to work at their own pace (Johnson, 2000; Van der Harstt and Maijers, 1999).

The guidelines stated above are applicable to all GUI design regardless of software application. Nevertheless, they are usually meant for software that enables the learner to perform a certain task, such as text editors and graphical editors. In the next section it is considered in which way the design of a GUI for educational purposes, that is, the design of a GUI for e-learning software, is different from the GUI design of task performance software.

GUI design in e-learning

In GUI design in e-learning, great emphasis is put on the user's model, which is the set of concepts and expectations a user has of the e-learning software. Although complete overlap of the user's model and the developer's model is an utopia, the developers should at least aim at the closest approximation. The central role of the user in GUI design for e-learning software leads to three more specific guidelines.

Guideline 5: do not neglect individual differences in ICT experience

A user judges a GUI based on earlier experiences with other computer programs or ICT experience in general. A GUI should take the differences in ICT experience between users into account. An inexperienced user will need more scaffolding than an experienced user, and the GUI should provide this.

Guideline 6: support different pedagogical scenarios equally

The goal of e-learning is to allow the user to learn as efficiently as possible. In order to reach this goal, different pedagogical scenarios can be provided. A pedagogical scenario is the range of activities carried out by the user in order to reach the learning goal. These scenarios are based on pedagogical models, in which theoretical principles and prescriptions from learning theories are stated. The user's individual characteristics determine which scenario suits the learning goals best. So a good GUI provides optimal support for each of these pedagogical scenarios.

Guideline 7: optimize individual freedom

In e-learning it is important to facilitate active and independent learning. The users of educational software are responsible for their own learning process. A GUI should therefore respond optimally to the users' initiatives.

Guideline 8: conform to the user's model

This is one of the most important guidelines in GUI design for e-learning. A good GUI uses a metaphor that is known to the user, and that is also suitable for the specific didactic scenario used. Moreover, the metaphor should adhere to the user's expectations, and should be adaptive to the user's needs.

In the next section an example is given in which some of the guidelines stated above are applied.

Casus: developing a GUI for the Edubox player

Edubox is used to deliver tailor-made education based on the functionalities of EML (the Educational Modelling Language, see Chapter 6). The educational potential of the GUI developed for the Web-based Edubox player comes from dynamically combining roles, activities and resources in order to enable personalization of learning in a variety of didactical models (guideline 6).

Users carry out activities according to roles (as either students or staff members) in environments (available tools and resources), all according to the metaphor of a theatrical play (guideline 8). As in a theatrical play, an act includes one or more role players that are 'on stage' at the same time. The activity description tells us what the role player should do with tools and resources included in the environment. An environment may include both learning objects and services such as e-mail and conference facilities.

From the activities section, users start their personalized learning path (guideline 7). While users are online, interaction is captured, conditions are evaluated and personal dossiers are constantly updated, triggering the Web player. Results can vary from displaying specific feedback to activating other users by sending announcements and/or assigning tasks.

Within the tools and resources section of the screen, resources become available, depending on activities, roles or even personalized dossier elements. Data stored in personal dossiers allow tutors to monitor and support the learning process. Based on individual student profiles (preferences, prior knowledge, and learning results, which are contained in student portfolios), the system can provide alternate feedback, content and interaction, as defined in the underlying educational model. For instance, students may want to receive either more theoretical information (like definitions) or more practical information (like cases) about the subject matter, or may require more or less support in learning to work with the user interface and its tools, and so on (guideline 5).

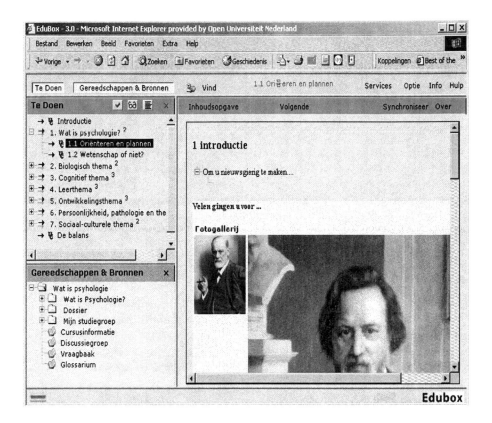

Figure 7.1   *Screen example of a digital workbook in the domain of psychology produced with an Edubox 3.0 player*

Figure 7.1 shows a screen example of a digital workbook produced with the Edubox player. It centres around a number of introductory psychological themes, each containing assignments for students. It shows an introductory section on 'What is psychology?' with learning content in the big window (pictures and information about famous psychologists), an activity tree in the upper left window, and available tools and resources (the student's personal dossier, information about the study group) in the lower left window.

Presenting multimedia content

An environment for e-learning is meant not only to be navigated through, or to provide the means for individuals communicating with each other, but also to present educational content. One of the main advantages of multimedia computers is that they can present this content in any form, from written text to video, and that these presentation modalities can be used simultaneously. However, because the learner has a limited capacity for processing information, overload can be a serious threat in e-learning environments. How to deal with presenting multimedia content in instructions is an important concern in the work of Richard Mayer (2001) on multimedia learning and the work on cognitive load theory by John Sweller (1999). Both researchers try to base their design guidelines on the cognitive architecture of the learner's mind. This mind consists, roughly speaking, of an unlimited long-term memory, in which all prior knowledge is stored, and a limited working memory, in which new information is processed and linked to information in long-term memory. The capacity limitations of working memory have some important consequences for the presentation of multimedia content in e-learning environments. This leads to the creation of guidelines, which are discussed in the following sections on split attention, multiple modalities and redundancy effects.

Prevent split attention

When learners have to integrate different information elements that cannot be understood on their own, such as a picture and an accompanying textual explanation, they have to switch from one element to the other. That means that they have to keep one information element active in working memory while searching for the other. Especially with multimedia, when people have to integrate verbal and pictorial information, like for example a graph and an on-screen explanation of how to read the graph, this can lead to a high working memory load, and sometimes even an overload that can hinder the learning process. This overload can be found in any situation in which learners have to split their attention between different sources of information. The main question is how to prevent this split attention.

Guideline 9: integrate information elements that refer to each other and cannot be understood separately

A very effective way of reducing split attention is to integrate physically the separate information elements that refer to each other. For example if explanatory text is placed inside a picture instead of under it, or the meaning of a foreign word is given directly above it instead of after the whole text, the amount of search is reduced, and mental integration of information elements will be much easier to accomplish. This way working memory load is reduced, and more capacity becomes available for the actual learning process. The positive effect of integrating information elements on learning has been demonstrated several times (Chandler and Sweller, 1991, 1992; Moreno and Mayer, 1999; Sweller *et al*, 1990; Tarmizi and Sweller, 1988; Yeung, Jin and Sweller, 1997). It is interesting that the same effect was also found when learners had to split their attention between a computer screen and an external source. Experiments showed that the use of either a written manual or an on-screen tutorial was superior to a mixed mode of learning, in which a combination of paper-based and on-screen information was used when learning a computer programming language (Cerpa, Chandler and Sweller, 1996; Chandler and Sweller, 1996; Sweller and Chandler, 1994). This implies that the designer of an integrated e-learning environment should take care that the learner who is working on a relatively limited task presented on the computer screen does not need any external sources like manuals to prevent working memory overload.

Information elements on a computer screen have to be not only physically integrated in order to prevent mental overload, but also synchronized. Information elements that are presented simultaneously can be integrated more easily, which leads to better learning results than when they are presented sequentially (Mayer and Anderson, 1992; Mayer *et al*, 1999; Mayer and Sims, 1994).

Use multiple modalities

Guideline 10: present text accompanying an animation as a narration

One alternative way of preventing learners from splitting their attention between a picture and text on a computer screen is presenting the text as a narration. This way the learner can simultaneously look at the picture or animation and listen to the text, so that working memory will not be overloaded. Moreover, as working memory has a separate subsystem for audio, its capacity is used more efficiently and overload is prevented. This 'modality effect' has been demonstrated in several experiments, in which better learning results were found when text was presented as audio rather than on-screen text (Jeung, Chandler and Sweller, 1997; Kalyuga, Chandler and Sweller, 1999, 2000; Mayer and Moreno, 1998; Moreno and Mayer, 1999; Mousavi, Low and Sweller, 1995; Tindall-Ford, Chandler and Sweller, 1997). However, it should be noted that this guideline to use audio only applies when time is limited and the instructions can only be studied once. With more time, or the possibility for the learner to set the pacing of the instruction, on-screen text is just as effective as audio (Tabbers, Martens and Van Merriënboer, 2001).

Prevent redundancy

So far, the guidelines for presenting multimedia content only apply to the situation in which two separate information sources like a picture and text cannot be understood separately. Sometimes this will not be the case. For example, some designers will present pictures that are self-contained, like a picture that shows the flow of current through an electrical circuit with arrows, and add some explanatory text to it that gives the same information about the current, only this time in words. In a comparable situation, text is presented on-screen and at the same time as a narration. Most designers think that this redundant information has a neutral effect, and will not be harmful to the learning process, so they decide to present the information twice, just to be sure. However, experiments have shown that presenting redundant information does have a negative impact on learning (Chandler and Sweller, 1991; Kalyuga, Chandler and Sweller, 1999; Sweller and Chandler, 1994), which leads to the following guidelines.

Guideline 11: remove any information that has already been presented in a way that can be understood on its own

The explanation is that all information has to be processed in working memory, which has a limited capacity. Processing redundant information will only overload the system, and will not be productive to learning.

Guideline 12: remove any information that is irrelevant to what has to be learnt

Not only can information that is presented in more than one way have a negative effect; adding 'nice' extra information elements, like illustrations or music or irrelevant sounds, can also lead to less learning (Harp and Mayer, 1998; Moreno and Mayer, 2000). Although the designer might think that decorating the interface with unnecessary extras will have a motivating effect on the learner, he or she should bear in mind that the learning process will be deteriorated, especially for novice learners.

Guideline 13: remove any information that the user already knows

Information that the user already knows can also be redundant, for example an on-screen explanation to a picture with which the user is already familiar. An expert in a certain area will not need the information that is essential to a novice. Having to process this unnecessary information increases the working memory load and also has a negative influence on learning (Kalyuga, Chandler and Sweller, 1998, 1999, 2000). This adds an interesting twist to the design of an e-learning environment, because the learner will gain expertise by studying the multimedia content. That implies that information will become redundant while working on a task. One way to deal with this is by scaffolding the multimedia content, in that all explanatory texts are gradually removed from the instructions. That leads to a final guideline for the presentation of multimedia content in integrated e-learning:

Guideline 14: build up the instructions by removing information that has become redundant as a result of increasing expertise

Discussion

So far, 14 guidelines have been discussed that should be applied when designing the computer interface in an integrated e-learning environment. The first eight are all related to the design of a GUI:

1. Do not complicate the user's task.
2. Promote mastering the GUI.
3. Deliver only relevant information.
4. Design for responsiveness.
5. Do not neglect individual differences in ICT experience.
6. Support different pedagogical scenarios equally.
7. Optimize individual freedom.
8 Conform to the user's model.

The next six are related to presenting multimedia content:

9. Integrate information elements that refer to each other and cannot be understood separately.
10. Present text accompanying an animation as a narration.
11. Remove any information that is already presented in a way that can be understood on its own.
12. Remove any information that is irrelevant to what has to be learnt.
13. Remove any information that the user already knows.
14. Build up the instructions by removing information that has become redundant as a result of increasing expertise.

All of these guidelines have an empirical basis, either in the human–computer interaction literature or in educational psychology. The two sets of guidelines are supplementary, as they are aimed at different elements of screen design. The main difference however between the guidelines for GUIs and the guidelines for the presentation of multimedia content is that the first are more aimed at adapting to the individual needs of the user, while the latter give us generic rules which can be applied to all users. On the other hand, the common theme in all guidelines is not to overload the learner with elements that can disrupt the learning process. Learning in an integrated e-learning environment should be enabled and not be hindered by what is presented on screen.

References

Cerpa, N, Chandler, P and Sweller, J (1996) Some conditions under which integrated computer-based training software can facilitate learning, *Journal of Educational Computing Research*, **15**, pp 345–67

Chandler, P and Sweller, J (1991) Cognitive load theory and the format of instruction, *Cognition and Instruction*, **8**, pp 293–332

Chandler, P and Sweller, J (1992) The split-attention effect as a factor in the design of instruction, *British Journal of Educational Psychology*, **62**, pp 233–46

Chandler, P and Sweller, J (1996) Cognitive load while learning to use a computer program, *Applied Cognitive Psychology*, **10**, pp 151–70

Galitz, W O (1997) *The Essential Guide to User Interface Design: An introduction to GUI design principles and techniques*, John Wiley, New York

Harp, S F and Mayer, R E (1998) How seductive details do their damage: a theory of cognitive interest in science learning, *Journal of Educational Psychology*, **90**, pp 414–34

Jeung, H, Chandler, P and Sweller, J (1997) The role of visual indicators in dual sensory mode instruction, *Educational Psychology*, **17**, pp 329–43

Johnson, J (2000) *GUI Bloopers: Don'ts and do's for software developers and web designers*, Morgan Kaufmann, San Francisco, CA

Kalyuga, S, Chandler, P and Sweller, J (1998) Levels of expertise and instructional design, *Human Factors*, **40**, pp 1–17

Kalyuga, S, Chandler, P and Sweller, J (1999) Managing split-attention and redundancy in multimedia instruction, *Applied Cognitive Psychology*, **13**, pp 351–71

Kalyuga, S, Chandler, P and Sweller, J (2000) Incorporating learner experience into the design of multimedia instruction, *Journal of Educational Psychology*, **92**, pp 126–36

Lynch, P J and Horton, S (1999) *Web Style Guide: Basic design principles for creating web sites*, Yale University Press, New Haven, CN and London

Mayer, R E (2001) *Multimedia Learning*, Cambridge University Press, New York

Mayer, R E and Anderson, R B (1992) The instructive animation: helping students build connections between words and pictures in multimedia learning, *Journal of Educational Psychology*, **84**, pp 444–52

Mayer, R E and Moreno, R (1998) A split-attention effect in multimedia learning: evidence for dual processing systems in working memory, *Journal of Educational Psychology*, **90**, pp 312–20

Mayer, R E and Sims, V K (1994) For whom is a picture worth a thousand words? Extensions of a dual-coding theory of multimedia learning, *Journal of Educational Psychology*, **86**, pp 389–401

Mayer, R E, Moreno, R, Boire, M and Vagge, S (1999) Maximizing constructivist learning from multimedia communications by minimizing cognitive load, *Journal of Educational Psychology*, **91**, pp 638–43

Moreno, R and Mayer, R E (1999) Cognitive principles of multimedia learning, *Journal of Educational Psychology*, **91**, pp 358–68

Moreno, R, and Mayer, R E (2000) A coherence effect in multimedia learning: the case for minimizing irrelevant sounds in the design of multimedia instructional messages, *Journal of Educational Psychology*, **92**, pp 117–25

Mousavi, S Y, Low, R and Sweller, J (1995) Reducing cognitive load by mixing auditory and visual presentation modes, *Journal of Educational Psychology*, **87**, pp 319–34

Park, I and Hannafin, M J (1994) Empirically-based guidelines for the design of interactive multimedia, *Educational Technology, Research and Development*, **41**, pp 66–85

Shneiderman, B (1992) *Designing the User Interface: Strategies for effective human–computer interaction* (2nd edn), Addison Wesley, Reading, MA

Sweller, J (1999) *Instructional Design in Technical Areas*, ACER Press, Camberwell, Victoria, Australia

Sweller, J and Chandler, P (1994) Why some material is difficult to learn, *Cognition and Instruction*, **12**, pp 185–233

Sweller, J, Chandler, P, Tierney, P and Cooper, M (1990) Cognitive load as a factor in the structuring of technical material, *Journal of Experimental Psychology*, **119** (2), pp 176–92

Tabbers, H K, Martens, R L and Van Merriënboer, J J G (2001) The modality effect in multimedia instructions, *Proceedings of the 23rd Annual Conference of the Cognitive Science Society*, pp 1024–29

Tarmizi, R A and Sweller, J (1988) Guidance during mathematical problem solving, *Journal of Experimental Psychology*, **80** (4), pp 424–36

Tindall-Ford, S, Chandler, P and Sweller, J (1997) When two sensory modes are better than one, *Journal of Experimental Psychology: Applied*, **3**, pp 257–87

Van der Harstt, G and Maijers, R (1999) *Effectief GUI ontwerp Een praktische ontwerpaanpak voor browser- en Windows interfaces* (Effective GUI design: a practical design approach to browser- and Windows interfaces) Academic Service, Schoonhoven, Netherlands

Yeung, A S, Jin, P and Sweller, J (1997) Cognitive load and learner expertise: split-attention and redundancy effects in reading with explanatory notes, *Contemporary Educational Psychology*, **23**, pp 1–21

Chapter 8

Usability evaluation of integrated e-learning

Fred Paas and Olga Firssova

Introduction

The adoption of innovative approaches to the design and delivery of education, such as integrated e-learning (IEL), requires a re-engineered vision of the educational process. For educational technologists the challenge becomes to produce competence for the individual student through embedding e-learning in a well designed student-centred educational system. This should consist of a carefully considered mix of classroom learning, distance education, self-study, Web-based learning and learning on the job. These changes exert pressure on educational technologists to develop IEL before empirically based guidelines and standards have been extensively developed and evaluated.

The process of evaluation is inherent in the course of any instructional systems development. As the demand for IEL grows, so too will the need for its systematic evaluation (Owston, 2000). Because of the rapid growth and technical development of the Internet and multimedia technology, virtually no comprehensive sources have emerged as guides for the design and evaluation of usable IEL. However, for each of the individual components of the integrated e-learning mix, a range of evaluation methodologies and tools and standards is available for the usability of human–computer interfaces, which may offer insight into achieving usable IEL. It is clear that apart from these existing methodologies and tools for the composition of the mix, an important focus of usability evaluation of IEL should be its unique characteristic, the integrative component.

Generally speaking, usability evaluation focuses on the whole system faced by the user. However, with IEL the whole system consists of a complex mix of interrelated multiple subsystems that have to be geared to one another to be effective in achieving specified educational goals. Because these subsystems are the foundation of the whole system, the usability of each subsystem can be considered a necessary but not sufficient condition of guaranteeing the usability of the whole system. It is possible that each component is very well designed and is rated as highly usable, but that the IEL system has unknown effects on learning.

This chapter presents a range of potential methodologies and tools that might enable evaluators of 'integrated' e-learning to identify usability strengths and weaknesses and rectify the latter. This chapter presents the concept of usability, the steps to be taken in usability evaluation, basic guidelines for the usability evaluation of IEL, and finally a discussion of the usability evaluation of IEL.

Usability

The fundamental tenet of usability is that a product (whether it is physical or virtual) or a system should be easy to use, effective and enjoyable from the user's perspective (Preece, Rogers and Sharp, 2002). Levi and Conrad (1996) refer to usability as the degree to which the system assists a user in completing a task. Norman (1998) considers products as usable and understandable when the user can understand what to do and can appreciate what is going on. In 1998, the International Organization for Standardization (ISO) presented a standard for the ergonomics requirements for office work with visual display terminals (ISO 9241). Part 11 of this international standard defines usability as 'the extent to which a product can be used by specified users to achieve specified goals with effectiveness, efficiency and satisfaction in a specified context of use'. On the basis of this standard and using guidelines from the field of human–computer interaction (see Dix *et al*,1998; Nielsen, 1994; Norman, 1998; Preece, Rogers and Sharp, 2002), the concept of usability can be argued to encompass the following eight attributes: effectiveness, efficiency, learnability, memorability, flexibility, robustness, error minimization and satisfaction.

- Effectiveness refers to the user performance of specific tasks in terms of task completion and accuracy.
- Efficiency refers to the temporal, mental, physical and financial resources used to achieve the level of effectiveness.
- Learnability refers to the extent to which the system is easy to learn, so that the user can rapidly begin effective interaction and achieve maximal performance.
- Memorability refers to the extent to which the users are required to learn the system over again each time they use it, with the implication that the system should be easy to remember.

- Flexibility refers to the multiplicity of ways the user and system exchange information.
- Robustness refers to the level of support provided to the user in determining successful achievement and assessment of goals.
- Error minimization refers to the extent to which the system is error-prone, and/or the extent to which the errors users make can be reduced and/or are not fatal.
- Satisfaction refers to the extent to which the users accept the system and are satisfied with their progress on completing a task by using the system.

Usability evaluation

This section describes the steps that are necessary to arrive at a reliable evaluation of the usability of IEL. The primary goal of usability evaluation is to improve the usability of the system. According to Lee (1999), usability evaluation represents the systematic process of determining whether a system meets predefined, quantifiable usability levels for specific types of real users carrying out specific real tasks. It can be conducted diagnostically during development to determine what is working well, with a view to continuing with it, or to identify and fix what is not working satisfactorily. It can also be conducted at the end of the development cycle to verify that everything is under control or to show to what extent the pre-set goals have been met. In addition, the IEL or its components can be compared to alternative designs at any point of the development cycle.

Traditionally, usability evaluation has had a strong focus on human–computer systems. Recently the concept of Web usability has received a great deal of attention (Corry, Frick and Hansen, 1997; Nielsen, 1999). Although the Web component of IEL can easily be subjected to usability evaluation, it is not common to refer to usability evaluation with regard to the other components of IEL such as classroom learning, distance education, self-study and learning on the job. In this chapter we discuss how the general approach of usability evaluation can be translated into the language of usability evaluation of IEL. A good starting point is provided by Söderberg (2000: 231) who has made an educational translation of the ISO definition of usability as 'the extent to which an educational product can be used by an individual student in order to achieve specified educational goals suited to their purpose with productivity and satisfaction in a given training situation'. Söderberg argues that the educational goals are the central factors for the training. Goals such as competence must be designed and formulated in such a way that the training can be measured against them.

As a first step in the process of usability evaluation of IEL, all components of the system need to be described in such a way that the evaluation can be reproduced. This means that the relevant characteristics of the learners (such as personal attributes, personal details, education, available skills and knowledge); the equipment (hardware, software and materials); and the physical and social environment (for example, workplace and family situation) have to be described. In addition, the usability goals and the task description in terms of the activities that need to be carried out to achieve the goals have to be described. Typically, a set of key users' tasks representing the overall task is selected from the results of a task analysis in which all user tasks and sub-tasks have been identified. However, in order to improve the usability of the whole system, any part of the system may be subject to evaluation in principle.

The usability goals or requirements are specified on the basis of the usability characteristics that have to be met by the learners. These include effectiveness, efficiency, satisfaction and learnability. It should be noted that for usability evaluation of the overall IEL system, measures can be specified for the whole system or for the components of the system individually. Overall usability measures with regard to effectiveness can relate to the percentage of goals achieved, the percentage of users successfully completing a task, or the average accuracy of completed tasks. With regard to efficiency, overall usability measures can relate to the time required to complete a task, tasks completed per unit time, or the monetary cost of performing the task. Satisfaction measures can be based on a rating scale for satisfaction, usage rate over time, or the frequency of complaints.

The next step in the usability evaluation process is defining the usability goals metrically by establishing the criterion values of the measures of usability. This is done on the basis of the requirements for the IEL and the needs of the organization setting the criteria. The following criteria are examples of overall and component usability goals for IEL in terms of criterion values of the efficiency and effectiveness measures:

- Overall system efficiency: learners will be able to successfully complete the course in less than 100 hours. The cost per learner should not exceed 250 euro.
- Component efficiency: learners will be able to successfully complete the study of the written materials of the course in less than 20 hours. The cost of the written materials of the course per learner should not exceed 40 euro.
- Overall effectiveness: at least 80 per cent of the learners should be able to complete the course satisfactorily.
- Component effectiveness: at least 90 per cent of the learners should be able to master the written course materials.

Following the definition of the usability goals, the evaluation can be planned and the type of evaluation method and data collection techniques selected. According to Preece (1993), the choice of a particular evaluation method depends upon various factors including the exact purpose of evaluation; the stage of design and development at which it is carried out; the question of ecological validity (permissibility of biases in data collection); the external limitations imposed on the evaluation process (time constraints, development cycle, cost and availability of equipment/ expertise); and the practical constraints of integrating evaluation with educational practice (expert evaluation and survey methods versus observational techniques and testing).

According to Rubin (1994), the next step in the usability evaluation process is to develop a plan which serves as a blueprint for the evaluation. As the main means of communication among the development team, it describes the required resources. Then, in the following order, representative participants need to be selected and recruited, the test materials need to be prepared, the test needs to be conducted, the participants have to be debriefed, and the data need to be transformed into findings and recommendations. For a detailed account of these steps, see Rubin (1994).

Usability evaluation methods

The different usability evaluation methods are presented in this section. A variety of evaluation methodologies can be found in the literature. The most general distinction is between analytical and empirical methods, with analytical evaluation focusing on characteristics and trade-offs of the system, while empirical evaluation provides facts on user interaction with the system (Rosson and Carroll, 2002). Both approaches can be combined in mediated evaluation, when the results of analytic evaluation throughout the design process become the source of empirical studies at later stages of the design and development cycle.

Generally, three main categories of usability evaluation methods can be distinguished: inspection, inquiry and testing (see Hom, nd).

The usability inspection approach examines usability-related aspects of a user interface. Commonly used inspection methods are cognitive walk-through, heuristic evaluation and pluralistic walk-through. This approach is also known as predictive evaluation (Preece, Rogers and Sharp, 2002).

In the usability inquiry approach, information is obtained about learners' likes, dislikes, needs and understanding of the system. The information is gathered by talking to them, observing them using the system in real work situations, or letting them answer questions, both orally and in writing. Inquiry methods include among others surveys, interviews, focus groups, panels and contextual inquiries.

The usability testing approach attempts to obtain information on how the user interface supports the users to do their tasks by analysing the results of representative users working on typical tasks using the system (or the prototype). Testing methods may include experiments, prototype evaluation, co-discovery and trial runs.

Whereas usability inspection is basically performed by experts early in the design and development process, inquiry and testing are performed by the end-users later in this process. Within each methodology a variety of data collection methods can be used to determine the usability of a system, including observation, interview/verbal reports, thinking aloud, questionnaires, audio–video recordings, auto data-logging programs, software support and expert reviews.

Table 8.1 presents a detailed overview of the different evaluation methods. It shows their purpose, data generation and collection techniques, the description of the method, the stage of the design and development when it is held, by whom it is performed, and the advantages and disadvantages of the technique.

Guidelines for usability evaluation of integrated e-learning

Due to the large number of components of IEL, the innumerable interactions between these components and the large number of available usability evaluation methods and techniques, it is impossible to present a complete picture of usability evaluation. However, with regard to the educational effectiveness of IEL, we can present some general guidelines for the whole system, and some specific guidelines, which are mainly related to the computer or the Web component of IEL.

With regard to the IEL system, it is important to recognize that IEL creates more 'affordances' and opportunities for learning than traditional learning environments. The learners frequently have to master different learning tools and materials, which have to be used separately or in combination under varying circumstances, and with different and continuously changing content (Collis and Moonen, 2001). This imposes a considerable burden on the cognitive system of the learners, and suggests that for IEL, additional principles such as the tuning of the different components of the IEL system are important. In general, there should be no redundancy in the components, that is, they should complement each other. Learners should never have to work with two or more components simultaneously, as this conflicts with our attentional system. Furthermore, the educational effectiveness of the IEL system is determined by the learners' perception of how easy a system is to use and how useful it proves to be; in other words, user satisfaction.

With regard to the components of the IEL system, it is important to check whether they are consistent with universal psychological facts. Chen *et al* (1997) note that many usability problems of Web applications are because of a lack of consideration of the cognitive limitations of working memory, attention and decision making. Similarly, Raskin (2000: 4) states that 'that crucial first step – making sure that the interface design accords with universal psychological facts – is customarily omitted in the design process'. For the usability evaluation situation, this means that one of the first steps in the usability test of the IEL system should be to check whether the IEL system is compatible with our cognitive system and the common mental attributes shared by the user population. For example, as it is generally accepted that Gestalt theory may be used to improve learning via the educational screen design (Preece *et al*, 1994), the usability evaluation of educational screen design could start by determining if the screens are consistent with the Gestalt laws of balance/symmetry, continuation, closure, figure/ground, focal point, isomorphic correspondence, proximity, similarity, simplicity and unity/harmony (see Chang, Dooley and Tuovinen, 2002).

With regard to the educational effectiveness of the Web component of IEL, Hall (1998) and Söderberg (2000) have identified several important specific success factors, such as the chance to study on one's own, tutors and mentors who support and follow up the training, time-delayed (asynchronous) delivery over the Internet and Intranets, multimedia applications delivered with time displacement, course and test administration, and training in real time (synchronously) using

Table 8.1 *Detailed overview of usability evaluation methods*

Type of evaluation	Evaluation method	Purpose of evaluation	Data generation and collection method techniques	Description of the method	Design and development stage	Evaluation performed by	Advantages	Disadvantages
				Usability inspection				
Analytic	Formal usability inspection	Examine usability of user interface; find design flaws early in design process	Specifications; questionnaires; observation; verbal protocols; video or audio recording	Inspectors walk through tasks with the user's goals and purpose in mind	Early in design and development process	Experts in the field, specially assigned inspectors	Can be held on early prototypes of design specifications or paper mock-ups	Does not provide insights into real user patterns of use and problems
Analytic	Heuristic evaluation	Find usability defects early in design process	Heuristics; checklists; verbal protocols; video or audio recording	Experts assess design guided by heuristics	Particularly well suited for earlier stages of the design process	Experts (usually 2–5)	Diagnostic; high potential return on investment; cost-effective	Subject to bias; locating experts may present a problem; no real users involved
Analytic	Cognitive walk-through	Find interaction design flaws and user difficulties	Usability specifications; checklists; verbal protocols; video or audio recording	Experts role play users performing the real tasks on early prototype	Early in design process	Expert evaluators	Cost-effective; can be held on design specifications; can provide a typical usage scenario	Restrictions in role playing; locating experts may be problematic; no real users involved

Analytic	Pluralistic walk-through	Evaluate user interface on interaction	Verbal protocols; observation; critical incident taking, questionnaires	Users, developers, and usability professionals collaborate to analyse the system	Early in development process	Users together with developers and usability professionals	Interaction between users and developers helps resolve usability problems faster	Requires special organization; involves high costs and time investments

Usability inquiry

Empirical	Survey	Obtain information about users' preferences or understanding of the system	Questionnaires; user interviews	Data collected from questionnaires or interviews	Implementation and evaluation stage (late in design process)	Users	Can be diagnostic; can be used for large groups; replicable	Information is subjective; low response rates; time-consuming
Empirical	Interview; focus group; panel	Obtain information on users' needs; get user feedback on the system	User interviews; retrospective verbal protocols	Data collected from user interviews, panels or focus groups	Analysis (formulation of users' needs); implementation and evaluation stage	Users	Flexible; allows in-depth attitude and experience probing	Information is subjective; time-consuming; requires special organization; data analysis may be complex
Empirical	Contextual inquiry	Gather information about problems experienced by users on product use	Contextual interviews; observation; verbal protocols; video or audio recording	Developers observe users performing real tasks and discuss the process with them	Early in development process	Users	Natural context of use; can help identify the causes of users' actions and decisions	High costs; difficult to analyse and interpret data

Table 8.1 *(Cont.)*

Type of evaluation	Evaluation method	Purpose of evaluation	Data generation and collection method techniques	Description of the method	Design and development stage	Evaluation performed by	Advantages	Disadvantages
				Usability testing				
Empirical	Experiments	Examine user performance on the structured tasks; gain insights into what users actually do	Logging of activities; performance measures; verbal protocols; observation; video-recording; questionnaires	Users perform clearly defined 'typical' user tasks in a controlled environment	Development, implementation and evaluation (late in the design process)	Users (5–20) or experts as user to distinguish patterns of use	Powerful; reliable; replicable; finds highly used (or unused) features	High costs; data analysis; time-consuming; low ecological validity; can affect users' performance level
Empirical	Co-discovery	Gather information about problems experienced by users on product use	Participant observation; verbal protocols; video or audio recording	Developers observe 2 users who work together and verbalize the process	Any stage of the design and development process	2 users	Can bring out more insights than a single participant vocalizing his or her thoughts	High costs; difficult to analyse and interpret data

Empirical	Prototype evaluation/testing	Get feedback from users on the system 'under construction'	Verbal or written protocols or notes; informal feedback	Designers let users try out the product and get their feedback	Any stage of the design and development process	1–2 users and/or experts	Provides data on user preferences and experiences; low costs; can be held in natural settings	Information can be subjective; provides incomplete picture
Empirical	Trial-run	Reveal problems and improve usability of the system before its release	Performance measures; logging of activities; questionnaires; interviews	Users perform the whole range of tasks and activities as they would in real life	Implementation and evaluation stages (late in the design process)	Users	Powerful; reliable; valid data; high ecological validity	High costs; time-consuming; requires special organization; user behaviour can be affected by evaluation

Sources: Preece, 1993; Preece, Rogers and Sharp, 2002; Hom, nd

video-conferencing systems. Based on these success factors, the following list of conditions can be constructed for the usability evaluation of the Web component of IEL:

- The content should be both relevant to the target group and of appropriate quality.
- The methodology should be designed in such a way that learning takes place.
- The operations require input from the learner. Motivating components are needed to stimulate student interaction.
- The learners receive feedback based on their interaction. In some cases the program adjusts the level of instruction to conform to the level of the learner.
- The use of media should have a design and tone that are aesthetically attractive and pleasing, and that are relevant to the target group.
- Navigation through the teaching material should facilitate overview and use.
- The student should be able to get his or her learning continuously evaluated by being able to log the teaching materials and activities.
- The objectives of each program are clearly defined.
- The operations for the use of the program are intuitively or clearly stated.
- The tone of the instruction is conversational rather than commanding.

In order to use these measures of usability in an evaluation, they need to be defined metrically (see the section on usability evaluation).

Discussion

In this chapter we have seen that in order to improve the usability of an IEL system by identifying and rectifying usability deficiencies, the following 10 steps need to be taken:

1. Describe all components of the system in such a way that the evaluation can be reproduced.
2. Describe the usability goals and the task description in terms of the activities that need to be carried out to achieve the goals.
3. Specify usability goals on the basis of the usability characteristics that must be met for the learners.
4. Define the usability goals metrically.
5. Select the type of usability evaluation method and data collection techniques.
6. Develop an evaluation plan.
7. Select representative participants.
8. Conduct the evaluation.
9. Debrief participants.
10. Transform data into findings and recommendations.

According to Rubin (1994), usability evaluation is most powerful and effective when implemented as part of an iterative product development process, that is, within a cycle of designing, testing, measuring and then redesigning throughout the product development life cycle. Two general approaches to the design and development of IEL systems can be distinguished that meet this criterion by incorporating evaluation and taking account of the learners' perceptions from the beginning to the end: usability engineering and participatory design.

In the usability engineering approach, a focus on usability more or less permeates the design and the development process, integrating usability heuristics with general design principles and guidelines (Nielsen, 1994). This approach incorporates results of usability studies into different stages of the engineering life cycle, from early analysis design through to final testing and follow-up studies. For IEL the usability engineering approach means that there should be a focus on usability throughout the design and the development process, integrating usability heuristics with other principles and guidelines that exist for educational products. Each component of the IEL system needs to be tested independently, bearing in mind that the integrated function of the whole system is the production of competence for the individual learner. Moreover, in the context of the market and economic aspects it is important to understand that the later in the design cycle the usability is tested, the higher the cost of solving problems. It is not possible to effectively test the usability of a product from the development process retrospectively (Wichanski, 2000).

Participatory design is an approach that focuses on collaborating with the intended users throughout the design and development process, rather than on designing a system for them. This means taking social and organizational requirements into account at an early stage in the development cycle (see Kensing and Blomberg, 1998).

It is clear that the challenges of IEL, as far as the use of the learning systems and tools is concerned, make the task of usability evaluation particularly important. It is not common practice today to engage in usability evaluation of new products within the educational establishment. Consequently, there is no in-depth understanding of the effort, time and resources needed for IEL. However, in line with developments in other fields, the payoffs that can be expected in this context from the strategic use of a participatory usability engineering approach are reduced production costs, reduced support costs, reduced costs in use and improved product quality.

To realize strategic usability evaluation within the educational field educational technologists should be able to anticipate two typical obstacles to strategic usability, namely, resource constraints (eg, perceiving usability as taking more time in schedule: 'too much to do and too few employees') and resistance to user-centred design/usability (eg, organizational inertia: 'we've always done things this way') (Rosenbaum, Rohn and Humburg, 2000). Only then there will be a good chance of educational technologists accepting usability evaluation as an essential component of the design–development–implementation cycle.

References

Chang, D, Dooley, L and Tuovinen, J E (2002) Gestalt theory in visual screen design: a new look at an old subject, in *Proceedings WCCE2001 Australian Topics: Selected Papers from the Seventh World Conference on Computers in Education, Copenhagen, Denmark. Conferences in Research and Practice in Information Technology, 8* (ACS. 5), ed A McDougall, J Murnane and D Chambers.

Chen, B, Wang, H, Proctor, R W and Salvandy, G (1997) A human-centered approach for designing world-wide Web browsers, *Behavior Research Methods, Instruments and Computers*, **29**, pp 172–79

Collis, B and Moonen J (2001) *Flexible Learning in A Digital World*, Kogan Page, London

Corry, M D, Frick, T W and Hansen, L (1997) User-centered design and usability testing of a Web site: an illustrative case study, *Educational Technology Research and Development*, **45**, pp 65–76

Dix, A, Finlay, J, Abowd, G and Beale, R (1998) *Human–Computer Interaction*, Prentice Hall Europe, London

Hall, B (1998) *Technology-Based Training: How to make it happen*, Brandon Hall Resources, Sunnyvale, CA

Hom, J (nd) The usability methods toolbox [Online] jthom.best.vwh.net/usability (accessed 6 December 2001)

International Standards Organization (ISO) (1998) *Ergonomic Requirements for Office Work with Visual Display Terminals - Part 11: Guidance on Usability*, ISO Standard 9241-11, ISO

Kensing, F and Blomberg, J (1998) Participatory design: issues and concerns, *Computer Supported Co-Operative Work*, **7** (3/4), pp 167–85

Lee, S H (1999) Usability testing for developing effective interactive multimedia software: concepts, dimensions, and procedures, *Educational Technology and Society*, **2** (2), pp 1–12

Levi, M D and Conrad, F G (1996) Usability testing of World Wide Web sites [Online] stats.bls.gov/ore/htm_papers/st960150.htm (accessed 23 August 2002)

Nielsen, J (1994) *Usability Engineering*, Morgan Kaufmann, San Francisco, CA

Nielsen, J (1999) *Designing Web Usability: The practice of simplicity*, New Reader, Indianapolis, IN

Norman, D A (1998) *The Design of Everyday Things*, MIT Press, London

Owston, R D (2000) Evaluating Web-based learning environments: strategies and insights, *CyberPsychology and Behavior*, **3**, pp 79–85

Preece, J (1993) (ed) *A Guide to Usability: Human factors in computing*, Addison-Wesley, Wokingham, UK

Preece, J, Rogers, Y and Sharp, H (2002) *Interaction Design: Beyond human–computer interaction*, John Wiley, New York

Preece, J, Rogers, Y, Sharp, H, Benyon, D, Holland, S and Carey, T (1994) *Human–Computer Interaction*, Addison-Wesley, Wokingham, UK

Raskin, J (2000) *The Human Interface*, Addison-Wesley, Reading, MA

Rosenbaum, S, Rohn, J A and Humburg, J (2000) A toolkit for strategic usability: results from workshops, panels, and surveys, in *Proceedings of the CHI 2000 Conference on Human Factors in Computing Systems*, pp 337–44, ACM Press, New York

Rosson, M B and Carroll, J M (2002) *Usability Engineering: Scenario-based development of human–computer interaction*, Morgan Kaufmann, San Francisco, CA

Rubin, J (1994) *Handbook of Usability Testing: How to plan, design, and conduct effective tests*, John Wiley, New York

Söderberg, U (2000) Competence via the web, *Behaviour and Information Technology*, **19**, pp 229–32

Wichanski, A M (2000) Usability testing in 2000 and beyond, *Ergonomics*, **43**, pp 998–1006

Chapter 9

Work processes for the development of integrated e-learning courses

Kathleen Schlusmans, Rob Koper and Wil Giesbertz

Introduction

A large number of institutes of higher education have decided on introducing e-learning by using a so-called 'learning management system'. Lecturers use this system to provide course information and to upload their PowerPoint presentations and additional reading texts on the Web. They use e-mail and newsgroup facilities in addition to their lectures and seminars. However, in most cases the learning management system and the digital materials are used in addition to the regular teaching activities, and the basic paradigm of teaching and learning has not changed at all.

By way of contrast, the introduction of integrated e-learning can radically change the entire outlook of education. It can offer flexibility of time, place and pace, and can enable students to follow their own personalized learning paths. Moreover, it offers great opportunities for self-directed learning and independent study. A radical change, however, entails more than using e-mail and PowerPoint presentations on the Web. It requires a complete rethinking of the educational system and, when it comes to quality, integrated e-learning courses that meet these challenges and live up to very high standards.

Developing these kinds of courses requires a great deal from the developers. They need a thorough knowledge of the subject matter, competency in instructional design and in Web design, technical skills, writing skills for the Web, and competency in graphic design and the use of multimedia. It is very rare to find one person who is an expert in all these fields. Developing integrated e-learning courses is not a job for one individual. It is an industrial process, which requires teamwork, cooperation between different specialists and a systematic workflow.

In this chapter we first describe the workflow in the development process of integrated e-learning courses that are suitable for the new paradigms of learning. We then go on to outline the different fields of expertise that are involved in the development process. Finally we give some examples of the course development process, and report on our experience.

The development of integrated e-learning courses: an industrial process

Traditionally, educational courses have been developed by the so-called 'artisan approach'. A lecturer is responsible for the entire development and delivery process. He or she is responsible for one or more groups of students, decides what to teach, designs the course, puts it on the Web or in print, and changes it whenever necessary. In addition, the lecturer tutors the students, answers their questions and corrects their assignments. There is a lot to be said for this approach. Courses can easily be adapted to the needs of the students, the time between design and actual realization is small, and the development costs are limited.

For developing high-quality reusable multimedia courses for large heterogeneous groups of students studying at different times and places, however, the artisan approach is not satisfactory. It does not produce the high quality required, the process is not efficient, the course components are not reusable and, moreover, the fields of expertise needed for developing these courses are seldom to be found in one person.

Institutes for distance education such as the British Open University and the Open University of the Netherlands (OUNL) adopted a new systematic approach for designing and developing courses as early as the 1970s and 1980s (Kaye and Rumble, 1981; Van den Boom and Schlusmans, 1995). This so-called 'industrial approach' allowed these institutes to develop written materials and audio-visual and computer programs on a large scale. First of all, this approach advocates working in course teams with a strong division of labour. In the traditional institutes for distance education, course teams consisted of subject matter specialists, educational technologists, layout specialists, producers of video materials, publishers, computer experts and so on. Second, there is also a clear distinction between the development process in which the courses are designed and developed, and the delivery process in which students study, interact with tutors and write exams. A third difference between the two approaches is the cost. In the industrial approach a great deal of time, effort and money is invested in the development phase, while the delivery is relatively inexpensive. In the case of the artisan approach, development and delivery merge with each other and more emphasis (time, effort and money) is often placed on delivery than on development. As the industrial approach is fairly expensive in the development phase, it is particularly suitable for courses with large groups of students and with reusable components (Koper, 2003).

With the introduction of the Internet in the mid-1990s, there was a tendency at the Open University of the Netherlands (OUNL) to move away from the industrial approach to course development. Individual tutors and lecturers started to experiment with the Web, and as it was comparatively easy to produce and change materials, many of the quality checks and the whole systematic workflow were abolished. It was felt that the quality of these e-learning courses did not live up to our traditional standards, and the new way of developing courses led to a large increase in exploitation costs. This is the reason we reintroduced the industrial approach to course development at the OUNL, and adapted it to the new challenges of e-learning courses.

Requirements of integrated e-learning courses

Students and staff alike have high expectations of integrated e-learning courses. The courses have to be attractive, effective and efficient. Students want user-friendly multimedia courses, which allow them to interact with the materials, with each other, and with the teachers. They want a fair measure of flexibility to organize their studies, and they want courses that can be adapted to their own learning needs. The teaching staff expect the courses to be user-friendly and decrease their teaching load. They should also be easy to adapt and update. Teachers and institutes want learning objects to be reusable and shareable. Moreover, educational institutes tend to use different learning management systems (LMS), and the staff expect the courses to be compatible with their own LMS and to allow interaction with their own administrative systems.

To meet all these expectations, integrated e-learning courses have to meet not only high educational standards but also several technical requirements. The most important ones concern the manner in which the courses are described and the way in which they are stored. When it comes to learning content, not only are technical standards such as graphics interchange formats required, so are formats for the way in which the packaging, sequencing, and other management of the software is handled in order for it to be transferred between platforms and environments.

To make integrated e-learning courses reusable and compatible with different systems, it is necessary to use a formal language that describes the course exhaustively. This includes the learning design, the learning objects and the services needed (Koper, 2001a, 2001b). Such a language is called an 'educational modelling language' (EML) (see also Chapter 6). The work on EML at the Open University of the Netherlands has led to the work on the IMS Learning Design specification that is now available as an independent open standard (IMSLD, 2003). Both EML and IMS Learning Design use XML to create highly structured course materials. A course described in EML might offer features such as reusable course material, personalized interaction for individual students and media independence. It allows the developers to model the pedagogical scenario (the learning design) of e-learning courses in such a way that students can interact with the educational environment. It also enables the course materials to be adapted to the individual needs of the students.

The course team

Developing integrated e-learning courses using EML requires specific skills and knowledge in several fields of expertise (see Table 9.1). There is not a one-to-one relationship between people and fields of expertise. Although some people combine several fields of expertise, it is unlikely that any one person will combine them all. These fields of expertise should all therefore be represented in a course development team (Duffy and Kirkley, 2002).

The instructional process: separation of development and delivery

To guarantee high-quality materials of a consistent standard, development and delivery are strictly separated. This is one of the main characteristics of the industrial approach. The whole instructional process can be divided into five phases (see Figure 9.1). These phases are the course definition (the task), course development, implementation, delivery and evaluation.

In the course definition phase, the curriculum committee or the planning advisory board decides that a particular course should be developed in a particular subject area for a specific target group. A course team is selected and the course is developed. There is an implementation phase between development and delivery. Here the tutors are trained, the authorization issues are resolved, and the course is incorporated into the curriculum. During the delivery phase, students study the course and write assignments and exams. The tutors give feedback and assess the students' progress. In the evaluation phase the quality of the whole course, including tutoring and support, is assessed.

Table 9.1 *Areas of expertise and examples of competencies*

Areas of expertise	Examples of competencies
Project management	Managing multidisciplinary teams
	Planning a project
	Reporting on the project's progress
	Managing time and finances
Instructional design	Developing a didactic scenario
	Developing learning activities
	Advising on using media
	Designing interactions
	Advising on writing instructional texts and assessments
Subject matter expertise	A good knowledge of educational modelling languages
	Translating the didactic scenario into an EML design
Content management	A good knowledge of content management learning systems
	Advising on the best data storage
	Developing a database of different educational materials
Editing	Editing educational materials
Developmental testing	Developing questionnaires for developmental testing
	Carrying out a user test
Publishing	Preparing materials for publication on the Web
Data entry	Using XML or EML authoring tools
	'Translating' educational materials into EML formats
Graphic design	Designing a user interface
	Preparing pictures and illustrations for Web publication
Media technology	Developing streaming audio and video

The course development process

The development process can in its turn also be divided into four phases: analysis, design, construction and developmental testing (see Figure 9.1).

Analysis

First of all, the course definition or task is analysed and the different course requirements are established. These requirements concern the following issues:

- course objectives;
- target groups;
- connection with other courses and programmes;

- study load;
- instructional model;
- financial and time constraints.

At the end of this phase the course requirements are clear and the development team can be established.

Development

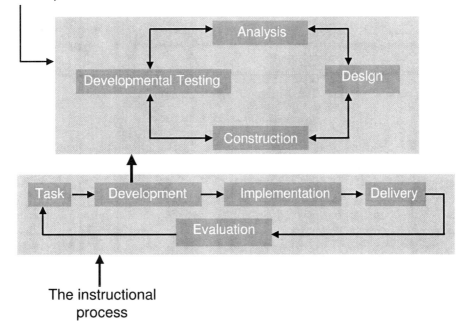

Figure 9.1 *Development and the instructional process*

Design

The design phases consist of three parts which are closely linked together, namely instructional design, technical design and test design, along with a fourth part, which deals with the planning and the budget.

The instructional design is based on the requirements from the analysis phase. In the instructional design the following issues are addressed:

- refinement of the course objectives;
- establishing the detailed entry level requirements and the consequences of not meeting these requirements;
- the assessment criteria for the course;

- the way in which students will be assessed during and at the end of the course;
- the way in which the course will be adaptable to different students' needs;
- the different roles of staff and students;
- the different learning activities students should undertake to meet the course objective;
- the order in which the learning activities will be presented;
- the materials the students will need to perform the activities;
- the way in which student progress will be monitored;
- the way in which tutors will give feedback;
- the interaction patterns between tutors and students;
- the media that will be used, that is to say, what will be printed and what will be Web-based.

Part of the instructional design is a description of the didactic scenario (see Table 9.2) and a description of the separate learning activities (see Table 9.3).

Table 9.2 *Example of part of the didactic scenario of a course in public administration*

	Learning activities	By whom	When completed	What is registered in port-folio	Support activities	By whom	What is registered in port-folio
1	Registration	Student	When form is filled in	All data			
2					Welcome	Tutor	
3	Reading Study Guide	Student	Unrestricted				
4	Practice assignment 1	Student	When feedback is positive	Result of Assignment 1			
5					Feedback	Tutor	Feedback

Designing a course is a creative, non-linear process in which subject matter specialists and instructional designers work closely together. It is important to refine the instructional design and to agree on every issue before even beginning to construct the course. The instructional design is the most important aspect of the whole development process. In our experience it is worth spending about a quarter of the development time on this phase.

Only when the instructional design of the course is completed can the technical design start. At the Open University of the Netherlands we use EML for the technical design of courses. The instructional design is translated into a 'course skeleton'. All activities and interactions are modelled in EML but without actual

Table 9.3   *Example of the design of a learning activity*

Number	1
Title	Practice Assignment 1
Description	Student writes a policy statement based on the case 'Pollution in Heerlen'
By whom	Student
Individual/group	Individual
Entry requirements	None
Completed	When feedback is positive
Registration	Assignment + feedback in portfolio
Resources in learning environment	Case materials Textbook Reference manual

content. This course skeleton allows us to test the run of the course, the interactions and so on. After a technical test, the course skeleton can be adapted. Expertise in the field of EML is required for the technical design.

The requirements for the course are set in the analysis phase. The test phase is to establish if the requirements have been met. The test design phase includes information on:

- the objective of the test;
- the stakeholders;
- the object which is tested;
- the manner in which data are gathered;
- the planning.

In the test design phase the subject matter specialist, the team manager, the instructional designer and the evaluation expert work closely together.

Finally, when the different parts of the design are ready, the course manager draws up the budget that is necessary to construct the course, including the developmental testing phase, and estimates what the exploitation costs of the course will be. The course manager also describes the activities planned, projects them on a timescale, and selects the course team that will be involved in the construction phase. In this phase editors, graphic designers and media specialists are frequently asked to join the team.

Construction

It might sound disrespectful, but if the instructional design phase were really successful, the construction phase would merely involve filling in the course skeleton. In this phase, the different tasks are divided according to the design of the course. Subject matter specialists write the learning activities, assessments and

Table 9.4 *Example of test design*

Objective	Stakeholders	Object	Method	Planning
Developmental testing	Students	Use; appreciation	Observation; logging; questionnaire	Week 12: students a, b, c; Week 13: students x, y, z
	Tutors	Use; appreciation	Questionnaire; interviews	Week 14: tutor x; Week 15: tutor y

learning texts. They select case materials and interesting hyperlinks. They work with media specialists to develop streaming audio and video materials. Data entry experts and content management experts ensure that all the materials are stored in the right formats for publication while EML experts integrate all the different aspects in the course skeleton. No matter how well the design has been thought out, minor changes might be required in the basic design in this phase.

Developmental testing

The developmental testing is mainly carried out by evaluation experts. The course is presented to a selected sample of students. Both the students and the tutors tackle the course as if it were real, but they are asked to fill out questionnaires, keep a time log, and report back on any problems they encounter (see Table 9.4). The test results are reported to the whole course team, then it is decided how the course needs to be adapted with reference to the test findings.

Cooperation between experts

We described a method for developing Web-based courses in which experts from different fields have to work closely together to achieve an optimal result. All these experts depend on each other's work as far as timing and quality is concerned. In Figure 9.2 we show how different experts have to work together in the analysis phase. In our systematic development method, all the different phases have been designed in this way.

Our experience

The Open University of the Netherlands (OUNL) has had considerable experience of working with course teams on the development and production of printed

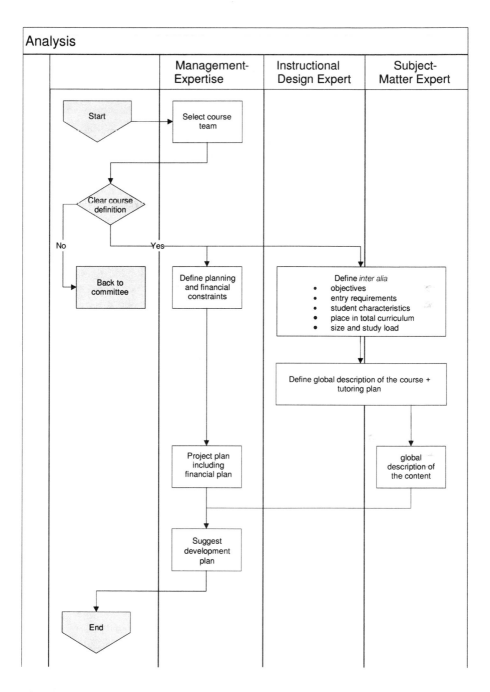

Figure 9.2   *A sequence diagram of the analysis phase*

courses. We have developed over 300 courses in this manner. Since 1997, we have also been using course teams to produce integrated e-learning courses. In the past we used HTML for course description but in 1998 we started developing and using EML.

Our first experiments with Web-based courses in EML were not at the OUNL itself but at the School of Higher Hotel Management in Maastricht. A form of dual education was introduced at this institute, so that students could combine study and work at the same time. All first year courses had to be redesigned from face-to-face courses to distance, Web-based courses. It was decided to use EML for this purpose. The development approach we described above was not used in the first instance. The lecturers in Maastricht developed course materials using a word processing programme and then handed the course over to the educational technologists at the OUNL. The courses were 'translated' into EML at the OUNL. However, this way of working proved to be rather problematical. The instructional design of the courses was implicit in the materials, and had to be deduced from the course in order to make an EML design. This quite often resulted in having to redesign the course, which required a great deal of communication. In the end it was concluded that a joint design phase and a more systematic development approach could have solved many problems (Janssen and van der Klink, 1999).

When we introduced working with EML at the OUNL, we also introduced the development approach described above. This approach was adopted in six course projects, and an extensive evaluation of the whole process of course development was carried out (Verreck et al, 2001). Most course teams were perfectly satisfied with the systematic approach for developing materials. It is useful to have a description of the whole process, and it seems to work in practice. Most course teams work according to the phases and task divisions explained in the approach. However, they observed that the description of the different phases is not as linear as is described in the approach. The development teams frequently wanted to perform a test after developing the first part of the material, to ascertain the look and feel of the course at an early stage. There also seem to be several ways of applying the systematic approach. For instance, one course team decided to design the whole course without taking technological constraints into account, and only afterwards did they adapt their initial design to the scope of the technology. Another team considered technological considerations to be an integral part of the instructional design, and started with an extended discussion of the technological constraints. At the moment it is difficult to decide which of the two approaches is the more effective.

Another point that emerged from the evaluation is the high degree of satisfaction as far as working together in teams is concerned. Each team member appreciated both the expertise of the others, and the added value of a range of points of view and of different fields of expertise. The cooperation between instructional designers, subject matter specialists, course managers and technological specialists was rated particularly highly. The position of editors, graphic designers and data entry experts still requires extra attention, and has not been thoroughly enough thought out yet.

One problem that was frequently reported was the feeling of the subject matter specialists that they had lost their freedom to change and adapt courses as they went along. Although theoretically they could appreciate the value of good design, they felt the need for more freedom and more adaptability. It was felt that the Web offers the opportunity to change materials quickly, and that by using an industrial development process, this opportunity seemed to get lost.

Finally it was established that although EML offers a high degree of flexibility in terms of course design and pedagogy, authoring tools for creating EML-based courses still require further refinement.

Conclusion

In this chapter we have described the industrial approach for developing integrated e-learning courses using EML, that is, IMS learning design. We have tried to show that the whole development process of integrated e-learning courses is rather complex and requires many fields of expertise. It is too much to leave the whole process to one teacher. Developing integrated e-learning courses requires teamwork, to which the experts each bring their own field of expertise. Moreover, we argued the case that designing the e-learning course is one of the most important phases in the development process. One of the issues that remains unresolved is that integrated e-learning courses should be easy to update and adapt. The tools and instruments we use at the moment do not permit this. A great deal of effort will have to be devoted to the development of tools and authoring systems in the near future.

References

Duffy, T M and Kirkley, J R (2002) Learning theory and pedagogy applied in distance learning: the case of Cardean University, in *Learner Centered Theory and Practice in Distance Education: Cases from higher education*, ed T M Duffy and J Kirkley, Lawrence Erlbaum, Mahwah, NJ

IMSLD (2003) *IMS Learning Design: Information model, best practice and implementation guide, binding document, schemas* [Online] imsglobal.org

Janssen, J P W and van der Klink, M R (1999) In de Praktijk Beproefd: Rapportage van een Pilot met een Prototype van de Elektronische Leeromgeving (ELO) (Tried and tested: a report of a pilot study using a prototype of an Electronic Learning Environment), OUNL-OTEC, Heerlen

Kaye, A and Rumble, G (1981) *Distance Teaching for Higher and Adult Education*, Croom Helm/Open University Press, London

Koper, E J R (2001a) Van verandering naar vernieuwing (From change to innovation), in *Handboek Effectief Opleiden* (Manual for effective training), 26, ed P Schramade, pp 45–86, Elsevier, The Hague, Netherlands

Koper, E J R (2001b) *Modelling Units of Study from a Pedagogical Perspective:The peda-gogical metamodel behind EML*, OUNL, Heerlen [Online] eml.ou.nl/introduction/docs/ped-metamodel.pdf

Koper, E J R (2003) Combining re-usable learning resources and services to pedagogical purposeful units of learning, in *Re-using Online Resources: A sustainable approach to e-learning*, ed A Littlejohn, pp 46–59, Kogan Page, London

Schlusmans, K (2001) *Het Inhoudelijk-Didactisch Ontwerp* (Content and didactic design), OUNL-OTEC, Heerlen

Van Den Boom, G and Schlusmans, K (1995) *Didactics and Course Development at the Open University of the Netherlands*, OUNL-OTEC, Heerlen

Verreck, W, De Craene, B, Poelmans, P and de Volder, M (2001) *Rapport Evaluatie Startprojecten. Project Evaluatie Digitale Open Universiteit* (Report on the evaluation of the Initial Projects: Project Evaluation Digital Open University), OUNL-OTEC, Heerlen

Further reading

Giesbertz, W, Schlusmans, K, Koper, R and Schuncken, R (2001) *Systematiek voor het organiseren van werkprocessen bij het ontwikkelen van onderwijs in EML*, (A systematic approach for the development of education materials in EML), OUNL-OTEC, Heerlen

Wagenmans, L and Poelmans, P (2001) *De Evaluatie van Projecten met Edubox* (The evaluation of Edubox projects), OUNL-OTEC, Heerlen

Chapter 10

Learning objects: are they the answer to the knowledge economy's predicament?

Peter Sloep

Introduction

This chapter is about a relatively recent addition to the learning technologist's vocabulary, the learning object. Putting it succinctly, learning objects are reusable bits of learning content. Their significance lies in their purported capacity to be flexibly reused, thus helping to create personalized learning materials, even at a reduced cost. This claim is voiced by many (Atkinson and Wilson, 1969) but particularly adamantly by the Advanced Distributed Learning Initiative (ADL) in its defence of the SCORM (Sharable Content Object Reference Model) approach (Dodds, 2001: 1–12). Learning objects, it would thus seem, are particularly helpful in sorting out the problems posed by the knowledge economy (Westera and Sloep, 2001; Downes, 2002). It is this thesis that I want to assess in this chapter.

First, I analyze how personalization and costs relate to each other and to the demands of the knowledge economy. As indicated, learning objects play a central role in this debate. Before delving into the question of what this role is, I look in detail at what learning objects are, and what they are not. The next sections of the chapter then tackle the questions of how and to what extent learning objects may assist in getting a knowledge economy off the ground. Finally I summarize the findings and discuss some practical inferences.

The predicament of the knowledge economy

The starting point of the analysis is the generally accepted maxim that as a matter of sound pedagogy an attractive, effective, efficient learning environment needs to meet a learner's needs and preferences (see Collis and Moonen, 2001: ch 1). It should present exactly the right materials in terms of complexity and subject matter ('just in case'), at exactly the moment a learner needs it ('just in time'), and it should perfectly match his or her learning style. The second premise, which also hardly needs defending, is that students do indeed differ in their demands and preferences. This implies that there is a need for customization of learning environments, which is usually referred to as the need for personalization.

Personalization comes at a price. Matching a learning environment with each and everybody's demands and needs is obviously more expensive than serving all the students with one learning environment only. More personalization implies increased costs per student, although clearly there is a limit. Someone has to shoulder the costs, irrespective of whether this is the student, the employer or the state. This presents us with a dilemma. The more personalization the better, we might almost say, but the degree to which a learning environment may be personalized is limited, as learning should also be kept affordable.

A strategy that has worked well in the past in lowering the costs of personalization is to increase the size of the group of students served by a particular learning environment. Suppose one practises face-to-face teaching in classrooms, or lecture halls. The costs are mainly delivery costs, which are determined by the teacher's salary. Delivery costs are dependent on the number of students served. For every so many students a new teacher needs to be hired. By increasing group sizes, the burden of the delivery costs may be shared by more students, thus lowering costs. Delivery costs are not the only costs; there are also development costs, but these may largely be ignored here, certainly if one works with experienced teachers. In distance teaching, increasing student numbers also helps lower the costs. By contrast with face-to-face teaching, distance teaching is based on course books or 'canned' lectures (in video format) and is usually mediated by asynchronous contacts between teachers and learners such as phone, fax and e-mail. Thus the delivery costs are low but the development costs are high. However, if the course books or videos are shared, the total costs may again be lowered.

This strategy of increasing group size works particularly well in initial education (that is, education of individuals before they enter the workforce, in contrast to further education), with its fixed degree programmes and rather homogeneous groups of students. Distance teaching, on the other hand, tends to serve rather more heterogeneous audiences. However, by setting entry requirements or, as in open distance learning, by suggesting ways to overcome student shortcomings, homogenous groups can be formed before commencement. Over the last two decades or so, with the advent of the knowledge economy, a new situation has arisen. It demands that we do not consider someone's education complete after graduating from, say, university. It requires us to establish forms of life-long learning in order to further educate people. The arguments are well known and have been articulated in various papers and books, academic and otherwise (Davis and Botkin, 1994; Westera and Sloep, 1998, 2001; Brown and Duguid, 2000). What they boil down to is that, mainly driven by the increasing role of the computer, societal change has quickened its pace to such an extent that ever more knowledge workers are needed. Moreover, these knowledge workers have to re-educate themselves continuously to stay abreast of societal change. Unfortunately, the rub is that in further education the strategy that worked so well in initial education now falls flat.

For each student, further education makes the same demands on personalization as initial education. Demands may even be a little more modest, as we are dealing with experienced learners who are better able to shape their learning environment. However, students in further education tend to be extremely heterogeneous, and all of them make significantly different demands on their learning environments (Bitter-Rijpkema, Sloep and Jansen, 2003). It is therefore impossible to have large groups of students jointly cover the delivery and development costs. To make matters worse, the investment each student is prepared to make in his or her education is likely to decrease with age. Life-long learners are by definition older than learners in initial education. The time to earn back their investments has contracted. Usually these investments have to come fully out of their own pockets or those of their employers. Unlike the situation in initial education, governments do not usually consider it their duty to pay for or even subsidize further education. Seen from the perspective of an educational institution, this means that further education needs about the same degree of personalization but at a lower cost. We submit that this is the predicament of the knowledge economy. The current literature suggests that learning objects represent a way of overcoming it.

Learning objects

According to a working definition proposed by the Learning Technology Standards Committee of the Institute of Electrical and Electronic Engineers (IEEE, 2000: 5):

> Learning Objects are defined here as any entity, digital or non-digital, which can be used, re-used, referenced during technology supported learning. . . . Examples of learning objects include multimedia content, instructional content, learning objectives, instructional software and software tools, and persons, organizations, or events referenced during technology supported learning.

Elementary logic dictates that proper definitions are required to obey a number of rules (Rescher, 1964). The first is that they should neither be too narrow nor too wide. This particular definition, however, seems to suffer from both these faults. It is too narrow, for why should one restrict a learning object's use to technology-supported learning only? They may be most beneficial in this case, but there seems to be no reason to rule out their use in situations of learning that are not technology-supported.

The definition seems too wide too, as almost anything used in support of technology-based learning counts as a learning object. This same point is made by various other authors (see Chapter 5; see also Sloep, 2002a, and most poignantly Wiley, 2002). It seems odd to count institutions and teachers as learning objects, and in fact there are sound reasons for excluding them. Use and reuse, the definition claims, are the defining characteristics of a learning object, and what makes them attractive as a possible solution for the knowledge economy's predicament in the first place. Unlike resources, persons and organizations have a fundamental limit to their ability to be shared. Resources, particularly digital ones, may be duplicated endlessly with little effort. This means that one person's usage of a particular resource does not affect someone else's opportunity to use that very same resource at all. Economists call goods with these characteristics 'non-rival' goods. Prime examples are a film in a cinema, a lighthouse, and indeed all sorts of digital resources such as texts, pictures, sound bytes and so forth (see Kohn, 2001). Note that this does not hold for non-digital resources, which deteriorate on duplication. Examples of rival goods are a bicycle and a computer. So too are persons. The time a tutor spends on one student cannot be spent on someone else. This means that there is a significant limit to a person's (and an organization's) ability to be used and reused. This immediately disqualifies persons and organizations as learning objects.

Taking this into account, the following amended definition would seem more appropriate: 'A learning object is any non-rival resource, digital or non-digital, that can be used, reused, or referenced in service of learning activities.' Will learning objects thus defined be adequate for the affordable personalization needed to sustain the knowledge economy? Unfortunately, not yet. In terms of the definition, the books and videos used in distance teaching are learning objects too, but adapting them to a particular learner's needs is rather expensive. We have learnt this from past experience. Objects such as books and videos are not really suitable for small-scale personalization. But suppose we restrict ourselves to digital resources only. Computers could then be used as an aid in the adaptation process. If this process could somehow be automated to some extent, the costs of adaptation would decrease immediately. Another reason it makes sense to restrict ourselves to digital learning objects is the worldwide cluster of networks, the Internet, through which computers are linked, and which fosters the emergence and growth of networks of people. As the networks are not bound by the limitations of physical space, they span the entire world, thus greatly increasing the number of people who could use a particular learning object in principle. The emergence of such a worldwide learning object market place ultimately creates a learning object economy, which is likely to result in cost reductions.

At this juncture we could either alter the definition of a learning object so that it only covers digital resources, or agree to restrict ourselves to digital resources in the remainder of the discussion. Either way, for the affordable personalization needed by the knowledge economy to become reality, various obstacles have to be surmounted. First, we need to establish how we can organize the reuse of learning objects on a worldwide scale, by groups of users who may not even know each other. Second, we need to establish how the costs of adaptation could be brought down with the help of computers. The next two sections will be devoted to these questions.

Reuse of learning objects

During the last five years or so, a number of technical means have been developed to ease the exchange of entire learning objects. The learning object metadata (LOM) specification and the content packaging (CP) specification stand out among them.

The LOM, according to its latest draft version (IEEE, 2002), seeks 'to facilitate search, evaluation, acquisition, and use of learning objects, for instance by learners or instructors or automated software processes'. Thus it is clearly about sharing learning objects. It tries to achieve this goal by providing highly structured descriptions of learning objects in such terms as the technical requirements for their deployment (the category 'Technical'), their educational and pedagogical characteristics (the category 'Pedagogy'), and their intellectual property rights and conditions for use (the category 'Rights'). There are at least two factors that may stand in the way of the LOM's success, though. First, it has become a rather large specification with over 80 data elements in nine categories. This may hinder its adoption. Second, its attempted certification as an official ISO standard seems to have become the subject of some political wrangling. Although the stamp of ISO approval would certainly lend the LOM a measure of credibility, a long-winded process of consensus building is not in the interests of the learning technology community, which needs a standard sooner rather than later.

Imagine someone had created a learning object and had dutifully provided LOM-compliant meta-data for it. Such a learning object would then be ready to be taken up and reused by others. How would that work in practice? More often than not a course, lecture or lesson will consist of several learning objects, organized in a particular fashion. The content packaging specification (IMS, 2003a) helps to capture this organization. This is not only useful in itself, but it also paves the way for the deployment of software that fosters reuse. Learning objects are processed by, for instance, authoring systems that assist their development, digital repositories that store them, and run-time systems that build the learner's learning environment, real or virtual, around them.

Thus the LOM and CP specifications show how the exchange of learning objects is technically feasible. A few wrinkles still have to be ironed out, such as the political issues surrounding the LOM (Kraan, 2003a). Clearly additional specifications are needed, such as those referring to the organization of digital repositories (IMS, 2003b). Existing specifications will need to be completed or revised, such as the current efforts to update CP. But this does not detract from the success of the specification efforts undertaken thus far. This success may suggest that once all the technical issues have been dealt with, nothing would prevent large-scale reuse from occurring. Claiming that much, however, would be a serious mistake.

In face-to-face teaching, all teachers are more or less alike in the responsibilities they bear and the tasks they have to carry out. They prepare for class, lecture, mark papers and assess their students' performance. In an educational system based on learning objects, this situation will change considerably. There will be extensive role differentiation. In a learning object's delivery phase, although the role of traditional teacher will still be recognizable for the most part, the details of the tasks will differ. Lecturing, for example, will become e-moderating (Salmon, 2000). During their development, however, a whole collection of new roles will emerge (see Chapter 9). Preparing for lecturing now becomes an authoring process, involving various professionals, not just content experts but also educational technologists, graphic designers, multimedia experts and perhaps programmers. This is a major change, over which teachers already have voiced their concerns, some in no uncertain terms (LeNoble, 1998).

I already noted that the LOM is a rather elaborate specification. Even the existing attempts at pruning it have resulted in large core sets (anonymous, 2003). Thus it takes considerable time and effort to fill out a meta-data form in full. It is crucial to note that it is not the person who fills out the meta-data form who benefits from this effort, but others who reuse the learning object in question. Indeed, creating a learning object in such a way that it may be used outside the context for which it was intended in the first place most likely requires an additional development effort. Once again, only others stand to benefit from this. No learning object economy will ever develop, let alone last, if the creators of learning objects are not somehow compensated for their efforts. A compensation system need not necessarily be based on the monetary system currently in use for books. Publishers may exploit learning object databases. They may see to it that these are filled with qualitatively good learning objects, or charge users of learning objects a fee and then compensate the authors for their creative efforts. Other systems might work equally well or perhaps even better, depending on the circumstances (Suber, 2003). Any solution that relies on closed communities, however, should be avoided as it limits the potential for reuse.

A no less significant obstacle to reuse is the current way of managing intellectual property rights. For one thing, laws and regulations differ between countries, sometimes to the extent that countries lack such regulations altogether or do not enforce them. Second, and no less important, according to a number of scholars current systems seem to err towards maximizing the profits of publishers rather than striking a just balance between compensating authors for their efforts and protecting larger cultural values such as fair use or access to the common cultural heritage (Kohn, 2001; Sholtz, 2001; Söderberg, 2002). Either way, reuse stands to suffer, as the incentive to make learning objects available to others is diminished.

There can be no doubt that current and future technical specifications foster the reuse of learning objects. However, this will occur only if the required social affordances also exist. In view of society's resistance to overthrowing its evolved institutions, the societal hurdles will probably turn out to be far more resistant to removal than the technical ones.

Adaptation of learning objects

I now turn to the adaptation of learning objects that is required for personaliza-tion. For simple reuse it suffices to look at a learning object externally, from the outside only, as is described by its meta-data. In this way one may do the searching, finding and retrieving needed for simple reuse. For adaptation that is for flexible reuse one needs to be able to alter a learning object's internal structure, though. How could this be done? And what precisely is the internal structure?

For reasons that will become clear shortly, I shall focus on compound learning objects only. Such learning objects themselves consist of learning objects, simple or also compound, that are organized in a particular way. One could swap one or more of these constituent learning objects for one or more others, change the route the learners are supposed to follow through them, offer alternative routes and so forth. All these alterations amount to a change in the compound learning object's internal structure. As I have already indicated, the content packaging specification is a means to record the way the learning objects combine in a compound learning object. This is formally called its organization. Compound learning objects may have multiple organizations.

The mechanism originally provided by the content packaging's organization element is not very adept at personalizing compound learning objects. It is really no more powerful than the table of contents in a book. Readers may decide to skip chapters, jump ahead and come back later, or whatever they like. Of late, more powerful tools have become available such as the IMS Simple Sequencing (SS) (IMS, 2003c) and IMS Learning Design (LD) (IMS, 2003d) specifications. Both substitute the CP's organizational element for one of their own. Both allow the designer to specify multiple routes through a collection of learning objects; to have routes split up and come together again; to affix conditions to these branching events; and to keep track of a learner's progress along the route chosen. Thus both allow personalization during the development phase, with the educational designer creating the entire 'routing system', and to some extent also during delivery through conditional branching. However, this is where the similarities end. Simple Sequencing is aimed at the training market and only provides for single-learner, single-role designs (Kraan and Wilson, 2003). Learning Design has been developed to support learning scenarios in which multiple learners feature in multiple roles, if so desired. Thus complex scenarios such as problem-based learning may be supported. In addition, its system of user variables (properties) and conditions is more flexible, as they may be entirely defined by the designer, whereas SS works with fixed sets (see Koper, 2003).

Do these specifications suffice to create the flexible reuse of compound learning objects we are in search of? Both specifications are still in their infancy. No software applications able to play learning objects marked up according to either SS or LD were on the market at the time of writing, let alone the authoring systems that are needed to develop learning objects powered by LD or SS. Hence even technically, major hurdles still have to be overcome. At the social level, the same obstacles that simple reuse stumbled over, such as teachers' resistance to change and the lack of suitable compensation and rights systems, hinder flexible reuse.

But there are additional problems. Thus far, authors of educational materials, whether they are textbooks as used in face-to-face teaching or course books as used in distance learning, have been admonished to fill their abstract texts with examples drawn from the students' previous experience or from their future working environment. They have also been advised to make regular cross-references in the text ('as we saw in Chapter 10. . .') to make it easier for the student to get an integral picture of the subject. (This became evident in personal experience as a former course developer and textbook writer.) All this advice, no matter how sound, should be ignored when developing learning objects. Learning objects need to be decontextualized as much as possible to enlarge their capacity for reuse. That seems to be feasible for examples used for illustrative purposes. Each example may be regarded a separate learning object, capable of being swapped for another one that provides a more fitting illustration. Thus one may imagine a statistics text that introduces descriptive statistical techniques such as histograms or pie charts to use different examples to illustrate the abstract instructions. But how should learning objects that are unaware of each other's existence cross-reference each other? Developers of learning objects will certainly have a hard time unlearning their 'bad habits'. The fact that CETIS, the UK Centre for Educational Technology Interoperability Standardization, went to great lengths to issue guidelines on how to develop decontextualized learning objects illustrates that we are dealing with a significant social hurdle here (Casey and McAlpine, 2002). This reinforces and amplifies the conclusion drawn at the end of the previous section. It will prove to be far easier to take down the technical barriers to simple and flexible reuse than the social ones.

Conclusion

The developed countries are moving in the direction of knowledge-based economies. In order to sustain a thriving knowledge economy, workers need to be educated before they enter the workforce (initial education) and particularly while they are part of it (post-initial or further education). We have seen that further education demands that we use learning objects, although their use still requires us to solve a variety of technical and social problems. The former are in the process of being solved, although many significant problems still exist. The latter have hardly been identified yet, let alone solved.

What role could our current educational institutions, whether distance or regular, play in further education? Traditionally, they have focused on initial education. However, because of their historical role as centres of knowledge and expertise, it seems plausible that they should also play a role in further education. To date, their solutions to the further education challenge are simple extensions of their approach to initial education. Regular educational institutions offer classes at more convenient hours and locations. Distance teaching universities recycle their materials for use in their degree programmes. I have argued above that this response is inadequate, as it leads to forms of education that are either affordable but insufficiently personalized (the most common approach in both distance and regular institutes) or forms that are sufficiently personalized but unaffordable, save for the happy few. An inevitable conclusion to draw from the arguments put forth in this chapter is that the current educational establishment needs to turn towards the use of learning objects if it wants to play a role in further education. In this way it could profit from the affordances for reuse, both simple and flexible, that learning objects offer.

Obviously such a move would be easier if learning objects could also play a role in initial education. In that case educational institutions could base their entire operation on a similar approach. In distance teaching, this poses a relatively small problem. Distance teaching may be said to have followed a learning object approach all along, albeit a deficient one, with its learning materials such as course books and canned lectures being perfectly reusable, but hardly adaptable. Adopting modern learning objects is just the next step on an already familiar road for them.

Things are different for the regular institutions that follow a face-to-face, classroom-based approach. At first sight, learning objects may seem to have no other use than perhaps to inspire teachers. Although this is a perfectly legitimate use, it is scarcely an argument for their introduction in initial education. Fortunately, face-to-face classroom teaching seems to be moving away from this traditional model (see Chapter 1). With the advent of constructivism students are far more often being left to their own devices. In approaches such as problem-based learning, case-based learning and project-based learning the students, whether alone or in groups, engage in learning activities and in doing so arrive at particular learning objectives (Oliver, 2000). In the course of their engagement in these activities they may consult various kinds of resource. Obvious candidates to fulfil the role of these resources are the learning objects discussed above. Thus learning objects would even seem to fit in with modern approaches to regular education. But note that particularly in this case the most difficult hurdle to face will be social rather than technical. It is teachers who need to be convinced of, or rather, convince themselves of the value of a learning-object-based approach to education.

The current situation regarding learning objects is rather precarious. As we saw above, both technical and social hurdles still need to be surmounted. With respect to their adoption, what strategy should one follow just now? Should one immediately invest heavily in their development: that is in authoring teams, in supporting software and the organizational change needed to work with them? Or would it be better to follow a more cautious course? In view of the instability of many of the required standards (efforts at harmonization, for instance, still need to be undertaken), caution would seem to be the best course to follow. In spite of the current marketing hype, there is no software available that fully complies with the current standards (IMS, 2003e). First, standards certified by accredited standardization bodies do not yet exist. The only one that is at least in the pipeline is the LOM. We only have specifications at various stages of their development. Second, with the exception of ADL's SCORM, there are no official compliance tests. 'Plug fests' organized by ADL and 'code bashes' organized by CETIS (Kraan, 2002) and 'Surf-SIX' (Kraan, 2003b) reveal that software applications show widely varying behaviours with respect to standards. Following a 'best-of-breed' approach when acquiring software may turn out to yield the best, although these applications may still not be good enough. It is therefore much wiser to follow a requirements-based approach. If no software exists that meets the requirements, one may wait for it to arrive, create it oneself, or become part of collaborative efforts to create it. Such collaboration, which also frequently follows an open source approach, may serve to spread the risk (Sloep, 2002b).

In conclusion then, publicly funded schools and universities should embark upon the learning object journey. They have little choice if they want to cater for both the initial and the further education demand. However, they should venture into this still little-known territory with great caution.

References

Anonymous (2003) *CanCore Learning Resource Meta-data Application Profile* [Online] www.cancore.ca (accessed 5 February 2003)

Atkinson, R C and Wilson, H A (1969) *Computer-Assisted Instruction: A book of readings*, Academic Press, New York

Bitter-Rijpkema, M E, Sloep, P B and Jansen, D (2003) Learning to change: the virtual business learning approach to professional workplace learning, *Educational Technology and Society*, (1) [Online] ifets.iece.org/periodicals/issues.html (accessed 5 June 2003)

Brown, J S and Duguid, P (2000) *The Social Life of Information*, Harvard Business School Press, Boston, MA

Casey, J and McAlpine, M (2002) *Writing and Using Re-usable Educational Materials: A beginners guide*, CETIS Educational Content Special Interest Group [Online] www.cetis.ac.uk/educational-content (accessed 12 May 2003)

Collis, B and Moonen, J (2001) *Flexible Learning in a Digital Word: Experiences and expectations*, Kogan Page, London

Davis, S M and Botkin, J (1994) *The Monster under the Bed: How business is mastering the opportunity of knowledge for profit*, Touchstone, New York

Dodds, P (2001) *Sharable Content Object Reference Model (SCORM™) Version 1.2, The Scorm overview*, Advanced Distributed Learning Initiative [Online] www. adlnet.org (accessed 12 May 2003)

Downes, S (2002) The Learning Object Economy, presentation at NAWeb 2002 [Online] naweb.unb.ca/02/Downes.ppt (accessed 5 February 2003)

IEEE (2000) *Draft Standard for Learning Object Meta-data IEEE P1484.12/D4.1*, IEEE, New York [Online] ltsc.ieee.org/doc/wg12/LOMv4.1.pdf (accessed 12 May 2003)

IEEE (2002*) Draft Standard for Learning Object Meta-data IEEE P1484.12.1/D6.4*, IEEE, New York [Online] ltsc.ieee.org/doc/wg12/LOM_WD6_4.pdf

IMS (2003a) *IMS Content Packaging Specification*, IMS Global Learning Consortium [Online] imsglobal.org/content/packaging/index.cfm (accessed 5 February 2003)

IMS (2003b) *IMS Digital Repositories Specification*, IMS Global Learning Consortium [Online] imsglobal.org/digitalrepositories/index.cfm (accessed 5 February 2003)

IMS (2003c) *IMS Simple Sequencing Specification*, IMS Global Learning Consortium [Online] imsglobal.org/simplesequencing/index.cfm (accessed 5 February 2003)

IMS (2003d) *IMS Learning Design Specification*, IMS Global Learning Consortium [Online] imsglobal.org/learningdesign/index.cfm (accessed 15 February 2003)

IMS (2003e) Panel Discussion 1: Conformance Issues Keynote Presentation [Online] www.imsglobal.org/otf/otfpresentations2002sheffield.cfm (accessed 5 February 2003)

Kohn, D (2001) *Steal This Essay*, Tidbits 602, 603, 605, 610 [Online] db.tidbits.com/getbits.acgi?tbart=06669 (accessed 12 May 2003)

Koper, E J R (2003) *Modelling Units of Study from A Pedagogical Perspective: The pedagogical meta-model behind EML*, document prepared for the IMS Learning Design Working Group, 2001 [Online] eml.ou.nl/introduction/docs/ped-metamodel.pdf (accessed 5 February 2003)

Kraan, W (2002) *Developers Content to Bash Code at CETIS* [Online] www.cetis.ac.uk/content/20021120030704 (accessed 5 February 2003)

Kraan, W (2003a) *IEEE to lift SCORM, IMS Content Packaging to Standard Status, Clarifies LOM Future* [Online] www.cetis.ac.uk/content/20030203181028 (accessed 5 February 2003)

Kraan, W (2003b) *SiX Plugfest Report: Encouraging, But Could Do Better* [Online] www.cetis.ac.uk/content/20030206174927 (accessed 6 February 2003)

Kraan, W and Wilson, S (2003) *Dan Rehak: 'SCORM is Not for Everyone'* [Online] www.cetis.ac.uk/content/20021002000737 (accessed 5 February 2003)

LeNoble, D F (1998) Digital diploma mills: the automation of higher education, *First Monday*, **3** (1) [Online] www.firstmonday.dk/issues/issue3_1/noble (accessed 12 May 2003)

Oliver, R (2000) When teaching meets learning: design principles and strategies for Web-based learning environments that support knowledge construction, Keynote speech at the ASCILITE 2000 Conference [Online] www.ascilite.org.au/conferences/coffs00/papers/ron_oliver_keynote.pdf (accessed 12 May 2003)

Rescher, N (1964) *Introduction to Logic*, St Martins Press, New York

Salmon, G (2000) *E-moderating: The key to teaching and learning online*, Kogan Page, London

Sholtz, P (2001) Transaction costs and the social cost of online privacy, *First Monday*, **6** (5) [Online]firstmonday.org/issues/issue6_5/sholtz (accessed 12 May 2003)

Sloep, P B (2002a) Necessary conditions for the flexible re-use of educational content conference, in *Proceedings of the 8th International Conference of European University Information Systems, EUNIS 2002, The Changing Universities: The Challenge of New Technologies*, ed L M Ribeiro and J M dos Santos, pp 114–17, FEUP Porto [Online] www.ou.nl/open/psl/Publicaties/EUNIS2002.pdf (accessed 12 May 2003)

Sloep, P B (2002b) *Learning Technology Standardization* [Online] eml.ou.nl/introduction/docs/LearningTechnologystandardization.pdf (accessed 12 May 2003)

Söderberg, J (2002) Copyleft vs. copyright: a Marxist critique, *First Monday*, **7** (3) [Online] firstmonday.org/issues/issue7_3/soderberg/index.html (accessed 12 May 2003)

Suber, P (2003) Removing the barriers to research: an introduction to open access for librarians, *College and Research Libraries News*, **64**, pp 92–113 [Online] www.earlham.edu/~peters/writing/acrl.htm (accessed 12 May 2003)

Westera, W and Sloep, P B (1998) The virtual company: towards a self-directed, competence-based learning environment in distance education, *Educational Technology*, **38** (1), pp 32–37

Westera, W and Sloep, P B (2001) The future of education in cyberspace, in *Provocative and Do-able Futures for CyberEducation: Leadership for the cutting edge*, ed L R Vandervert and L V Shavinina, pp 115–37, Mary Ann Liebert, Larchmont, NY

Wiley, D A (2002) Connecting learning objects to instructional design theory: a definition, a metaphor, and a taxonomy, in *The Instructional Use of Learning Objects*, ed D A Wiley, pp 1–23, Agency for Instructional Technology and Association for Educational Communications of Technology, Bloomington, IN [Online] reusability.org/read/chapters/wiley.doc (accessed 12 May 2003)

Chapter 11

Management and organization of integrated e-learning

Marcel van der Klink and Wim Jochems

Introduction

There is a general awareness in the world of education that integrated e-learning (IEL) is a strategic topic of paramount importance that needs to be addressed by faculty management. At the same time, however, it is unclear what exactly the advantages will be. The future is rather fuzzy. Electronic learning environments still have many limitations, and standardization issues remain unresolved. All in all, this has created an extremely uncertain atmosphere when it comes down to the basic questions: What? Why? and How? Nevertheless, IEL has to be managed and organized.

In this chapter we concentrate on the topic of IEL from a managerial point of view, particularly from the perspective of faculty management of institutes for higher education. Faculty management faces many questions, challenges and uncertainties when it comes to decisions on IEL and its implementation. This chapter aims to provide food for thought when it comes to this issue. It commences with a short description of the state of the art. The current situation can be best described as high-level ambitions with poor implementation. We recognize that the true value of IEL lies in its potential to reform education in the direction of new pedagogical approaches that promise to be able to meet future challenges such as competency-based education. Accordingly, we have paid attention to innovation in educational practice by means of IEL. Striving for more innovative types of education implies an approach in which technological, strategic, pedagogical and organizational views of implementation are integrated. These views will be discussed below. We then go on to discuss the various phases of the process of implementation. The last section summarizes and reflects on the main insights of the previous sections.

The state of the art

In many universities the use of ICT depends on the commitment of small groups or single faculty members who are convinced of the advantages of electronic learning. This is what Bates (2000) defines as the 'Lone Ranger approach'. This approach is typified by the fact that the departure of one single faculty member may severely damage the use of ICT within that faculty. Moreover, the lack of standardization and collective agreements leads to considerable costs, which might give the impression that IEL cannot perhaps be afforded on a larger scale. Collis (1999) describes the current situation at universities as one in which a thousand flowers bloom, meaning that there are a large number of experiments, small groups and solitary enthusiastic teachers using ICT in courses, although generally speaking, there is no broad approach from the faculty as a whole. Examples of the successful use of ICT are on the level of single courses, and to date there are not many examples of these with regard to IEL integrated into the whole curriculum. Only a few European universities have started to develop a strategy towards the large-scale application of IEL (Hendrikx, 1999). While it could be the faculty's purpose to maintain a *laissez-faire* policy, many universities strive for a more comprehensive use of IEL. However, in order to achieve use on a large scale, it is becoming increasingly clear that this requires an integrated approach (Collis and Van der Wende, 1999). A single teacher's enthusiastic use of ICT without the support of the faculty will almost certainly fail, as shown in the boxed example.

The large-scale usage of IEL depends on so many variables and processes, and requires the involvement of such a variety of actors, that an integrated approach on the faculty level is a necessary condition for successful implementation. The nature of the integrated approach for large-scale usage of IEL will depend, however, on the faculty's goals concerning the use of IEL. These goals may differ, and we will discuss three types: substitution, innovation and transformation. The essence of *substitution* lies in the replacement of conventional learning materials by electronic materials. Nothing actually changes fundamentally. The content and pedagogical approach remain unchanged, and no alternative learning activities are offered. In most cases it is the individual teacher who decides to what extent electronic materials can replace written materials. When the purpose is substitution, the technical aspects of ICT attract the most attention. Pedagogical and organizational

The teacher as Don Quixote

A teacher decided to use ICT in his course to support students' learning outside the classroom. In this course the focus shifted from teaching towards self-directed learning using ICT. However, when students experience that traditional teaching is the dominant means of learning expected in the curriculum, they find it difficult to take on one single course with an approach that requires self-directed learning. In this case, many students ultimately resisted the approach to that specific course. They found it difficult to cope with the different expectations of learning and assessment. Any individual teacher whose ambition it is to improve learning processes may therefore find it extremely challenging to do so.

aspects are hardly considered at all, because substitution is perceived to be merely a matter of replacing an old facility by a new one, leaving all the other aspects of education unchanged.

This is not the case when *innovation* is the goal. Innovation assumes rethinking the pedagogical approach as the starting point. A characteristic feature of innovation is that more than one teacher is involved. The innovation has impact on more courses or even on the whole curriculum. It requires the participation of teachers, tutors and managers. Compared to substitution, when the goal is innovation there is more focus on the pedagogical advantages of IEL and it is perceived as an investment in improving the quality of courses.

Transformation assumes a radical change. Not only must the pedagogical approach alter profoundly but so too must the processes, structures and staff roles, for instance by shifting towards competency-based learning. Transformation could be required to meet the demands of our postmodern knowledge society. The result is that IEL becomes a necessary condition: without the potential advantages of IEL this transformation could not succeed, with the result that IEL becomes a catalyst in improving the quality of education.

Three levels

From the perspective of management it is necessary to have a clear view of the change aimed at by introducing IEL, as to a large extent it determines the work that has to be done in order to implement that change. At the same time, we should realize that 'management' operates at different levels. At the *organizational* level the board manages, for instance, by providing a specific infrastructure with respect to information and communication technology; stating the mission with respect to education and educational policy; making technical support available; and possibly by providing additional means and training in the use of the new facilities. At the *curricular* level the director of studies manages the programme by planning the types of course to be delivered by the teachers; structuring the programme; and defining the sequencing of courses. Finally, at the *course* level teachers develop and deliver courses, and in so doing actually manage the learning activities of the students. Work has to be done at each of these three levels, and it has to be done in such a way that it is in line with the other two levels. Thus from a managerial perspective the change we are aiming at by introducing IEL also has to be clarified in order for all the parties concerned to appreciate what is expected in order to implement the change. This means that an important step is developing an educational concept or model that clearly expresses in what way IEL will be used within the programme.

An educational concept can be described as a coherent set of guiding principles. Concepts may be student-centred, problem-based, case-based, project-based and competence-based education. A concept provides a general model, a blueprint of the type of instructions or learning arrangements to be provided to students, and it therefore affects education on the same three levels we mentioned above. At the *organizational* level it influences the educational organization of the institute or faculty. The concept could have impact on the roles and accountabilities of all those who are involved in the educational processes. It could influence the course production and course delivery processes. In this case, the concept demands different approaches from the former situation, and thus might require changes in the infrastructure of the institute. At the *curricular* level the director of studies will use the concept as a format with respect to shaping a curriculum or an educational programme. It defines types of course, the structure of the programme, the rhythm of the curriculum (for example the timetable, the way in which learning and testing or assessing alternate, and the preferred interactions with the students), the sequencing of modules and so forth. At the *course* level the concept provides guidelines for course developers and teachers, for example with respect to the preferred types of learning arrangements, types of learning activities, instructional settings to be realized, prescribed testing or assessing procedures, and the educational media allowed. An important aspect of the concept of a 'course' will be the specific way IEL plays a part in them.

Let us consider competency-based education with IEL as a means of intensifying self-study and homework. We will use this example to explain the impact of an educational concept on the levels mentioned. In competency-based education the curriculum is not organized according to the subject matter domains to be mastered, but according to the competencies that are perceived to be characteristic of a particular profession. Thus, for instance, a course is not 'owned' by a specific teacher who has a great deal of expertise in that particular topic, but by a group of experts who together cover the competency under consideration. The roles and responsibilities of the experts involved will change because this concept demands teamwork, with the director of studies in the lead. Competency-based learning also stresses the use of rich, meaningful, realistic learning tasks as the driving force in learning (Merrill, 2002). This means that teachers are expected to maximize active learning by creating learning arrangements in which theory and practice are well integrated, and in which e-learning should support the learning arrangements such as tasks and information sources. The result is that a model of learning and instruction that has been preferred is defined at the course level.

The essence of an educational concept is that a curriculum is not perceived as the sum of a series of more or less independent courses that have to be completed in a prescribed order, but as an integrated whole. The concept describes the way the integration should be organized and managed. In other words, a curriculum should be more than the sum of the performances of individual teachers. It is considered to be a team performance, and the concept indicates the principles the team members will use in developing and delivering the learning arrangements. An educational concept contributes to the quality of a curriculum by improving the consistency and coherence of an educational programme, because it expresses the intended relations between the components in the programmes (at the curricular level), explains the roles to be performed by the various players (at the organizational level), and indicates an approach to be realized (at the course level). Thus an important step is to exteriorize the educational concept that characterizes the kind of IEL you would like to implement.

Managing the change: an integrated approach

Davis and Botkin (1995) maintain that when educators use technology to do their same old job better, they generally fail. We can only agree with their conclusion. The central question to be addressed in this section is how to manage the change process using IEL innovatively in higher education. Implementation aiming at the usage of IEL on a large scale requires a holistic approach from the outset. Any faculty seriously considering the use of technology for teaching and learning really needs to go through some form of planning exercise before it makes any major commitments, particularly if it is recognized that technology is not just an adjunct but can genuinely bring about fundamental change (Bates, 2000). Four perspectives need to be taken into consideration here: technological, strategic, pedagogical and organizational. These perspectives will be discussed below.

A technological view

'Based on technological optimism, there is a strong tendency to distribute as much as possible technological equipment in the educational system' (Elen, Lowyck and Van den Berg, 1999: 191). When one surveys the last few years, it is evident that higher education institutes have made substantial investments in technological infrastructure, but that the benefits have been rather disappointing. The premise was that supplying staff and students with an adequate infrastructure would be sufficient to boost the innovation of educational programmes. This premise has not been upheld. The technological aspects were too strongly focused on, without it being clear how the technological infrastructure relates to the strategic faculty goals and how the technology must support the programmes to ensure pedagogical quality, as shown in the box.

Technology and the quality of education

A faculty decided to introduce using SMS messages as a learning aid, by inviting students to send SMS messages containing questions and remarks to the teacher during a lecture. After reading the messages in the coffee break the teacher was obliged to respond to these questions and remarks during the second half of the lecture.

At first sight we could see this as a valuable technological contribution to the quality of lectures. But this is not a foregone conclusion. There are many ways to improve the level of interaction between students and teachers during lectures. The students could simply be encouraged to raise their hands if they have something to say. It seems that the only real beneficiaries of this particular initiative were probably the telecom industries.

Moreover, the world of e-learning is still in its infancy, meaning for instance that agreement on internationally accepted standards has not yet been achieved, and that learning platforms might evolve rather rapidly. New investments in infrastructure might be needed in the near future. At the same time, the costs of systems maintenance and technical support have been underestimated. The costs of content development and content maintenance are not usually taken into consideration at all, particularly when the implementation of e-learning is viewed from a technological point of view, in which case the following considerations are essential:

- Use as much as possible existing technology that has already proven its value, and is generally accepted and recognized by the educational community.
- Consult other educational institutes that have already implemented IEL and use their expertise in reaching your decision.
- Preferably use technology standards such as XML that support open standards, so that the exchangeability of the infrastructure is guaranteed.
- Avoid systems that do not allow you to convert instructional materials to other or new systems. After a number of years, the e-learning materials developed by the teachers represent a considerable sum of money that should not be wasted in the event of a switch to a new version or system.
- A consortium or association of institutes sharing expertise and experience is in a better position to evaluate technological facilities, and might be able to negotiate better conditions from the providers.
- There is nothing wrong with small-scale pilot projects that are gradually introduced. Problems raised by the integration of the process of developing instructional materials, administrative processes such as student admission and registration, and storage and content management processes need not all be solved at once.

In many cases people are aware of the technical problems but not of strategic, pedagogical or organizational difficulties. It follows that technical problems in general are not the most difficult ones to solve.

A strategic view

IEL cannot be regarded as an isolated issue. It is expensive and impinges on a large number of processes. We need a considerable number of good reasons to aim for IEL. Raising strategic questions supports the faculty in gaining insight into the expectations and the priority of IEL on the faculty's agenda. From this perspective we have to ask whether it will contribute to the faculty's strategic goals. This raises the following questions:

● Will IEL contribute positively to the faculty's reputation, and if so, in what way?
● To what extent will IEL enhance the development of new, flexible educational programmes?
● Does it demand closer cooperation with fellow faculties, and if so, what are the possibilities and what are the pros and cons of cooperation?
● What funds (whether internal or external) are available or can be made available to the university?
● Could IEL serve as an attractive, valuable asset in marketing directed towards recruiting potential students, and if it could, would it do so in practice?
● What are the expectations of employers and professional bodies in this respect?

Exploring these issues contributes to the view of the possibilities connected with the implementation of IEL. Moreover, it increases the level of awareness concerning the concrete expectations of IEL. Finally, it clarifies to what extent IEL relates to the faculty's strategic goals, both current and future. Table 11.1 provides an overview of the strategic arguments that have been advanced by the universities to underpin their decision to implement ICT. It shows a range of arguments that vary considerably and are linked to various internal and external conditions. Drawing on the results from literature reviews and case studies, Fisser (2001) identified nine factors that are related to the implementation of ICT in universities.

Although developing a strategy is generally linked to selection and the cogency of the arguments, in practice fewer rational arguments play a significant role. Nevertheless, faculty management has to provide a grounded, convincing, clear picture of the most appropriate strategy, given the internal strengths and weaknesses, and the external threats and opportunities.

A pedagogical view

An approach driven by sheer technology does not necessarily improve the quality of education. A pedagogical view is required to determine the sensible use of

Table 11.1   *Factors enhancing the implementation of ICT*

Factors	Explication
The new marketplace	Universities use ICT to deliver education for new markets, which are striving for cooperation with partners, including students from business and industry
The pedagogy of flexible learning	Universities use ICT to offer flexibility in time and/or place and to alter the pedagogical view aiming at more student-centred types of education
The technology for flexible learning	Universities use ICT because it is available
Students in a dynamic world	Universities use ICT to anticipate the need for life-long learning and student demographics
Concrete vision	Sharing a vision, and with concrete plans, universities hope to benefit from the implementation of ICT
Workplace demands the use of ICT	Students and employers expect universities to use ICT because IT plays an important role in many professions
Individualization	Universities use ICT to meet the needs of specific groups of students and to increase access to university education programmes
Cost-effectiveness	Universities expect to increase efficiency by implementing ICT
Funding	Universities implement ICT because they receive additional funding for it

Source: Fisser, 2001

technology in an appropriate, efficient, effective manner. In order to reach a conclusion, a considerable number of questions have to be answered:

- What is the role of classroom-based activities and what other learning activities such as individual study, small group work and e-learning are important? What exactly is the role of e-learning in this mix of methods? What is the role of collaborative learning and of computer-supported collaborative learning, and how are we going to enhance this type of learning?
- To what extent have discipline-based courses to be replaced by courses that integrate knowledge, skills and attitudes?
- How are we going to promote our students to become more independent, self-directed learners?

- How can we assess the students' progress in an integrated manner, and what new forms of assessment including e-portfolio do we need to achieve that?
- How will we promote the use of rich, meaningful, realistic learning tasks as the driving force for learning?

To develop a pedagogical view of education and IEL, it is advisable to start with rethinking the views on learning, instruction and teaching to encourage staff to think beyond the contemporary framework. Some issues that have been mentioned previously may be helpful in getting started.

A simple example of a pedagogical view

Suppose you wanted to introduce e-learning in competency-based dual learning. The core concept could be to mix educational methods such as classroom activities (collaborative learning), self-study of written course materials, and e-learning as a means of structuring students' learning activities. The backbone of such a course would be a series of tasks (provided by the Web), together with background information (books and electronic sources). The beginning of a task would be prepared in the classroom, but it would have to be finished individually at home and the feedback provided at the next meeting.

At the same time, authentic learning is considered to be of importance in order to promote transfer from theory to practice. Accordingly, learning arrangements would be needed in which students learn to solve real-life problems and perform real-life tasks.

The following guidelines (Bates, 2000) will enhance the process of adapting a new pedagogical view:

- It is important to gain insight into the faculty's degree of autonomy to alter the pedagogical view. What is the campus policy regarding the 'pedagogical flavour'? We need to clarify the boundaries in which the faculty's pedagogical view must 'nest'.
- Draw on those staff members who have some experience with new technologies, so that information becomes available about the potential and limitations of this technology.
- Foster a sense of urgency, stressing that change is inevitable for the continuation of the institute, as it will enhance the development of creative, original views.
- Invite external speakers such as alumni, business people, and members of fellow institutes with progressive views on technology, learning and teaching to give lectures and demonstrations.

Although participation of staff members is necessary, strong leadership by the faculty management in the development of a new pedagogical view is even more essential. Faculty management should steer the process, guard its continuation, and strive for concrete, detailed statements about the pedagogical view and its consequences for the technological infrastructure. Leadership is also required for the final agreement on the pedagogical view. It is unrealistic to expect that every single staff member will fully adopt the new view. However, considering objections and looking for alternatives to overcome problems in collaboration with staff members is always advisable. Many innovations in education fail because they do not sufficiently address the needs and concerns of staff (see Van den Berg and Vandenberghe, 1999). A successful innovation requires ownership, vision and enthusiasm at all levels of the faculty, but in the final analysis it is the faculty management who have to bear the responsibility for the pedagogical view.

An organizational view

The introduction of IEL will be either an innovation or a transformation, and will therefore definitely have a strong impact on various aspects of the faculty as an organizational unit. We should like to mention some issues that need to be addressed.

First of all, the workflow will change. The introduction of IEL will influence developing and delivering instruction and instructional materials. As a result, new procedures and methods will have to be designed and organized in order to enable all the staff members involved (teachers, technologists and educational designers), to cooperate effectively (see Chapter 9). Whatever the technological infrastructure becomes, support for staff members will be necessary to learn to cope with the technology. Support is also needed with respect to the pedagogical aspects of IEL. How do we develop learning material that is rich and effective from an instructional point of view? This can be realized by training and coaching teachers, but also by providing examples of 'best practice' that can function as models. As long as the organizational structure is unclear and not in harmony with the innovation, its implementation becomes a 'mission impossible'.

The roles and responsibilities of staff members will change to a certain extent, depending on the educational concept chosen. Cooperation between teachers becomes more important, and the work of faculty members becomes more team-based instead of in the traditional mould with the teacher as a 'stand-alone' staff member. Another point is that the director of studies will need a more prominent position in order to be able to guide and manage the teachers. These new roles and responsibilities have to be made explicit to all concerned. But an even more important point is that staff members become convinced of the need to work in teams, and have a positive attitude towards cooperation in delivering high-quality, attractive educational programmes.

One of the major organizational issues concerns the faculty's human resources management (HRM) policy. When the aim is, for instance, to integrate competency-based education and IEL at the heart of teaching and learning, it is necessary to reconsider the roles and responsibilities of the staff, including those of teachers.

Staff development is crucial so that it is made clear to all the participants that implementing IEL is not merely an adjunct. The essential issue to address is to what extent all staff members, and teachers in particular, will have to perform new roles and responsibilities. What will become the minimum level of staff competencies that can be agreed on? Finally, to what extent do IEL higher levels require more specialized competencies that probably cannot be mastered by the average staff member? Thus, great changes in many aspects of the HRM policy are required, for instance with respect to job descriptions, recruitment criteria, tenure tracks, incentives, career management, training and so on.

Towards a coherent plan for implementation

In the previous sections we discussed the strategic, technological, pedagogical and organizational perspectives. These four views provide the cornerstones of outlining the innovation plan. It is our opinion that the design of a coherent plan demands a synthesis of the information delivered by each of these views. At the same time, choices have to be made because the views are to a large extent closely interrelated. Moreover, a number of issues with respect to the specific faculty have to be taken into consideration, for example past experience, the availability of expertise, educational culture, ambitions, budgets and educational leadership.

An innovation plan should address the following additional issues:

- the implementation objectives in measurable terms (targets);
- the projects and phases for the intended outcomes (deliverables);
- the time schedule (deadlines);
- the appointment of a change manager;
- the appointment of project managers for particular initiatives;
- the budgets and support available to staff members;
- the monitoring and evaluation of the implementation.

To improve the feasibility of the implementation, the following guidelines may be helpful (Inglis, Ling and Joosten, 1999; Fisser, 2001):

- Prioritize the tasks and do the planning in detail. This will cover, for instance, who is responsible for the actions; who will help rethink the critical factors necessary step by step; and who will be in charge.
- Identify pioneers with experience in use of ICT who also have a positive attitude towards the new educational concept. These pioneers can be invited to become members of the first projects that are launched. They will serve as models and advisors to their peers.
- Cultivate the influence of the faculty management, for example if the dean of the faculty has a positive effect on staff members to adopt an innovation. However, this only holds if the faculty management really does have authority and power.

- Find as many ways as possible to spread the word about the implementation. Make sure that information about innovations becomes a regular topic on the agenda of every staff meeting.
- Celebrate milestones. Never let achievements pass unacknowledged.
- Start with projects aiming at the development of new initiatives, for example new programmes. This has major advantages. Innovation in existing programmes is much more difficult.
- Be explicit about what type of electronic content is redundant. Enthusiastic staff members sometimes have the tendency to make whole textbooks electronically available. This does not contribute to high-quality learning. It is much more appropriate, particularly in the case of competency-based education, to focus on the development of interesting, challenging assignments and study tasks.
- Be realistic about the possibilities for the development of interactive multimedia courseware. This can be quite costly. It is better to look for opportunities for collaboration with other providers with mutual interests.
- Keep focusing on the objectives and avoid technological determinism. There is a real danger that staff members will use all the possibilities the technological infrastructure offers, not because it is necessary from a pedagogical point of view but just because it is available.

Conclusions

It is common practice for institutes of higher education to have technologically driven motives to adopt new types of technological infrastructure. The availability of the infrastructure and the fear of lagging behind create an atmosphere that can be defined as the 'me too syndrome'. In most cases this results in substitution, in other words replacement of written materials by electronic delivery without substantial improvement or benefits, making the me-too syndrome potentially rather expensive. Real innovation in education with the use of IEL requires an approach that ensures different aspects are taken into account. It goes without saying that it requires a long-term plan. In addition, there are no roadmaps available that will unfailingly lead to successful implementation. However, the examples and guidelines cited above will provide the faculty management with considerable food for thought in determining its own road.

References

Bates, A W (2000) *Managing Technological Change: Strategies for college and university leaders*, Jossey-Bass, San Francisco, CA

Collis, B A (1999) Implementing ICT in the faculty: letting a 1000 flowers bloom or managing change? in *De Digitale Leeromgeving* (The electronic learning environment), ed M Mirande, J Riemersma and W Veen, pp 121–36, Wolters-Noordhoff, Groningen, Netherlands

Collis, B A and Van der Wende, M (1999) *The Use of Information and Communication Technologies in Higher Education: An international orientation on trends and issues*, University of Twente/CHEPS, Twente, Netherlands

Davis, S and Botkin, J (1995) *The Monster under the Bed*, Simon and Schuster, New York

Elen, J, Lowyck, J and Van den Berg, B (1999) Virtual university: will learning benefit? in *Socio-Economics of Virtual Universities; Experiences from open and distance higher education in Europe*, ed G E Ortner and F Nickolmann, pp 185–211, Deutscher Studien Verlag, Weinheim, Germany

Fisser, P H G (2001) *Using Information and Communication Technology. A process of change in higher education*, doctoral dissertation, Twente University Press, Enschede, Netherlands

Hendrikx, P (1999) On the way to virtual universities: open and distance higher education in Europe, in *Socio-economics of Virtual Universities; Experiences from open and distance higher education in Europe*, ed G E Ortner and F Nickolmann, pp 29–51, Deutscher Studien Verlag, Weinheim, Germany

Inglis, A, Ling, P and Joosten, V (1999) *Delivering Digitally. Managing the transition to the knowledge media*, Kogan Page, London

Merrill, M D (2002) First principles of instruction, *Educational Technology Research and Development*, **50** (3), pp 43–59

Van den Berg, R and Vandenberghe, R (1999) *Succesvol leidinggeven aan onderwijsinnovaties* (Successfully managing innovations in education), Samson, Alphen aan den Rijn, Netherlands

Chapter 12

Coaching and training in integrated electronic learning environments (IELEs)

Henny Boshuizen and Paul Kirschner

Introduction

The terms 'coaching' and 'training' almost inevitably conjure up a sporting connotation. Some teams have trainers, some have coaches and some have both. Although coaches and trainers have a great deal in common, they are also quite different. Both coaches and trainers help either an individual or a team to develop skills, strategies and tactics. Moreover, both coaches and trainers determine goals, assess ability and performance, measure the gap between the present state and the required or desired performance levels, and develop plans on how to bridge that gap. The difference is that coaches focus on the whole, including attitude, mental fitness, lifestyle, diet and so on. Their responsibility does not stop once the match begins. It remains their task to continue pointing to shortcomings with respect to skills, modifying strategies or replacing players. In other words, coaches take a holistic approach toward the development of competence.

Trainers, on the other hand, concentrate on developing isolated skills and tactics, or they deal with one aspect of the player's well-being (they are the dietician, weight trainer or masseur, for instance) and they do this primarily between the matches played. In other words, trainers focus on a part of that competency that has to be trained separately. In soccer, for example, the coach determines who does or does not play, gives directions from the sideline during the game, and decides when and who to substitute. The trainer, on the other hand, observes the players and draws conclusions as to the ways in which they need to be trained in the coming period. This division of work and responsibility can also be seen in other fields. In human resources management, a coach is like a big brother or sister who counsels a trainee or a new employee with respect to all aspects of work, while a trainer usually gives specific courses (hence the name, 'training') on specific aspects of a job. In this chapter we discuss how these two concepts relate to the field of human learning, and particularly to learning in integrated electronic learning environments (IELEs).

A two-tier system

The previous paragraph focused implicitly on how a coach and a trainer work at developing competencies, which is the role of all institutions that profess to strive towards competency-based education. Competencies are more than just the sum of knowledge and skills needed for a specific field or profession. They are an integrated whole of knowledge, skills and attitudes that can be used to make adequate, effective decisions and/or take adequate, effective action in a specific setting or situation (Kirschner *et al*, 1997).

This focus on competencies has strong implications for the way coaching and training in IELEs can and should take place. For example, it assumes that it is the students themselves who invest in the acquisition of knowledge and skills. They have to do the work. The teachers, in this case in the role of trainers, can only help them attain the required knowledge and skills by the time they graduate. But if we as educators in a competency-based learning system do our work well, the knowledge learnt and skills acquired must be part of a larger whole of competencies that allows graduates to apply the knowledge and skills in varying, previously unencountered situations. It also allows them to maintain the acquired knowledge and skills, to develop new knowledge and skills in the light of developments in science and society, and to accommodate new insights and developments in their professional domain, in their work and in society in general into their repertoire.

This means that graduates also need the assistance of a coach to achieve this integration. Thus training and coaching make up a two-tier system in competency-based education. First, academic, professional and personal knowledge, skills and attitudes in a specific domain have to be developed, as do the soft skills which have so often been neglected. For this, new kinds of assignments and work forms have been developed that stimulate critical thinking, creative problem solving, collaboration and information skills. This is discussed in Chapters 1 and 2. For students who lack experience in working in this way, help and support in the form of coaching and training are needed.

Second, these all have to be integrated into competencies which allow the learner to make use of the knowledge, skills and attitudes to make satisfactory, effective decisions in a specific setting or situation (Kirschner *et al*, 1997). Another factor is that they should have confidence in their ability to take effective and appropriate actions, explain what they are about, live and work effectively with others, and continue to learn from experience (Stephenson and Weil, 1992). This requires a far more implicit way of learning, and coaches who have comprehensive information about the students' performance. The possibilities of these two tiers are discussed in this chapter.

The roles of the teacher in competence-based education

Competencies are not learnt, but are acquired through sufficient practice in a variety of situations. Competencies, along with their constituent knowledge, skills and attitudes are best acquired through rich learning environments (Collins, 1988) where experiences are provided that 'mimic' the experiences of practitioners. Although it is not possible to immerse the learner in practitioner environments, IELEs that, for example, make use of simulations and virtual working environments (see Chapter 4) and meaningful experiences help learners learn an expert's ways of knowing. Reflexivity is essential and must be nurtured (Barnett, 1997a, 1997b). Finally, all this is best achieved when learning takes place in ill-structured situations (Spiro *et al*, 1988).

In focusing on such competencies the genie is released from the bottle, and in this case the genie is 'practice', which must be carried out in situations that are as similar to professional practice as possible, so that students acquire relevant skills (both soft and hard), have relevant learning experiences, build up integrated knowledge, skills and attitudes, and know when and how to apply what. The traditional breakdown of education into isolated knowledge domains (which defend their own position in a curriculum) and skills is superseded.

Similarly De Vijlder (2002), based upon work by Gibbons *et al* (1994), observed that teaching and learning is moving away from a traditional 'didactic', solitary educational model towards a more 'constructive', interconnected educational model (see Table 12.1).

A model emerges in which learning is embedded in a context of direct application. Knowledge, skills, attitudes and competencies are not reduced to separate, hierarchically organized subject domains. Methods and organization are heterogeneous, depending on the features and constraints of the topic area. Learning is integrated with other activities, and quality is also judged by the impact on the organization involved.

This change in focus also implies a change in the teacher's role. The learning of students who have to develop their own skills becomes the focus, rather than the

Table 12.1   *Modes of learning*

Mode 1 learning	Mode 2 learning
Learning is based upon methodology and content conventions developed in education	Learning takes place in the context of the immediate application
Learning is organized in content domains, possibly based upon 'projects'	Knowledge and skills cannot be reduced to separate content domains
Learning is homogeneous and predictable in its methods and organization	Learning is heterogeneous and idiosyncratic in its methods and organization
The relationship between learning and society is sequential and indirect	Learning is related to other activities with respect to both time and direct impact
Quality criteria are based upon internal 'educational' standards	Quality is determined by the effect of what is learnt on society

Source: based on De Vijlder, 2002

academic subject matter to be mastered. The role of the teacher develops accordingly, from being 'merely' the expert, the transmission medium and the examiner and/or grader, to one of guide, knowledge intermediary and assessor. In addition to all this, the teacher becomes the learning processes coach. Some people would even say that the teacher becomes a coach, first and foremost.

Many of the things said in the previous paragraphs concern instructional design as well as teaching, coaching and training. The model used in this volume (see Chapter 1) explicitly focuses on competency acquisition via whole-task training (which requires coaching), sub-skill training (which requires training), and just-in-time information and supporting information (both requiring primarily teaching in the classical sense). All four of these components need to be planned and prepared as well as possible. The kind of support needed during the learning process depends not only on this level of preparation in advance, but also on how well the four elements can be separated, prepared and trained in isolation.

This view of the teaching and learning process, and the role of teachers in it, raises a number of questions, of which the most important ones are, if the task of trainers and coaches is not the transmission of knowledge and skills, what is it and what should they do?

Skills training

The Four Component Instructional Design (4C/ID) model assumes that at least part of the competency to be trained consists of recurrent skills that can be separately trained and automated. Examples are asking open questions and summarizing the information given in interviewing skills, doing certain physical examinations as part of the diagnostic skills of a medical practitioner, and fitting pipes in a new house being built. Acquiring these skills through training requires careful analysis of the knowledge and skills needed, to determine whether they really are recurrent, and determining the facts that constitute the skills and the knowledge necessary for carrying them out. This means that training and automating them cannot be done without simultaneous knowledge acquisition and skills training (Van Merriënboer, Kirschner and Kester, 2003). Once the design has been made and all the necessary materials have been collected and made available to the learner, the role of the trainer in face-to-face situations is basically to demonstrate the skill to the students and give feedback on the way the skill is performed by the learner. Whether this trainer needs any special skills depends on the kind of skill being trained, and more exactly on the kind of feedback required. Sometimes both demonstration and feedback can be prepared and at least partially built into the training materials. The trainers themselves may not be required at all – for example, it is possible to learn to knit from a video or printed instructions – or training can be carried out by a peer or layperson who can give feedback, with the eventual help of a checklist.

However, when the quality of the performance at successive moments during the learning process is important, a skilled trainer with an understanding of expert performance, who can identify significant deviations and knows how they can be remedied, can make a significant contribution to the learning process. Patrick (1992) differentiated between four types of guidance (adapted from Holding, 1965):

- *Physical guidance*, particularly in the field of motor learning, and including physical restriction.
- *Demonstrations*, including modelling situations in which a learner learns by observing or imitating an expert.
- *Verbal guidance or advice*, such as explaining and prompting to help selection of a correct or adequate response.
- *Cueing*, whereby the learner is made aware of signals and their relevance.

Guidance by a trainer in a face-to-face situation is even more important when skills are trained that can have a major impact on the mental and physical well-being of the student or others. Examples can be found in health care, where the trainer has to ensure that the learner and the subject of examination (the patient) are not injured or harmed, while at the same time evaluating performance and advising on ways to improve, if necessary by adapting the training to the specific difficulties this learner may be having. Conversely, the better potentially harmful situations can be prevented, and the better mistakes and errors can be foreseen, the easier it is to design instruction that can be done at a distance or through other media.

Coaching and coaches

Not surprisingly, the role of the coach is less clear cut than the trainer's, since coaching is an interpersonal process to help individuals and/or teams reach their highest levels of performance. Whitmore (2002) presents a model (GROW) consisting of four stages: 1) setting Goals; 2) doing a Reality check; 3) identifying Options and alternative strategies; and 4) determining What needs to be done, when, and by whom. In other words, coaching is an integral process involving the learners, their cognitive and affective state, what needs to be learnt and the learning environment or situation.

In our definition the coach's focus is the competency itself. Since a coach's task is to help students to develop competencies, his or her way of working consists of observing students' behaviour in whole-task situations and skills that are typically non-recurrent, that is, specific to certain situations. He or she does this by collecting further information, diagnosing the level of mastery, giving feedback, and advising and guiding students to adjust their learning strategies, depending on their individual style and problems.

Coaching is also a social process. With respect to a task, the coach must provide personal encouragement and motivational assistance (Gunawardena and Zittle, 1997; McDonald and Gibson, 1998). Social interaction can contribute to learner satisfaction and frequency of interaction in an online learning environment (Gunawardena and Zittle, 1997; Kanuka and Anderson, 1998). Such coaching in whole-task situations can be threatening, because it concerns the student as a person and not his or her abstract knowledge acquisition or isolated skills. In such situations, feelings of safety, commitment and mutual trust are required between student and coach. When more students are involved, which can be required when an authentic situation is defined by several roles that are taken by a group of students, this safety, commitment and trust must be guaranteed by the group as a whole.

These cognitive and affective aspects of coaching mean that a coach must fulfil the following functions in an educational situation:

- *Tutoring*, involving a large range of situations that help learners gain knowledge, skills and competency.
- *Mentoring*, for helping learners develop such things as savvy, understanding how culture affects choice, and insight into how to advance oneself.
- *Confronting or challenging*, so that clear performance standards are established, actual performance is compared against those standards, and performance that does not meet those standards is addressed.
- *Counselling*, to help the learner recognize, talk about, gain insight into, and solve either real or perceived problems that affect performance. This also involves dealing with frustrations, insecurities, anger, resentment and lack of commitment.

When we survey the variety of functions, poignant questions to ask are, who can be a coach, and is it necessary for a coach to also be an expert in the domain? These questions have been the subject of heated discussions within the realm of sports. When it comes to who is best suited to be a coach, is it the star player, past or present, who is an acknowledged expert and has reached the pinnacle of success, or the average player who has experienced how hard it is to reach a certain level, albeit not the top?

This question cannot be answered without taking into consideration the questions raised earlier. A coach must be able to make observations, compare them with a standard of mastery, give feedback, create safe situations and so forth. In certain fields and situations, both expert tutors and advanced students who act as tutors have been found to be effective, with each having their advantages and disadvantages. Student tutors were best in assessing the specific problems students have with the process of learning (such as working in groups on a problem or project), in building up specific competencies, and in creating a safe atmosphere. Expert tutors were better in stimulating students to reach higher levels of mastery. The best expert tutors were able to do both (Moust and Schmidt, 1994; Schmidt and Moust, 1995).

IELEs add an extra dimension to these questions since they include cases where students and teachers interact primarily or exclusively through communication channels that are much narrower than those in face-to-face interaction, and which are asynchronous with respect to learning and training or coaching. According to Moore (1993: 22), this 'transactional distance' – the psychological and communications space between learners and instructors – can lead 'to a psychological and communications gap, a space of potential misunderstanding between inputs of instructor and those of the learner'. The implication of these two factors (narrow communication and asynchronicity) for training and coaching will be discussed in the final section of this chapter. But first, we should like to turn to the role of the coach in skill acquisition via whole-task learning.

Role of the coach in skill acquisition via whole-task learning

By definition, students are novices who do not have a clear view of their level of understanding and mastery as compared with experts. Wagenaar *et al* (2001), for example, found that students in training as counsellors could deal with only one aspect while doing an intake interview with a new client, namely how to ask open, emphatic questions. Experts could focus on at least three separate aspects simultaneously, for example gathering enough information to make a preliminary diagnosis, dealing with the patient in such a way that a future relationship with this patient would not be jeopardized, and monitoring their own emotional reactions. It is a very long way from novice to expert, and it is no use requiring students to be able to maintain these three perspectives before they are aware of their importance and have accumulated enough skills in the basics. Coaches should be aware of this gap, and should adapt their coaching and feedback to the estimated level of student mastery, and aim at the zone of proximal development (Vygotsky, 1978).

Another complication that both student and coach should be aware of is that they may disagree about the exact nature of the competency that has to be developed, which can result in a tension between the coaches' role in assessing and maintaining standards, and students' self-image and sense of integrity. In teacher training, for example, students (that is, student teachers) and coaches (that is, their faculty advisors) may disagree on how much discipline is required in classrooms and how it should be maintained. In counselling, the two may disagree on how a counsellor should deal with his or her own emotions toward the client, or his or her behaviour. In medicine, intern and doctor may have different ethical standards and opinions which influence their choice of treatment. These differences may seem an acceptable difference of taste to the student closely connected to his or her personality and value system, while the coach perceives it as a stage in the learning process that must be overcome.

In general, the coach can choose one of two roles, stimulator/facilitator or advisor/assessor. These different roles of coaches are summarized in Table 12.2.

Table 12.2 *Actions of coaches depending on their role*

Coach stimulates and facilitates	Coach advises and evaluates
The student's experience is the point of departure for action	The coach's experience is the point of departure for action
The coach is a stimulator and as such is process-directed	The coach is an expert and as such is product-directed
The student sets the agenda	The coach sets the agenda
Personal development of the student (both hard and soft skills) is of central importance	Professional development of the student (both hard and soft skills) is of central importance
The coach asks questions	The coach gives guidance and advice
Development of reflection on learning and experiences by the student	Development of reflection on skills and competencies by the student

Source: based on Crasborn and Henning, 2001

Conclusion and discussion

In our treatment of the training and coaching of competency acquisition, we have taken our examples primarily from face-to-face situations. At the time of writing, more and more institutes of learning are making use of electronic learning environments, either in an exclusive way (distributed education and learning settings, often called distance education) or in a blended way (where both face-to-face and distributed education complement and suppiement each other). Rather than present an in-depth study of what is and is not possible in face-to-face and distributed education with the aid of IELEs, we will devote the rest of this chapter to a number of examples of the different forms of electronic coaching and training.

As we have seen, coaches and trainers carry out a number of activities in their work. Among those activities are in the first instance designing, delivering, observing, collecting information, diagnosing, giving feedback, advising, guiding or restraining (with respect to learning strategies and problems). Further activities include providing safety, creating or demanding commitment, building mutual trust, asking questions and stimulating reflection. The question is then whether IELEs are capable of carrying out these functions. The answer is both yes and no.

With respect to the training of the recurrent skills and the teaching of the necessary prerequisite and supportive knowledge and skills, the answer is a definite yes. There are many electronic environments, beginning with traditional computer-based training programmes and computer-assisted instruction systems, and advancing to more 'modern' integrated e-learning systems, that have proved to be capable of allowing students to achieve the knowledge, skills and even attitudes needed in their further learning and professional life. These systems can present information (sometimes just-in-time), supply the learners with variable problems (sometimes based upon dynamic task selection), and give the learners tailor-made feedback. The Open University of the Netherlands has even designed and implemented a number of stand-alone experimental practicals not only aimed at the acquisition of knowledge and skills, but also intended to help students develop important attitudes towards their chosen discipline. The trainer's role has been built in (see Kirschner and Huisman, 1998). Examples are:

- A practical that confronts learners with the reality and/or complexity of environmental problems where they experience the dilemmas of the environmental scientist and apply theoretical concepts learnt. They do this through the use of interactive cases in which they follow a game-like structure, through which the case evolves according to decisions made by the student (Huisman *et al*, 1993).
- A soil and environment practical where learners, in the context of an environmental case study, learn to judge the relevance of resources and decide in what phase of the case research particular resources should be studied (Lansu *et al*, 1994). This multimedia programme presents students with a large volume of diverse, sometimes contradictory resources on cases about soil and environment. The student is placed in the role of an environmental scientist who has to solve three problems using these resources, which include case introductions, interviews, landscape views, legal texts, data tables, soil profiles, maps, aerial photographs, newspaper articles, scientific reports and results of computations with a geographical information system.
- A practical where students may use a laboratory in which they learn to design experiments (behavioural toxicological research; Niesink *et al*, 1997). In this

practical students analyze research questions, formulate hypotheses, search through literature, set up an experimental protocol, and analyze and interpret experimental results. A great deal of effort has been invested in the early phase of research involving translation of a research question into a testable hypothesis. Students enter their formulation of the hypothesis in full text. An intelligent procedure interprets this and comments on unknown or inaccurate elements until the student has amended and reformulated the hypothesis into an acceptable form. Based on the hypothesis, students set up an experimental protocol by choosing between a large number of options on methods, materials, techniques and parameters. A built-in tutor comments on the relation between protocol and hypothesis. Students do not perform the experiments. The results are drawn from a database and are presented for analysis and interpretation. This interpretation, again with the aid of the electronic tutor, takes place on two levels, namely: 'Has my hypothesis been confirmed or rejected?' and 'Is my experimental design appropriate?'

It is far more difficult to 'cram' the coach into an electronic environment. Such an attempt is hindered by two factors. The first is inherent in the role and function of the coach, the second in the limitations of (or experience of) computer-mediated communication. That the coach always deals with non-recurrent, often unpredictable events is inherent in the role and function itself. A baseball coach, working with the same 28 players, in the 162nd, last game of a baseball season, against a team that he or she has played against 15 times earlier that season, will still be confronted with a situation that has not been encountered before. This is the same in the educational context, particularly in cases involving learning in groups (see Chapter 2), where each new learner, each new day presents the coach with new, unforeseen challenges. Intelligent agents which are often used in intelligent tutoring systems might provide the first solutions to this problem, although the artificial intelligence community has been promising this for more than 20 years and has still not delivered the goods.

The fact that participants in IELEs interact primarily or exclusively through communication channels that are much narrower than those in face-to-face interaction, and that are asynchronous, is inherent in the limitations of a computer-mediated environment. This leads to an increase in transactional distance and thus to 'a psychological and communications gap, a space of potential misunderstanding' (Moore, 1993: 22). This is not beneficial in fostering the necessary trust, intimacy and feelings of proximity needed for the rather 'threatening' role that a coach must fulfil. This is compounded by the fact that, although some IELEs are capable of supporting the necessary social interaction the stimulation of such social interaction, is usually restricted to the cognitive aspects of learning (Kreijns, Kirschner and Jochems, 2003). Designers and educators ignore or forget that social interaction is equally important for the socio-emotional processes responsible for the development of a community of learning in which a social space can be found that is characterized by trust and belonging, where social relationships are strong, and where a sense of community exists. These qualities are necessary for open dialogues and reinforcement of the social interaction that benefits learning (Rourke, 2000; Wegerif, 1998). Wegerif (1998: 48), for example notes that 'Without a feeling of community people are on their own, likely to be anxious, defensive and unwilling to take the risks involved in learning'.

Training and coaching require integrating or blending face-to-face personal contact into the concept of integrated electronic learning environments. Coaching in IELEs and developing automated coaches is one step farther than we are capable of at the moment.

References

Barnett, R (1997a) *Towards a Higher Education for a New Century*, University of London, Institute of Education, London

Barnett, R (1997b) *Higher Education: A critical business*, Open University Press, Buckingham, UK

Collins, A (1988) *Cognitive Apprenticeship and Instructional Technology*, Technical Report No 6899, BBN Labs Inc, Cambridge, MA

Crasborn, F and Henning, P (2001) *Leren Voetballen met Het Linkerbeen; Kun Je Coaches Leren Coachen?*, (Learning to Play Left-Legged Soccer; is It Possible to Teach Coaching to Coaches?), Programmamanagement EPS, Utrecht

De Vijlder, F (2002) Leren organizeren (Learning to organize), *Adviesraad voor het Wetenschaps- en Technologiebeleid / Commissie van Overleg Sectorraden Onderzoek en Ontwikkeling. Schoolagenda 2010, 2* – Essays, pp 175–232, Adviesraad voor het Wetenschaps- en Technologiebeleid, The Hague

Gibbons, M, Limoges, C, Nowotny, H, Schwartzman, S, Scott, P and Trow, M (1994) *The New Production of Knowledge: The dynamics of science and research in contemporary societies*, Sage, London

Gunawardena, C N and Zittle, F J (1997) Social presence as a predictor of satisfaction within a computer-mediated conferencing environment, *American Journal of Distance Education*, **11** (3), pp 8–26

Huisman, W, Martens, H, Mulleneers, E and van Dijk, J (1993) *LAVI-leed* (Computer software), Open University of the Netherlands, Heerlen

Kanuka, H and Anderson, T (1998) Online social interchange, discord, and knowledge construction, *Journal of Distance Education*, **13** (1), pp 57–74

Kirschner, P A and Huisman, W (1998) Dry laboratories in science education: computer-based practical work, *International Journal of Science Education*, **20** (6), pp 665–82

Kirschner, P A, Vilsteren, P, van Hummel, H and Wigman, M (1997) A study environment for acquiring academic and professional competence, *Studies of Higher Education*, **22** (2), pp 151–71

Kreijns, K, Kirschner, P A and Jochems, W (2003) Identifying the pitfalls for social interaction in computer-supported collaborative learning environments: a review of the research, *Computers in Human Behavior*, in press

Lansu, A, Ivens, W, Westera, W, Hummel, H, Huisman, W, Slootmaker, A, Martens, H and Berkhout, J (1994) *Soil and Environment* (Computer software), Open University of the Netherlands, Heerlen

McDonald, J and Gibson, C C (1998) Interpersonal dynamics and group development in computer conferencing, *American Journal of Distance Education*, **12** (1), pp 7–25

Moore, M G (1993) Theory of transactional distance, in *Theoretical Principles of Distance Education*, ed D Keegan, pp 22–38, Routledge, New York

Moust, J H C and Schmidt, H G (1994) Facilitating small-group learning: a comparison of student and staff tutor's behavior, *Instructional Science*, **22** (4), pp 287–301

Niesink, R, Westera, W, Hoefakker, R, Kornet, L, Jaspers, R, van Wilgenburg, H Gubbels, I, Vos, M, Delsing, R and Berkhout, J (1997) *Behavioural Toxicological Research* (Computer software), Open University of the Netherlands, Heerlen

Patrick, J (1992) *Training: Research and practice*, Academic Press, London

Rourke, L (2000) Operationalizing social interaction in computer conferencing, *Proceedings of the 16th Annual Conference of the Canadian Association for Distance Education, Quebec City* [Online] www.ulaval.ca/aced2000cade/english/proceedings.html (accessed 31 January 2001)

Schmidt, H G and Moust, J H C (1995) What makes a tutor effective? A structural equations modelling approach to learning in problem-based curricula, *Academic Medicine*, **70** (8), pp 708–14

Spiro, R J, Coulson R L, Feltovich, P J and Anderson, D K (1988) *Cognitive Flexibility Theory: Advanced knowledge acquisition in ill-structured domains*, Technical Report No. 441, University of Illinois, Center for the Study of Reading, Champaign, IL

Stephenson, J and Weil, S (1992) *Quality in Learning: A capability approach in higher education*, Kogan Page, London

Van Merriënboer, J J G, Kirschner, P A and Kester, L (2003) Taking the load off the learner's mind: instructional design for complex learning, *Educational Psychologist*, **38** (1), pp 5–13

Vygotsky, L (1978) *Mind in Society*, Harvard University Press, Cambridge, MA

Wagenaar, A, Boshuizen, H P A, Muijtjens, A, Scherpbier, A J J A, Bögels, S M, Dik, K and Vleuten, C P M (2001) Diagnostic expertise: communication in health care, paper presented at the biennial meeting of European Association for Research in Learning and Instruction, 28 August–1 September 2001, Fribourg, Switzerland

Wegerif, R (1998) The social dimension of asynchronous learning networks, *Journal of Asynchronous Learning Networks*, **2** (1), pp 34–49

Whitmore, J (2002) *Coaching for Performance: Growing people, performance and purpose*, Brealey Publishing, London

Chapter 13

Implementing integrated e-learning: lessons learnt from the OUNL case

Wim Westera

Introduction

The problem of technology is not technology, but rather its implementation. From the 1970s, a worldwide technology euphoria started proclaiming the indisputable benefits of computer automation. Computers were the magic spell to improve economic productivity and production efficiency. They promised radical changes in society, and ultimately a radical change to life itself. Even though this seems to have come true to a certain extent, establishing automation projects in the 1970s and 1980s was highly problematic (Tapscott and Caston, 1993; Forester, 1989). When, occasionally, such projects were concluded successfully and the systems and software were working satisfactorily technically, users often turned out to be unwilling or unable to handle them appropriately. Inadequate business process analyses, technocratic problem solving, cryptic human–computer interaction, and grossly lacking involvement of user groups (whether they were systems administrators, office staff or consumers), caused a surfeit of insurmountable problems as soon as the systems had been installed.

As yet, the processes associated with the implementation of new technologies are complex and highly unpredictable. A number of theoretical frameworks have been developed to describe the processes by which technologies are adopted and deployed. These include the theory of reasoned action, the theory of planned behaviour, and classical diffusion and innovation theory (Fichman, 2000; Pantano and Cardew-Hall, 2002; Rogers, 1995). All of these frameworks start from the premise that the adoption of innovations is determined by individual beliefs and perceptions. It is also assumed that the adoption decision is taken by the individual, which is unfortunately rarely the case when implementing e-learning. Various authors therefore question the validity of these frameworks (Pantano and Cardew-Hall, 2002; Gallivan, 2000). Theoretical frameworks for organizational change like total quality management, business process redesign, process change management and Kaizen certainly may offer something to hold on to, but their predictive value is poor. Success but also failure are part and parcel of them all (Grotevant, 1998; Utterbeck, 1994).

This chapter takes a pragmatic perspective. We highlight and discuss some relevant implementation issues with reference to the Open University of the Netherlands (OUNL) as an illustrative case. To deal with the complexity and multidimensionality of the implementation process we consider it from different angles in order to identify and assess the relevant difficulties, decisions and critical factors for success or failure. In close connection with the OUNL case, we focus on three relevant questions for technology-based innovations, and try to give an account of the lessons we learnt with reference to each of these questions. The questions are:

- *Vision on innovation*: how is integrated e-learning substantiated by the institute's mission and strategic goals?
- *Organizational change strategy*: what strategy should be used to assimilate integrated e-learning?
- *People*: how should we treat the 'human factor', the people who have to accept and carry out the innovation?

It is claimed that each implementation should explicitly think these issues through, and that disregarding any one of them may cause serious problems (Silius and Pohjolainen, 2002; Bates, 1997). Before we elaborate on these issues we briefly describe the OUNL context.

The OUNL case

The context of distance education places high demands on an educational system. At the OUNL, each course rests on an explicit instructional design and is delivered in a balanced mix of different media. The OUNL's pedagogical model is strongly based on mediated instruction. Its learning materials are designed for self-instruction, at times supplemented by some tutoring. From its inception, the OUNL has always built up considerable expertise to develop self-contained virtual practicals for the training of skills and competencies. In addition to print, these practicals use audio, courseware and both linear and interactive video. They often focus on offering complex, authentic training tasks. The pedagogy of this sort of self-instruction ('independent learning') seems to suit the population of adult students, who for the most part have a job and study at their homes at times of their own choosing.

We are forced to admit that the OUNL's choice of an independent learning pedagogy has been more or less obligatory, having been dictated by the restrictions of distance education. When in the 1990s the World Wide Web and its TCP/IP protocol seemed to become a world standard for communication, the OUNL realized that these Internet-technologies might be the vehicle for a revolutionary reassessment of distance education (Itzkan, 1994). The Internet might overcome the drawbacks of common distance education while enabling computer-supported communication between teachers and students, instant access to learning resources, file exchange and collaborative learning (Westera and Sloep, 2001). In fact since 1997, the 'Studienet' ('Study Web'), the Web-based virtual campus of the OUNL, has been used to facilitate communication among the students, and between students and teachers. It is the OUNL's first step towards integrated e-learning.

Notwithstanding the fact the OUNL had implemented many new methods, tools and technologies to enhance the quality and efficiency of learning since it opened in 1984, the introduction of the Studienet was different in both size and impact. It not only demanded the involvement of all departments, it also fundamentally affected the institution's primary processes. The management, being well aware of the risks of such radical technology-based innovation, set up this project most professionally and meticulously, while generously covering many relevant issues such as resources, communication, project management, involvement of users, testing, professionalization and support. Although the implementation of the *Studienet* may ultimately be considered a success, a large number of difficulties were encountered that threatened the project's prosperity. In the rest of this chapter, we will use the OUNL as an informative case to illustrate the introduction of new technologies in education, including distance education. We do not profess to offer an exhaustive analysis, and will select only a few relevant occurrences to illustrate and review the implementation issues mentioned above.

Vision on innovation

Before starting any e-learning activities or projects one needs a clear vision of education and innovation. It is obviously not sufficient to substantiate a simple e-learning pilot study by saying that it is important to gain e-learning experience and know-how. Such an *ad hoc* approach runs the risk of being outstripped by another *ad hoc* idea soon afterwards. An adequate vision should cover the *what* and the *why* of innovation, and should go into the processes, structures and staff roles that are envisioned. This is dealt with in Chapter 11. It should preferably start at the pedagogical level. Indeed, any educational provider should go for a pedagogical means rather than a technological one.

It goes without saying that the vision should be made explicit and set out in a document that is widely circulated. It should be made known throughout the organization, and be discussed not only by the management, but also, as it were, by the workers on the shop floor. Moreover, all levels should be involved in the decision making. A vision should make the innovation objectives concrete by explicitly describing what innovative education should look like.

For the OUNL, the anticipated role of e-learning is characterized by the integral incorporation of information and communication technologies (that is, integrated e-learning) in order to reassess the meaning of 'distance', 'contact' and 'educational services'. It addresses vast digitized reusable content, the 'atoms' of which can be managed electronically in order to compose tailor-made individualized training programmes. Such programmes can take into account the individual's prior knowledge, capabilities and personal goals. The educational system envisioned assumes a drastic redesign of the OUNL's business processes, and seems to require that the infrastructure be approached top-down rather than bottom-up. It requires a change of focus from mere instructional design of learning materials towards educational design at the organizational level. Over the years, this view of the importance of integrated e-learning for the OUNL appears to have been adequate.

Sharing the vision

The thoroughness of this view does not necessarily make it a view that is shared. Despite a series of plenary discussions with the staff, the internalization of the innovation view turned out to be a laborious, time-consuming process. Both the OUNL Management Board and the communication department underestimated the effort that is necessary to achieve sufficient acceptance and support (see Chapter 11 for additional suggestions). Plenary sessions are extremely important to this end. At certain stages, however, the management should state its position clearly and demarcate the issues that are still open to discussion from those that have been completed. This requires a subtle balance between directive and non-directive modes of leadership, which reflects the need to alternate between authoritarian and democratic management styles, readiness to listen patiently, consistent reasoning, careful timing and persuasiveness. We have to confess that the OUNL management could have done better in this respect, particularly by pointing to the impact of this view on the organization, its processes and existing roles.

Nevertheless, full acceptance of the innovation view has not been established. Many discussion issues have continued to slumber while nothing has been explicitly finalized. This is amplified by the culture of debate connected with the academic context of the OUNL. Special attention should be paid to the premises and starting points. A tendency of technology-push (introducing an overall, dominant e-learning system) may give rise to long-lasting disputes that can never be resolved. A final weakness in the OUNL's view of innovation, and perhaps in any futuristic view, is that no one could really foresee the radical consequences for the organization, the arrangement of working processes and job descriptions, and take them into account. As was the case at the OUNL, such uncertainty should also be shared. By stressing the pioneering role for all those involved in innovation, unforeseen problems and questions should be received as collective challenges rather than unwanted setbacks. Innovation can be exciting in itself.

Lessons learnt about developing a vision

These are the lessons we learnt with respect to developing a vision:

- Develop a vision based on educational motives rather than technological, advertising or other motives.
- Make the vision explicit and accessible by releasing a vision statement.
- Make the vision a shared vision. Arrange discussions about key issues, particularly about the starting points.
- Combine directive and non-directive modes of leadership.
- Make explicit decisions to finalize discussion topics step by step.
- Create a collective sense of pioneering by pointing to the uncertain, challenging path to innovation.

Organizational change strategy

A clear vision of innovation does not automatically guarantee successful innovation. The vision should be interpreted and translated into a strategy for organizational change. To effect such a strategy, projects have to be defined to redesign, test and introduce new organizational structures, business processes and role descriptions (see Chapter 9).

According to its view on innovative distance education, it followed that the OUNL had to incorporate e-learning technologies into its educational services. In 1995, the challenge was whether the OUNL would be able to launch a Web-based virtual campus that would be accessible from all over the world to the staff and the registered students. It is important to note that at that time the Internet was still in its infancy. Turnkey solutions were not available, to say nothing of Web-based learning platforms. All the Web facilities for the OUNL had to be designed, developed and implemented by internal experts. In fact, the OUNL set itself the task of developing a Web-based learning platform before the term had even been coined. Considerable effort was put into creating favourable conditions to realize this idea. Budgets were earmarked and staff were allocated to develop the *Studienet*. Various projects were defined, in which progress was guarded and controlled by a steering committee. These projects were separated from other, everyday business. The focus of each project was essentially on both the technological development of a Web-based environment and the organizational structure necessary to run and maintain it. Today, the development of the technical system is of less importance, as many off-the-shelf solutions for e-learning are commercially available. In this chapter we only touch on the technical aspects incidentally, and focus on the implications on the organizational level.

Preparation

All in all, the preparation of the *Studienet* turned out to be a major operation that claimed a substantial proportion of the budget and human resources from the primary processes for a period of one and a half years. After this period of intense effort the technical part, the Web-based learning environment, was delivered satisfactorily. This was one of the first operational Web-based learning environments in the world. It was innovative, impressive and trend setting, particularly for other educational providers.

The organizational support structure had also been prepared in great detail. To warrant the adequate creation, use and management of hundreds of course sites in the *Studienet*, existing structures had to be redesigned, taking into account new tasks, new responsibilities, operational procedures and proper management. Because of its impact across the organization, a functional unit transacting all the existing departments was set up. Such an approach signifies collective responsibility, and promotes support and acceptance throughout the organization.

At the OUNL, the *Studienet* Management Board, which is composed of representatives of all the OUNL departments, is responsible for the quality, reliability and accessibility of all the Internet services. It allocates Web masters for each course, and issues editorial directions with respect to topicality, style, correctness, integrity and representativeness of the information. In addition, the *Studienet* Management Board guards against malpractice and breaking the law. In particular, it keeps an eye on infringements of copyright, criminal law, privacy regulations and the law covering computer crime. To stress the site ownership of Web masters, each *Studienet* page displays the author's name and an e-mail link to promote approachability. Several procedures and protocols have been introduced to allow swift processing of standard transactions, for example the allocation of discussion groups, the declaration of new Webs, authorization requests, password problems, reporting and fixing of bugs and so on.

The launch

To introduce all this, the OUNL management chose a strategy that relied on generating a small number of successes by the early adopters. It was hesitant to change common processes abruptly, and at the beginning persisted in considering the *Studienet* as an additional facility for devotees. A coherent implementation plan for integrated e-learning was not available (see Chapter 11). The management supposed that gradual growth of the use of the *Studienet* by both faculty and students would occur more or less autonomously, alongside modest incentives. To this end, all editorial staff were trained extensively to become acquainted with the basic ideas of the *Studienet*, its structure, procedures and data entry tools. Additional support was rendered through an extended instructional site, which acted as an online manual and which presented answers to FAQs. A help desk was made available in case of emergencies.

Effects

Even though the OUNL management was prepared for the widespread use of the *Studienet* by both educational staff and students to take quite some time, it still fell short in practice. Despite splendid facilities, extensive information, and proper training and support, for a long time the *Studienet* was used by only a limited number of early adopters. The majority of staff showed reserve and reluctance. The OUNL management relied strongly on organic, autonomous change. Although such a strategy might work at the beginning by attracting an enthusiastic, highly motivated group of early adopters, it will gradually fail because, unintentionally, it is precisely these early adopters who tend to restrain the other staff from joining in, which thus serves as an excuse for the majority of the staff to remain uncommitted.

In 2001, four years after the launch, an internal survey showed that the *Studienet* had become an important source of information for both students and staff. The *Studienet* had been quite successful thus far. Yet as a means of delivering education, things were different. It appeared that only 10 per cent of the 400 OUNL courses in the *Studienet* actually offered any online content and associated computer-mediated communication. One may sense some reserve on the part of the staff here, which is quite understandable. Despite all the organizational, precautionary measures, we should realize that the introduction of a Web-based infrastructure at the OUNL meant breaking the old habit of bottom-up innovation. It implied a top-down strategy, which was strongly stimulated by technology. Such innovation strategies can be observed anywhere, often causing implementation problems (Bates, 1997). From one day to the next, new facilities were made available, which forced the staff into new patterns and the use of new tools, while existing innovation patterns still remained worthwhile.

This full launch stressed the technical dimensions and the almost overwhelming nature of the *Studienet*, and created anxiety rather than enthusiasm. Staff remained highly noncommittal, while re-establishing existing patterns. As a consequence, very little e-learning content was developed or delivered during the initial years, and students could not always establish any surplus value when visiting the *Studienet*. Moreover, the sudden availability of the *Studienet* greatly interfered with current business, which further restricted the possibilities of instant adoption and habituation.

A gradual introduction using confined pilot projects might have worked better. It would have supported a smooth transition to new business processes, and it would probably have generated readier commitment and acceptance by the staff. To stimulate the use of such a system, the management should define explicit targets that include clear incentives and reward mechanisms (Bates, 1995). The failure of the organic approach to organizational change could perhaps have been anticipated. If the management fail to specify explicit goals, targets, migration schedules, incentives, a sense of urgency, and criteria to assess the implementation, the staff are likely to remain passive and uncommitted. To achieve successful organizational change, the management should explicitly facilitate the necessary redistribution of roles and responsibilities.

Yet as the years went by, the *Studienet* experienced substantial growth. Faculty and students gradually seem to have become acquainted with the Web environment, and surprisingly, seem to have exchanged positions with the management. Some five years after the launch of the *Studienet*, staff and students are urging the management to extend the e-learning facilities. One might even conclude that the cautious change strategy actually worked in the end. Everything comes to him who waits.

Lessons learnt about organizational change

With respect to organizational change we learnt the following lessons:

- Develop and communicate a change strategy.
- Do not underplay the organizational impact.
- Clarify the redistribution of roles and responsibilities.
- Take enough time for staff to get acquainted.
- Develop a coherent implementation plan to cover all the relevant issues.
- Set explicit targets with respect to actual use and available content.
- Set up an operational support unit that works with all the existing departments.
- Arrange adequate support facilities such as training, manuals and a help desk.
- Apply incentives and reward mechanisms to promote growth.
- Reposition the status of common business with respect to innovation.
- Involve students and other users.
- Arrange significant pilot projects.
- Generate, communicate and extend early successes.
- Arrange evaluations (see Chapter 14) and be receptive to user requests.
- Take maintenance and upgrading into account.

People

Any organizational change in pursuit of innovation obviously has an impact on people. Tension may easily arise between organizational demands and individual beliefs, perceptions, needs, visions and attitudes, particularly in a knowledge-intensive context with highly educated professional staff. We should like to select and elaborate two issues in this connection, training and the empowerment of staff.

Training

As indicated above, training is necessary to provide sufficient knowledge and skills among the users. When considering training it is important to distinguish carefully between different types of user. With respect to the *Studienet*, tutors, course designers, authors, content editors, graphic designers, PR officers, IT engineers, maintenance staff and, last but not least, the students will all have their particular views, tasks and interests.

To prepare the OUNL staff for working with the *Studienet* a range of training courses was set up. This training could roughly be divided into functional training and technical training. Functional training focuses on the role of the *Studienet* as a channel for educational delivery, by emphasizing its conceptual and pedagogical possibilities. Technical training concerns general IT skills and the practical operation of software applications. A frequent pitfall is to focus on technical training only. Basic IT training, 'studying by mouse', is also offered to OUNL students. It is worth noting that all this training has been offered with no obligation. Although new roles and tasks were defined with respect to course development in the *Studienet*, course teams and individuals could decide for themselves what training was appropriate for them. The required competence levels for the various tasks have not been formalized and established in human resources management. Nevertheless, making training compulsory might have adverse effects as it neglects the possible complaints, beliefs, attitudes and fears that make people keep their distance. Training on the job may be a better alternative.

Empowerment

Empowerment from as low a point as possible in the organizational hierarchy is assumed to be a critical condition for successful implementation, particularly in a community of academics. Empowerment concerns the right to decide on one's own training, the choice of tools for Web-based content, and even the right to develop private layouts that deviate in style and approach from the institutional formats. Such decentralized empowerment may well conflict with the idea that the introduction of a Web-based infrastructure by definition represents a top-down approach.

The fixed format of the database-published Web sites, the associated style sheets and the prescribed software for communication actually raised many objections. In fact content development at the OUNL is rather decentralized, and many a content developer claims that the freedom of movement and independence – not to say anarchy – are prerequisites for creativity, innovation and quality. Restrictive facilities like the *Studienet* and its rigid prescriptions and regulations are easily perceived as a threat to quality and flexibility.

To accommodate these objections the OUNL made a sweeping concession by lifting the rule that OUNL style sheets should be used for content pages, and allowing faculty members to design their own Web sites, or to install and host different server software at will. There is obviously a discrepancy between the need for cost-efficient management and the desire for unlimited exploration. The need for cost-efficiency represents the long-term goal of innovation, namely the creation of new products and services or a new approach to the design, production or marketing of goods at an acceptable price. The desire for unlimited exploration represents exactly the means of arriving at this goal by promoting creativity and reflectivity.

The *Studienet* was originally supposed to be the only Web-based learning facility. Today, some 10 different Web-based delivery platforms are operational. However, the OUNL has begun to reverse its liberal policy slightly. It must be clear to anyone that such a policy is hardly cost-effective. The ideals of harmonization and uniformity, both in pedagogy and when it comes to 'look and feel', have recently been gaining popularity. One might conclude that the OUNL has successfully completed the initial phase of exploration and acceptance, which took a number of years, and that it is now ready to enter the phase of the wide diffusion of a uniform approach to the creation and delivery of Web-based content.

Lessons learnt regarding the human factor

With respect to the human factor we learnt the following lessons:

- Emphasize functional training rather than technical training (see Chapter 12).
- Customize training for different target groups, including students.
- Press for sufficient skills. Interrelate training and human resource management (see Chapter 11).
- Preferably make training compulsory, but cater for those who reject training by offering training on the job.
- Empower staff from as low a point as possible in the organizational hierarchy.
- Allow a measure of deviation from institutional formats and tooling, particularly during the start-up phase of e-learning.
- Beware of the call for unrestrained creativity. Be sure to balance the costs against the envisioned gains.
- Offer outstanding author environments.

Conclusion

This chapter has explained how the introduction of a Web-based learning environment is a complex operation across an organization. From the start, the implementation of the *Studienet* has been taken very seriously by the OUNL, which has been only too aware of the hazards of introducing new technologies. The Board of Management, a help desk, editorial directions, procedures for operation and maintenance, and extensive staff training have all been arranged. However, we cannot but conclude that the implementation of the *Studienet* has been a lengthy, laborious process, which has still not been altogether completed.

This chapter reviewed a number of relevant topics and reported on a number of the lessons we learnt. To a certain extent these lessons may appear self-evident, but for a full understanding of their significance it is necessary to think meticulously through the underlying patterns and pitfalls as described above. The lessons we learnt indicate how we could have done better at various points. Yet it would be a mistake to think that these lessons will protect us from every conceivable difficulty. Thus, the ultimate lesson learnt is also a challenge: whatever problems are anticipated, be prepared for the implementation to fall short of solving them easily.

References

Bates, A (1995) *Technology, Open Learning and Distance Education*, Routledge, London/New York

Bates, A W (1997) Restructuring the university for technological change, paper presented to the Carnegie Foundation for the Advancement of Teaching, 18–20 June 1997, London [Online] bates.cstudies.ubc.ca (accessed 12 December 2002)

Fichman, R G (2000) The diffusion and assimilation of information technology innovations, in *Framing the Domains of IT Management: Projecting the future through the past*, ed R W Zmud, pp 105–27, Pinnaflex Educational Resources, Cincinnati, OH

Forester, T (1989) *Computers in The Human Context: Information technology, productivity and people*, Blackwell, Oxford

Gallivan, M J (2000) Organizational adoption and assimilation of complex technological innovations: development and application of a new framework, *Database for Advances in Information Systems*, **32** (3), pp 57–85

Grotevant, S M (1998) Business engineering and process redesign in higher education: art or science?, paper presented at CAUSE 98 Seattle, Washington, 1998 [Online] www.educause.edu/ir/library/html/cnc9857/cnc9857.html (accessed 12 May 2003)

Itzkan, S J (1994) Assessing the future of tele-computing environments: implications for instruction and administration, *The Computing Teacher*, **22** (4), pp 60–64

Pantano, V and Cardew-Hall, M J (2002) Technology diffusion and organizational culture: preliminary findings from the implementation of a knowledge management system, *Proceedings of the IEEE International Engineering Management Conference 2002*, pp 1–6, Centre for Technology Management, Cambridge, UK

Rogers, E M (1995) *Diffusion of Innovations*, 4th edn, Free Press, New York

Silius, K and Pohjolainen, S (2002) Strategic planning for web-based learning and teaching at Tampere University of Technology, *Proceedings of European Conference on the New Benefits of ICT in Higher Education, 2002*, pp 182–89, Erasmus-Plus, Rotterdam

Tapscott, D and Caston, A (1993) *Paradigm Shift: The new promise of information technology*, McGraw-Hill, New York

Utterbeck, J M (1994) *Mastering the Dynamics of Innovation*, Harvard Business School Press, Boston, MA

Westera, W and Sloep, P B (2001) Into the future of networked education, in *Cybereducation: The future of long distance learning*, ed L R Vandervert, L V Shavinina and R A Cornell, pp 115–36, Mary Ann Liebert, New York

Chapter 14

Evaluating integrated e-learning

Theo Bastiaens, Jo Boon and Rob Martens

Introduction

More and more aspects of formal classroom training and e-learning have become merged into hybrid learning environments which contain a combination of face-to-face and Web-based formats (Benson, Johnson and Kuchinke, 2002), often referred to as 'blended learning' (Bastiaens, Martens and Stijnen, 2002). The electronic part of this blended learning is at the forefront of this book, making the term 'integrated e-learning' more appropriate. Evaluation plays an important role in identifying the issues involved in integrating e-learning in education and training. Evaluation is needed to improve the quality and effectiveness of the e-learning initiative and check the design assumptions. In other words, does the curriculum, course or task succeed in achieving the intended learning goals or the desired improvement of student competencies? Does the media mix work as intended? What are the organizational consequences?

This chapter tries to identify important questions when it comes to the evaluation of integrated e-learning. Although it is not possible to treat this subject exhaustively, we have introduced a framework for the evaluation of integrated e-learning and have illustrated it with an example.

Evaluation framework

The evaluation of educational innovations occupies a pre-eminent part in the evaluation literature. In higher education a switch of focus can be seen from measuring student performance to a more structural approach that measures the impact of education and the success of educational programmes as a whole. Evaluation of e-learning is a relatively new topic in the field, requiring an approach on different levels at the same time. There are many different stakeholders, and a range of problem areas extending from content to technological questions. Concerns about the quality of the content, the learning access level, technological features, costs and sustainability call for a broad evaluation design.

This chapter looks at evaluation from a much more general perspective than only student assessment. The focus is on evaluating the effectiveness and efficiency of e-learning components as part of a lesson plan, curriculum or a course administered by an educational institute. For this reason we propose to use Kirkpatrick's (1998) four-level evaluation framework. It offers a simple, logical way for a general conceptual framework, which is applicable to integrated e-learning (Walker 1998; Singh, 2001). Kirkpatrick's framework has been popular mainly in the commercial training world for about 40 years, offering a useful scheme for evaluation. The framework was originally designed to be used by human resources management divisions in enterprises that developed or outsourced training. The straightforward structure of the framework made it most suitable for the evaluation of training even in the pre-e-learning age.

Kirkpatrick's framework describes four levels of evaluation. Level 1, the reaction level, is defined as what the participants think of the course or training: in a word, do they like the initiative? Level 2 is concerned with measuring the learning results, and raises the question of what participants learn. Level 3, behaviour, determines to what extent the participants change their behaviour on the job. What is the transfer of what was learned? Level 4, results, monitors the organizational improvement such as quality changes, effectiveness and costs. Did the initiative affect the organization? To further operationalize the four levels the goal, design and arrangement are defined for each level (based on Rummler and Brache, 1995; Swanson, 1994). Table 14.1 shows the different levels. The grey areas anticipate the application of the scheme which is discussed later in the chapter.

Of course, as with all evaluation activities, the evaluation of integrated e-learning requires a clear plan describing the goal, the object and the criteria for the evaluation. The description refers to the ways the results will be used. The definition of the object is a refinement of the goal, and concentrates on the main topics of importance, for example the user-friendliness of an e-learning initiative. The criteria are standards used for making judgements (Valdez, 1996). For example, a criterion for 'flexible working and learning when using integrated e-learning' can be 'independence of place' as demonstrated in Table 14.1.

The evaluation design, which describes the questions to be answered, is complemented by a description of the design specifying the evaluation set-up, the validity measures assuring the reliability of the data, the instruments, the indicators

(Valdez, 1996), the technique for the data analysis, and the ways of reporting the conclusions of the study (see Table 14.1 and the elaboration of the framework). The project plan also contains management and organizational issues such as costs and evaluators, which are summarized in the topic arrangement.

The media mix and the levels of evaluation

The evaluation framework described is a useful tool for structuring different evaluation questions, thereby making the evaluation of integrated e-learning more manageable. The central question is the quality of the final product, which results from the mix of the different media and their combination in specific applications. Quality is measured against the constraints (such as resources available and the desirability of flexible delivery independent of time and place); task requirements (such as media attributes required by the task and the necessary response modes of the learner); and features of the target group (such as the learners' ability level and the learning processes aimed at) (see Chapter 1).

All these considerations are essentially the foundation for evaluation research aiming at assessing the quality of integrated e-learning. We need to ask whether the learners accept the media mix, and if they like it. In general the variables here focus on user satisfaction and the desirability of flexible delivery independent of time and place (level 1). When we consider learning effects, what we want to know is whether the media mix supports the learning process adequately. Here the variables focus on the learners' ability and the learning processes aimed at (level 2). The performance level of the evaluation concerns issues such as whether the media mix supports and allows learners to work on tasks in a highly 'authentic' context. The variables focus on media attributes required by the task (level 3). On the organizational level the key question is whether the media mix contributes to the organizational goals and results that are aimed at. The variables here focus on the resources used. The different evaluation questions exemplifying the level concerned fit into the framework (see the grey areas in Table 14.1; based on Ravet and Layete, 1997).

Developing the framework

This section describes an evaluation design using the framework as a structuring principle. For example, the section uses a virtual business e-learning environment (VbeL) as the context for the design (see Chapter 4). A VBeL is a good example of e-learning resulting from a mix of different media. The learning environment is closely modelled on real companies, but is located on the Internet. It aims at bridging the gap between learning and work by situating learning in a real-life business setting. Students have to perform tasks with real clients (Westera, Sloep and Gerrissen, 2000). Students are stimulated to act autonomously and to take

Table 14.1 *A framework for the evaluation of integrated e-learning*

	Goal	Design	Arrangement
1. Reaction	What is the purpose of the satisfaction measurement? What is the object of the evaluation? What are the criteria for the evaluation?	What is the design? How valid is it? What are the instruments? What are the indicators for the criteria? What techniques are used for data analysis?	Who are the subjects? Who is the evaluator? What are the costs of the evaluation? How is the data collection done?
	Do learners accept and like the media mix?		
Use; learner acceptance; instructional validity	Is the e-learning used as intended? Are they satisfied? Are the activities and material consistent with the goals?	Observations, tracking reports; questionnaires; analysis, eg jigsaw	
2. Learning	What is the purpose of the measurement at the learning level? What is the object of the evaluation? What are the criteria for the evaluation?	What is the design? How valid is it? What are the instruments? What are the indicators for the criteria? What techniques are used for data analysis?	Who are the subjects? Who is the evaluator? What are the costs of the evaluation? How is the data collection done?
	Does the media mix support the learning process sufficiently?		
Knowledge; skills; attitude; competence	Do they know the facts, concepts and rules? Do they use their new skills? Have the desired competencies been developed?	Multiple choice questions; simulations; cases; reports; assignments	

Table 14.1   *(Cont.)*

	Goal	Design	Arrangement
3. Performance	What is the purpose of the performance measurement? What is the object of the evaluation? What are the criteria for the evaluation?	What is the design? How valid is it? What are the instruments? What are the indicators for the criteria? What techniques are used for data analysis?	Who are the subjects? Who is the evaluator? What are the costs of the evaluation? How is the data collection done?
	Does the media mix support and allow learners to work on tasks in a highly 'authentic' context?		
Integration of knowledge, skills and attitude; performance	Can they do the job?	Simulations; on-the-job assessment; observations	
4. Organization	What is the purpose of the organizational impact measurement? What is the object of the evaluation? What are the criteria for the evaluation?	What is the design? How valid is it? What are the instruments? What are the indicators for the criteria? What techniques are used for data analysis?	Who are the subjects? Who is the evaluator? What are the costs of the evaluation? How is the data collection done?
	Does the media mix contribute to the organizational goals and results aimed at?		
Business results; productivity increase	Has the business benefited from the e-learning? How efficient is the programme?	Observations; reports; performance tracking system	

Source: based on Kirkpatrick, 1998; Rummler and Brache, 1995; Swanson, 1994

responsibility for the accomplishment of their study goals. The educator's task is mainly to monitor the efficacy and quality of learning, giving feedback when students need it. It is clear that the evaluation of this e-learning experience requires careful planning, taking into account the educational design, the technological features, the effects on learning, and the managerial aspects such as costs and efficiency. This plan will be described in the following section using the Kirk-patrick framework as a starting point. In the description each level is represented by an example of one evaluation question. We discuss all the areas, starting with the goal, design and arrangement on the reaction level.

Level 1: Reaction

The first step required at this level is providing a definition of general aspects concerning the goal. We need to be clear about the purpose of the evaluation. In the example of the VBeL, students learn innovatively and combine work and learning in an electronic environment supported by different media. The goal of an evaluation at this level may be to gather information about the combination of the different media in optimizing the media mix. The objective is then the actual use of the different media sources. The criteria for the evaluation also have to be determined. The evaluators have certain expectations when they commence. For example, they may have included an electronic discussion group in the media mix, with the expectation that it will be useful for the communication between learners. Criteria based on those expectations have to be developed to test the evaluation. Two sample criteria for the VBeL are the intensity of the use of the discussion group and the quality of the contributions. Strijbos, Martens and Jochems (in press) stress the importance of using functional role models, as well as coordinating learning goals and tasks in computer supported collaborative learning (CSCL). Other researchers stress the importance of tools to increase social awareness in CSCL. These are examples of design characteristics that may influence the effectiveness and efficiency of CSCL in a VBeL.

At the reaction level, the design depends on the goals of the evaluation. In the present VBeL example, a logging design has been opted for. Students are monitored in the electronic environment and every step they take is recorded in a database.

The validity of the content of the evaluation is of primary importance. Does the evaluation measure what it is supposed to measure? An example of an action to assure validity is the participation of two experts as quality assessors in a discussion group. The evaluators also have to construct and use instruments such as question-naires or interview protocols that are not open to misinterpretation. In our example the instrument is monitoring software which records every action and every contribution. The indicators for the criteria are generally quantified. An indication of the intensity, that is the extent to which the discussion group is used, is the number of contributions. Longitudinal and frequency analyses provide the techniques for data analysis in our example.

The arrangement involves the subjects, the evaluators, the costs and the data collection. It is obvious in this context that the subjects are the students working and learning in the VBeL. Depending on the evaluation, other people (the stake-holders), such as their bosses or clients can also be involved as subjects. A detailed description of the evaluators is also required. Who are going to do the interviews? Do they require training in interview techniques? Who is carrying out the statistical analysis? In the example of the VBeL, several external evaluators are responsible for the total evaluation process. The tutors or coaches are also evaluators who assess the quality of the contributions. Depending on the scope of the evaluation (aspects such as the number of people and the degree of support and effort required) and the consequences involved (for example, training the evaluators and the time needed to carry out the evaluation) the costs can be considerable. In our example, however, the costs are relatively low because of the automatic data collection of the monitoring software. How the data is collected gives a description of the different evaluation stages (that is, in what order the evaluation questions should be answered) in a time frame including the individual responsibilities of the evaluators.

Level 2: Learning

Once again, we should state the goals of the level 2 evaluation. What learning results are important? In our example of the VBeL, we want to know more about the media mix and its contribution to learning. We should then define the object. In the case of the VBeL the object is the knowledge gained while using the electronic environment. Another point to consider is the criteria for the learning test. In the case of the VBeL, the criterion is a knowledge test. For the design of the level 2 evaluation, it is important when the evaluation is carried out and how it is compared with other data. Most of the time the evaluators want to know not only whether students fulfil the criteria as defined, but whether they learn more, or better, than before. For this reason the results on the learning test have to be compared with other data from the same group before the e-learning initiative (pre-test and post-test design), or with an identical group who learned the same content in another more traditional way. In our example we use a pre-test and post-test on knowledge. The validity is assured by the involvement of two experts grading the knowledge test independently. The next step is the translation of the criterion into an indicator. With the VBeL the indicator is defined as the grade gained on the knowledge test. The data analysis technique is a statistical analysis of the learners' results and variables on the knowledge test. The arrangement is comparable with the first level.

Level 3: Performance

We need to examine the goal of this level 3 evaluation. Why is the evaluation of the performance important? At this level evaluators look at performance on the job. The main goal in the VBeL example is whether the students can use what they learn in their jobs. The object of the evaluation is, for example, project management skills. In our example students are evaluated while actually performing during a period of two months. The criterion used for the evaluation is performance-based. Take the criterion 'to manage deadlines'. The design on this level is often rather complicated. The measurement of the participant's increase in performance on the job might involve observations of peers or statistical comparisons. We used a so-called '360 degree' evaluation, which allows each employee to be evaluated by a group of individuals ranging from supervisors to customers and peers.

Validity is a point of particular concern. When it comes to measuring, the opinions of several people often involve the use of more than one instrument for a single question. This is also known as 'triangulation'. The indicator for the criterion of being able to manage deadlines can be the extent to which the deadlines are not met. The sorts of instruments employed here are checklists, templates and guidelines. The technique for data analysis involves a more qualitative analysis, for example of evaluation reports. The arrangement is comparable with the other levels. At this level the costs of the evaluation can be rather high, as performance evaluation often involves many evaluators.

Level 4: Organization

Organizational improvement can be measured in several ways, including cost savings (factors here are time, travel and reduced employee turnover); work output improvement (increased sales); or quality changes. In the case of educational institutions one can think of a better match between future work places and the competencies students acquire. This may result in more success on the labour market for graduates. Once again the goal of this level 4 evaluation has to be stated. This is often in tune with a so called 'front-end' analysis: in order to define evaluation goals, organizational goals and performance gaps have to be analyzed. The front-end analysis includes determining key business issues, business goals, performance indicators and so on. In the VBeL example the business goal was the introduction of collaborative learning. The object of evaluation is flexibility. In the example, the criteria for flexibility are independence of place and time, meaning that employees can learn at any moment in any location.

The design of the level 4 evaluation is very difficult. It is not easy to measure the impact of training at an organizational level, so that this part of the evaluation of innovative e-learning approaches is frequently neglected. It is advisable to associate causal factors, such as lack of skills and knowledge, with performance indicators that could be tracked at intervals before and after the training to judge the impact of the training (Singh, 2001). In our example we keep it relatively simple. The flexibility of collaborative learning is defined as independence of place and time, and can be logged. It is designed to be able to record the learners' behaviour. From which location and at what time do learners log into the electronic environment? The arrangement is again comparable, although at this level it tends to be a group evaluation. The more people who contribute to a change, the more easily the organizational impact can be measured.

Lessons learnt and recommendations

In addition to a detailed elaboration of the framework, it is advisable to take more general aspects of the evaluation of integrated e-learning into account. Regarding the goal of the evaluation, Oliver and Conole (1998: 1) describe three general qualities, which they refer to as authenticity, exploration and scale. Authenticity describes the notion of how closely an evaluation captures the context of an e-learning initiative. An evaluation of an entire e-learning environment, taking into account the learning of a large group of learners and looking at the influences on their on-the-job performance, would be considered highly authentic. A two-hour evaluation of the user-friendliness of the interface at a laboratory would have a low level of authenticity. Exploration refers to whether the study has a well-defined initial hypothesis or is tackling an open problem. An evaluation that aims to gather data on the influences of e-learning at an organizational level would involve a high degree of exploration. An evaluation that tests well-defined hypotheses on the learning of two groups of e-learners would be less explorative. Scale refers to the number of participants.

Regarding the design, important general factors are time requirements (how long it takes to gather the data); the objectivity required by a hypothesis (comparison of the fact that whereas at the reaction level low objectivity might be appropriate, at the learning level for example, a highly objective form of data gathering would be preferable); and focus (the concept that considers the state of the data, meaning for example that while an unstructured interview could generate almost any data, a structured one would restrict responses to a narrow range of topics) (see Oliver and Conole, 1998: 4).

In the application of the Kirkpatrick framework the central question is how specific the evaluation of e-learning is. One can maintain that an e-learning environment makes evaluation technologically easier, at least the evaluation of the first two levels of the scheme, as the medium itself can be used to gather evaluative data from students and tutors. At the same time, however, we would like to argue that the approach proposed by Kirkpatrick is partial and has to be revised conceptually to be applicable, particularly in e-learning environments today.

For level 1, this means that one has to realize that in spite of the popularity of the framework, organizations rarely if ever evaluate training. At the same time, they pretend to carry out evaluation by accentuating the first step in Kirkpatrick's scheme. Using the first and most popular step of the scheme (sometimes called the 'happy sheet') to measure the reaction of the trainees means primarily measuring learners' immediate reactions to training or a course. A mixture of social and emotional or rational satisfaction or dissatisfaction immediately on completing a course generally determines the scores on the evaluation sheet. The main problem with the evaluation of satisfaction is the atheoretical approach, leading to a mere description of different aspects.

At level 2, the framework recommends measuring pre-test and post-test results. In practice the former are often omitted in training evaluation. A pre-test and post-test differential is particularly suitable for very specific types of courses accentuating mostly cognitive and factual content, as in the example of the evaluation of the VBeL. Moreover, post-course testing tends to stress merely the learners' short-term memory. In the case of e-learning courses or programmes designed to increase students' competencies, the effects of a course cannot be measured by a simple test or questionnaire just after completion of the course, but should be measured in an authentic situation or in the professional context of the student. The assessment of acquired competencies does not focus on individuals but on functioning in teams. In a competency-based curriculum, interweaving assessment and learning content is important from a student perspective. More information on this can be found in Chapter 3.

The most difficult aspect of evaluation of e-learning is the question whether the media mix is successful. Do the different media support the learning process optimally? This brings us to the third level of the model, namely performance. At this level, the transfer of learning to actual performance, it is very difficult to measure the impact of learning. In the first place, in the organizational context factors such as communication and performance in a team should be considered without only focusing on individual performance. This stresses the value of non-randomized quasi-experimental or other non-experimental approaches to measuring the impact of training.

It is clear that a complete impact assessment is demanding, and should be carried out only when there is a high probability that the evidence will be used as the basis for significant policy or, for instance, when it is part of an educational research programme. This might be the case when training is innovative or when it is set up as a pilot project to test a specific concept. We do not believe that impact assessment is relevant in every evaluation process. In some e-learning contexts this step is clearly of high importance in the phase where the course development has been completed and the technological setting is stable.

Finally, level 4 of the framework considers the results of the evaluation on the organizational level, considering questions of costs, improvement of work or of interpersonal communication for the organization as a whole. As a result of the high expectations of the cost-effectiveness of e-learning, the demand for this aspect of evaluation is considerable. In fact this level is oriented toward the management level. The differences with the previous steps lie in the purposes to which the findings are put. The emphasis is not on implementation but on accountability, which is needed to judge whether e-learning activities should be continued, expanded or reduced. As for the previous level, this one is also important during the implementation of innovative programmes. However, the same methodological problems arise as with the impact evaluation. Perhaps the cost factor is the least difficult when administered properly. Organizational changes in performance or communication are harder to measure because it is difficult to isolate the effects of training.

Conclusion

In general, evaluation is a basic component of good innovation design and implementation (Tavistock Institute and Open University, 1998). It is important to take multiple topics into account. In general, these topics can be categorized into technical, educational, institutional, economic and implementation aspects, and can be evaluated at different levels. We recommend that Occam's razor be applied. It is not wise to perform a four-level evaluation for every e-learning event, but only for each new type of medium that is adopted, or for each new course type (Walker, 1998) for otherwise the evaluation costs would probably exceed the development costs of many e-learning initiatives. As a minimum we recommend performing an evaluation at the reaction level every time the e-learning event takes place.

Kirkpatrick's model, which for 40 years has proved its worth for the evaluation of training and courses, is a useful tool for the evaluation of e-learning. This mainly results from the fact that the model suggests considering a range of questions and stakeholders, ranging from the students themselves to tutors, employers and managers. However, the evaluation of e-learning differs in some crucial respects from the evaluation of face-to-face learning, one of the main differences being the fact that the medium itself can be used to gather evaluative data from students and tutors. This results in data collection being easier, quicker, cheaper, and possible to carry out at an early phase of the learning process.

Nevertheless, we believe that the similarities of the evaluation of e-learning and face-to-face learning are more important than the differences. The most important similarity is the fact that more data do not automatically result in more relevance. Evaluation has to be based on a well-considered theoretical model, describing hypotheses relating to the research field and criteria to judge results. The same holds true when the aim is more practical than theoretical. Evaluation has to be based on a well-designed mode that makes it possible to assess objective, relevant data. Obviously this model has to be constructed at the forefront of the process during the e-learning design. Assumptions and expectations about learning, the effects of different media on learning, and the mixture of these media in a learning environment should all be made explicit at this stage.

References

Bastiaens, T, Martens, R and Stijnen, P (2002) ICT en onderwijs: inleiding op het themanummer (Introduction to the special issue ICT and education), *Pedagogische Studiën*, **79**, pp 431–35

Benson, A D, Johnson, S D and Kuchinke, K P (2002) The use of technology in the digital workplace: a framework for human resource development, in Advances in *Developing Human Resources: Information technology in human resource development*, ed A D Benson and S D Johnson, **4** (4), pp 392–405

Kirkpatrick, D L (1998) *Evaluating Training Programs: The four levels*, Berreth-Koehler, San Francisco, CA

Oliver, M and Conole, G (1998) Evaluating communication and information technologies: a toolkit for practitioners, *Active-Learning*, **8**, pp 3–8

Ravet, S and Layete, M (1997) Technology-based training, in *A Comprehensive Guide to Chosing, Implementing, Managing and Developing New Technologies in Training*, pp 147–58, Kogan Page, London

Rummler, G A and Brache, A P (1995) *Improving Performance: How to manage the white space on the organizational chart*, Jossey-Bass, San Francisco, CA

Singh, H (2001) Online implementation of Kirkpatrick's four levels of evaluation using Web databases, in *Web-Based Training*, ed B H Khan, pp 523–36, Educational Technology Publications, Englewood Cliffs, NJ

Strijbos, J W, Martens, R L and Jochems, W M G (in press) Classifying group-based learning, *Computers and Education*

Swanson, R A (1994) *Analysis for Improving Performance: Tools for diagnosing organizations and documenting workplace expertise*, Berreth-Koehler, San Francisco, CA

Tavistock Institute and Open University (1998) *Teaching and Learning Technology Programme: Guidelines for project evaluation, version 1.2*, Tavistock Institute, London [Online] iet.open.ac.uk/TLTP/bs031doc.html (accessed 15 February 2003)

Valdez, G (1996) *Evaluation Design and Tools*, North Central Regional Educational Laboratory [Online] www.ncrel.org/tandl/eval2.htm (accessed 15 February 2003)

Walker, S (1998) The value of building skills with online technology: online training costs and evaluation at the Texas natural resource conservation commission, in *Distance Training: How innovative organizations are using technology to maximize learning and meet business objectives*, ed D Schreiber and A Berge, pp 270–87, Jossey-Bass, San Francisco, CA

Westera, W, Sloep, P B and Gerrissen, J (2000) The design of the virtual company: synergism of learning and working in a networked environment, *Innovations in Education and Training, International*, **37** (1), pp 23–33

Chapter 15

Epilogue

Wim Jochems, Jeroen van Merriënboer and Rob Koper

Introduction

We started this book with the statement that higher education is changing as a result of technological and societal developments. It was suggested that an integrated approach to e-learning could help to cope with these changes. We mentioned three essential elements of integrated e-learning, and pointed out that pedagogical, technological and organizational aspects have to be taken into account in order to be successful in implementing e-learning. A design perspective on instructional systems is also needed, meaning that it will often be necessary to combine Web-based instruction with face-to-face instruction, classroom training, and written self-study materials (the so-called 'media mix'). Finally, student learning has to occupy the central position. We argued that this leads to a concept of learning that can be characterized as complex, flexible and dual.

In integrated e-learning a variety of coherent measures at the pedagogical, technological and organizational levels are needed. A large number of issues have been presented and discussed in the preceding chapters. Nevertheless, a lot of questions remain unanswered and there are still many barriers and limitations to be overcome. In this final chapter we address a number of problematic aspects with respect to integrated e-learning from four different perspectives (see Table 15.1).

The first is the perspective of the student or life-long learner. What kinds of problems with respect to the student, student behaviour, or interaction with the student can be expected in introducing integrated e-learning? In the second section of this chapter we discuss these problems in relation to the three dimensions of this book, namely pedagogy, technology and organization. The second perspective is that of the teacher and/or designer. The third section addresses potential problems with respect to teachers involved as a result of changing roles and work processes related to integrated e-learning. The third perspective concerns the instructional or learning materials used in integrated e-learning, and specifically the e-learning parts of it. These are discussed in the fourth section. The fourth perspective refers to the context, the setting in which integrated e-learning is implemented. This affects not only the educational institute but also, for instance, the study environment and inter-institutional aspects in cases of networked collaboration between institutes. This perspective is focused on in the next section of the chapter. Finally, we present some concluding remarks.

Table 15.1   *An overview of the main barriers for implementing integrated e-learning*

Perspective	Three dimensions of integrated e-learning		
	Pedagogical	*Technological*	*Organizational*
1. Student/lifelong learner	Self-management; individualization	Student tools; navigation	Training; acceptance
2. Teacher/designer	E-pedagogy; feedback	Tools for work processes	Teamwork and roles
3. Learning materials	Input-output requirements	Sharing and reuse	Learning object economy
4. Context/setting	Social presence; social control	Inter-institutional interoperability	Change management; Quality

The life-long learner's perspective

Integrated e-learning as described in this book is strongly learner-centred. The traditional student who is carefully guided through a well-defined curriculum is replaced by a life-long learner, who is self-directed with regard to the selection of learning tasks and contents, the use of different media, and cooperation with teachers, tutors and peers. This places additional demands on students' higher-order skills, such as metacognitive and self-regulatory skills (like planning, monitoring and evaluating one's own learning processes), interpersonal skills (such as cooperating with others using new communication techniques), and problem solving skills (such as dealing with unexpected situations which are an integral part of an open learning environment). Accordingly, well-designed environments for integrated e-learning must offer the opportunity to develop such skills, and provide the necessary support structures for learners who are able and willing to do so. At the same time it should be acknowledged that integrated e-learning is probably not the best approach for low-ability learners, learners suffering from severe motivational problems, or maybe even learners from cultures where the traditional school system does not allow for any form of self-directed learning or its development.

Technology is the factor that enables integrated e-learning, but it also presents most of its constraints, not least to life-long learners. In this book we have drawn a distinction between the underlying ICT technologies (in bandwidth, mobile accessibility, security and so forth) and the more specific learning technologies. We focus on the constraints that current learning technologies place on the ambitions of integrated e-learning. This more specifically applies in terms of the lack of useful tools and necessary interoperability specifications, the so-called learning technology standards.

From a learner's perspective the first point is that the user-friendliness of the applications for learning must be improved in a variety of aspects. The quality of the user interfaces is still rather poor, and the support computers provide to facilitate learning could be improved, for example through agent technologies. User interfaces require better support for interactivity, and their ability to represent non-textual complex real-life situations, including powerful group communication and collaboration facilities, must be improved.

Besides the problems in the quality of the user interfaces, there is a lack of a large number of tools that would better support learners during the learning process in integrated e-learning, for instance tools for study management, navigation, personalization, searching through relevant study materials, or tools for co-development and evaluation and/or feedback to course developers. Another serious problem for learners today is the lack of interoperability between different educational institutes, especially when seen from a life-long learning perspective. For example, it is very difficult for learners to keep records of a portfolio or dossier of study accomplishments that is portable and can be used in different educational and training institutes. Given the availability of computer networks in integrated e-learning this is rather strange, as it implicitly makes solving the problem possible. One of the reasons is that real interoperability specifications for portable dossier data are still not very easy to get hold of. As far as they are available (as with IMS LIP), this is not on a very wide scale. From a broader perspective, the tools for more advanced student assessment in integrated e-learning are underdeveloped in terms of standards and software implementations.

Integrated e-learning might contain some new aspects for students that demand specific study skills. Thus attention has to be paid to equipping students in using e-learning facilities by providing both technical and functional training in 'studying with a mouse'. We need to ask whether students appreciate or at least accept the new media mix. A specific element is that a great deal of communication will be computer-mediated, which might cause problems, for instance how to manage the communication between students, teachers and staff in supporting units. This is not just a matter of the number of messages to be processed but also of forwarding the right message to the right person. This problem has to be faced in the design of learning tasks, and more specifically the design of collaborative components in

CSCL (computer supported collaborative learning). Procedures have to be developed to ensure that students get a reply from the right person within a limited period of time.

The teacher's and designer's perspective

Currently, the most important issue with regard to integrated e-learning is the almost complete absence of a useful pedagogy. As a result, instructional designers and teachers tend to fall back on traditional pedagogies, leading to forms of e-learning that offer little more than turning Web pages and filling out boxes, or provide only a surrogate for classroom teaching. For distance teaching universities such as open universities in Europe, many teachers are struggling with the opportunities and limitations of the Internet as a new medium. But for teachers at traditional institutes, a new pedagogy of integrated e-learning implies a basic paradigm shift in their view on teaching.

One of the main reasons for this is probably the absence of direct student feedback. In classroom teaching, lesson planning sets out the basic outline for lectures, seminars or practicals. Any imperfections in the plan show up during the lesson. Blank faces from students in the front row or a restless audience are enough to induce the lecturer to change the plan and provide additional examples, start a discussion, explain a concept for the second time and so forth. There is no such direct feedback in the case of integrated e-learning. It requires a systematic design and development of instruction beforehand, and for this reason the development of dedicated instructional design models for integrated e-learning deserves the highest priority.

Another problem for the teacher and designer is that a large number of tools are not available. Current integrated e-learning is still too weak in its support for the development of content of a more complex character which is interoperable, reusable and which can be aggregated. This means content consisting of advanced instructional designs, multimedia adaptive content and high-quality user inter-actions such as real world simulations.

Yet another problem is that advanced learning designs currently increase the activities of tutors, particularly in more open collaborative environments. This makes integrated e-learning less cost-effective to implement and hinders its acceptance. A direction in trying to solve this problem in future is by looking to autonomous agents to support the work of tutors. Teachers and designers still lack many more advanced tools. Moreover, tools to support the learning design process, to support monitoring student progress, or assess students conveniently are still underdeveloped. In the field of sharing and reuse, there is a lack of incentives for reuse. Learning object economies and implementations are underdeveloped, some standards are missing, and genuinely user-friendly tools for advanced tutoring tasks still have to be developed.

Finally, the introduction of integrated e-learning demands a new view on learning which has to be expressed in terms of an educational concept, and has to be clarified and accepted by all those involved. This is usually very difficult to achieve within higher education institutes. The next thing is that educational processes have to change. For instance, the move towards the development of instructional materials in course teams will affect roles, responsibilities, work processes and so on, in short the collaboration between teachers, educational designers, technologists and other staff members involved. The most essential aspect is probably that the work has to become more team-based instead of the traditional 'stand alone' mode. Moreover, new procedures and methods have to be developed and implemented with respect to design, production, maintenance and the renewal of materials. New expertise might be needed, which requires training, both functional and technical, and finally, cooperation within multidisciplinary teams has to be managed. This means that strong educational leadership is essential.

Instructional and learning materials

The way we envisioned integrated e-learning encompasses a deliberate use of different media, yielding a 'media mix' that provides an optimal solution for the specific context, target group, and tasks and contents that need to be mastered. However, the heart of integrated e-learning is the Internet, which drives the learning process by setting tasks for the learners. It provides a kind of 'simulated' environment in which learners can work on their learning tasks, or at least provides the tasks that can subsequently be worked on in another setting (for example, on the job). If e-learning is not used to set tasks for the learners, but only to provide information or communication facilities, it should not be seen as integrated e-learning but as 'blended e-learning' or another form of technology-enhanced learning. This viewpoint also indicates an important limitation of current integrated e-learning. For many tasks with particular input and output requirements, and especially for more advanced learners, integrated e-learning may lack the necessary input–output facilities needed for the learning process to occur. Putting it simply, integrated e-learning is not the best solution to train individuals in negotiating with clients in face-to-face situations, holding pleas in court or performing surgical operations.

In order to make learning materials reusable within and between institutions, much attention has been paid to so-called 'meta-data' standards (such as RDF and LOM) during the last few years. In addition, today there are more specific content specifications (such as XML, XHTML and Topic Maps) and learning technology specifications (such as IMS Content Packaging). These are important first steps, but in order for real reuse and sharing to occur, specific user-friendly tools that comply with these standards also have to be developed. With respect to the learning object economy, that is to say the use and exchange of learning materials, the situation still is very problematic. Many of the required certified standards are unstable, so we have to be cautious. Besides, procedures and mechanisms for exchanging materials (including copyrights) have not been elaborated yet. There are still many un-answered questions with respect to so-called active, personalized learning content such as simulations and advanced hypermedia. This is specifically true for content that is not 'frozen', but is constantly being adapted and improved by different users over a period of time. Aspects of the tooling are the shared, distributed repositories where teachers can add, search, find, edit, aggregate and redefine the purpose of learning objects.

Because most of the learning takes place outside the classroom and outside the institute, quality control with respect to the learning materials is another important element in integrated e-learning. A specific, problematic aspect here is the media mix. Two key questions are whether the mix of media supports the learning processes sufficiently (and even optimally) and precisely what an optimal mix is. These questions are very difficult to answer because of the large number of factors involved. In any case, feedback has to be organized, for instance by using question-naires, tests, progress reports and so on, in order to ensure that the learning takes place more or less according to plan.

Context and setting

Integrated e-learning as discussed in this book has been primarily situated in the field of higher education and life-long learning. This is an ideal setting for e-learning for several reasons. There is a clear connection between the contents of the programme and the profession that it leads to, making it relatively easy to define learning tasks. The target group consists mainly of high-ability students, who are well able to direct their own learning. These students have reached an age where their social development is no longer of prime importance. However, it should be clear that integrated e-learning as discussed in this book is not very useful in primary education, where play and social development are central issues, and probably – to a lesser degree – also not for secondary education. This is not to say that the Internet should not be used in these settings. On the contrary, we think that an appropriate use of new technologies is very important and may improve learning in primary and secondary school settings, but not in a way where the Internet is used to set the learning tasks and to steer the learning process.

One of the promises of integrated e-learning is to connect different educational institutes and other providers such as educational publishers, libraries, research institutes and training companies with each other, to strengthen what they can offer in terms of quality, quantity and flexibility in learning-related services. In addition to the organizational consequences these collaborations have, there are still many technical interoperability problems in putting these networks into practice. Anyone with experience of collaboration outside their own institute knows how difficult it is to get access to data and tools from other institutes. Firewalls and different standards may restrict the collaboration possibilities to e-mail and Web sites. This problem area motivates current approaches such as peer-to-peer networks and the GRID. However, when these more generic technological constraints have disappeared is just the moment that the problem for collaboration standards in the field of learning begins. This raises a vast number of questions. What is the granularity of reusable learning objects? To what extent can learning materials be exchanged? How do we redefine the purpose of materials made by others to fit our own context and purpose? How can we calculate the value of each other's contributions as a basis for payment?

Finally, from an innovative point of view the introduction of integrated e-learning is not unique. The transformation from traditional face-to-face or distance education towards competency-based or problem-based education also is a major transition that has to be organized carefully. Like any large-scale educational innovation, the introduction of integrated e-learning is a difficult expedition in which organization, management, implementation and evaluation are not simply important, but are also problematic elements to be taken into account. The expedition will become even more problematic when there is an inter-institutional network, for instance a consortium of institutes, in which students might take courses from each of the participating organizations. Under these circumstances educational leadership becomes extremely important. Another issue is quality management, especially in cases of a network approach in which a number of institutes is involved. We have to clarify who takes care of what, who is accountable for the quality, and of course, who awards the certificates.

Concluding remarks

Integrated e-learning is still in its infancy but is developing rapidly. E-learning is a trend, and as such a selling point in the competition between higher education institutes in the eyes of many managers in higher education. It is common practice for these institutes to have technology-driven motives to adopt new types of ICT infrastructures. In the Introduction we called this phenomenon 'technological optimism'. At the same time, the preceding chapters have shown that integrated e-learning, despite the problems that remain, provides a promising perspective and will no doubt play an important part in the mix of educational media, particularly because of the flexibility it can provide to educational systems.

We should like to conclude this book by presenting the following three deliberations. In the first place, educational technology is directed at the improvement of the effectiveness, efficiency, attractiveness and accessibility of education. The core of integrated e-learning is not that it will necessarily improve the effectiveness of education in the first place, but that it makes education:

- more accessible (other target groups; freedom of time and place; support for the mobility of learners; and access to unique or single source or rare information and/or environments);
- more flexible (individualized delivery);
- more productive (for example, through reuse and sharing);
- more attractive for life-long learners as a result.

Although integrated e-learning has this potential, there is still a long way to go before all these benefits have been further developed and achieved in practice.

The second point is that this book takes the stance that integrated e-learning environments have to be considered from a wider, organizational, systemic perspective. They are based on network technologies that connect distributed life-long learners, tutors and learning materials. One often reduces this perspective, for example by taking only the interaction of the learner with the computer and its applications into account. However, the computer is nothing more or less than a means of connecting the different actors and resources in education. The organization of this network in terms of the processes (development and delivery; evaluation and management of education; the roles of the different persons involved; the learning resources and the media) provides a better and more complete perspective to understand, improve and implement integrated e-learning. Another common type of reduction is to look at integrated e-learning only from the perspective of course delivery. However, the justification for the use of integrated e-learning is not to be found in the question of whether it improves the delivery of certain courses or not. Its added value lies in the addition of the several factors mentioned above, which are directed at the achievement of learner-centred life-long learning in practice.

Last but not least, it is necessary to adopt a more balanced approach towards integrated e-learning on several dimensions simultaneously. This book sets out to provide a contribution to this area by showing that the dimensions can be viewed coherently. There are innumerable questions that have yet to be answered and learning technologies that have still to be developed. Nevertheless, some of the pieces of the puzzle are already in place, and we hope that this will make it easier to find the remaining ones in the not too distant future.

Index

4C/ID model   14–15, 17–19, 31, 43, 167
  and performance assessment   43–46

adaptation   57, 66
  of learning objects   145–46
  see also computer adaptive testing;
    personalization
ADDIE model (analysis, design, development,
  implementation, and evaluation)   22, 55, 56
affordance
  educational   25, 28–29
  social   25, 28
  technological   25, 28
aggregation and repurposing   73
ALOYS (always looking over your shoulder)
  18
Argyris, C and Schön, D A   62
artisan approach   127
assessment   70, 74–75
  peer   47–48
  performance   9–10, 16, 39–50
    definition of purpose   41–42
    design   41
    instructional design framework   45–47
    tasks   42, 45
  Web-based tools   39–40, 48
Atkinson, R C and Wilson, H A   139
Axelrod, R   67

Baker, E L and Mayer, R E   39, 48
Banathy, B H   7
Barkai, D   67
Barnett, R   166
Baskett, H K M and Marsick, V J   51
Bastiaens, T *et al*   18
Bastiaens, T and Martens, R   41
Bastiaens, T, Martens, R and Stijnen, P   187
Bates, A W   3, 152, 155, 159, 177, 182
Beijaard, D *et al*   48

Bennett, R E   41
Benson, A D, Johnson, S D and Kuchinke, K
  P   187
Bereiter, C   3
Biggs, J   40
Bitter-Rijpkema, M, Sloep, P B and Jansen
  D   62, 141
blended learning   22, 172, 187
Booch, G, Rumbaugh, J and Jacobson, I   67
Bray, T, Paoli, J and Sperberg-McQueen, C
  M   85
Brown, J S, Collins, A and Duguid, P   82
Brown, J S and Duguid, P   141
Brown, S and Glasner, A   74
Brush, T A   32

Campbell, L M   73
Carley, K M   67
Carroll, J M   116
case studies   16, 19
case-based teaching   19–21
Casey, J and McAlpine, M   146
causal design view   26
causal models   16
Cerpa, N, Chandler, P and Sweller, J   107
CETIS   146, 148
Chandler, P and Sweller, J   106, 107, 108
Chang, D, Dooley, L and Tuovinen, J E   117
change management
  organizational view   160–61
  pedagogical view   157–60
  strategic view   157
  technological view   155–57
Chen, B *et al*   117
Clark, R E   13, 24
Clark, R E and Estes, F   14
coaching and training   11, 164–75
  affective aspect   169
  coach as role advisor   171

coach as role stimulator   171
  cognitive aspect   169
  role of coach   169
Coffield, F   51
cognitive feedback   16
cognitive skills   41
collaboration, affording   25–29
collaborative learning   24–38, 47
Collins, A   166
Collis, B A   152
Collis, B A and Van der Wende, M   152
Collis, B and Moonen, J   117, 140
competence-based education   154, 165–66
  role of teacher   166–67
competencies   3
complex learning   3–4
  instructional design for   14–17
complexity theory   66
computer supported collaborative learning
    (CSCL)   2, 9, 24, 28, 192, 202
computerised adaptive testing (CAT)   39
conceptual models   16
concurrent learning   51
Conklin, E J and Weil, W   33
constructive alignment   40–41
content packaging (CP) specification   143
context and settings   204–05
coordination   3
Corry, M D, Frick, T W and Hansen, I   114
course   14, 154
  definition   129
  design   131–33
  development as an industrial process
    127–28
  development process   130–34
  industrial approach   127–28
  requirements   128–29
  team   129, 134–37
Crasborn, F and Henning, P   171
CSPT (computer supported page turning)   14
Curran, C. and Fox, S   6
curricular level   154, 155

Daft, R L   66, 68, 69
data bases   144
data collection   115
Davis, S M and Botkin, J   141, 155
De Boer, W and Collis, B   19
De Vijlder, F   166, 167
delivery   70, 128, 129–30, 144
  costs   140
  systems   73–74
designer's perspective   202–03
development issues   70–72
Dick, W and Carey, L   55

didactic scenario   132, 166
differentiation   3
digital courses, interface design for   100–11
digital repositories   144
Dillenbourg, P and Schneider, D   82
disaggregation   73
distributed learning systems   7
Dix, A et al   113
Dodds, P   139
dossier   68, 74
double loop learning   62
Downes, S   72, 139
drill and practice computer programmes   46
dual learning   4–5
Duffy, T M and Cunningham, D J   71
Duffy, T M and Kirkley, J R   129
Duncan, C   72

e-learning, definition   5
e-mail   126
Edubox-player   81, 86, 90, 91, 92, 94, 96
  graphical user interface for   104–05
educational modelling   10
educational modelling language see EML
electronic performance support systems
    (EPSS)   18
Elen, J, Lowyck, J and Van den Berg, B   2, 155
EML   7, 10, 71, 80–99, 129, 136
  activities   87–89
  conceptual structure   84–85
  curricula   95
  definition   80
  designing within   85–87
  environment   89–90
  evaluation   96
  formalization   82
  interoperability   82–83
  method   90–95
  pedagogical flexibility   82
  pedagogical meta-model   83–85
  requirements   81–83
  roles   86–87
  XML binding   85
empowerment   184–85
epistemic fluency   33–34
evaluation   11, 187–98
  analytical   116, 118–19
  authenticity   195
  course   196
  empirical   116, 119–21
  framework   188–91
  learning   193
  and media mix   189
  mediated   116
  organization   194

performance   193–94
reaction   192–93
usability   10, 112–25
experiential learning   4

faculty management   10, 151, 160
'fading'   16
Ferber, J   67
Fichman, R G   177
Fisser, P H G   157, 158, 161
flexible learning   4
Forester, T   176
Forte, E *et al*   73
Foster, I, Kesselman, C and Tuecke, S   67
four-component instructional design model *see*
    4C/ID model
Fowler, M   67
Frederiksen, N   40

Galitz, W O   101, 102
Gallivan, M J   177
gaming   53
Gamma, E *et al*   67
Gaver, W   28
Gibbons, M *et al*   166
Gibson, J J   26
Goodyear, P   1, 4
granularization, of learning artefacts   72
GRID   67, 69, 204
Grotevant, S M   177
group size   24, 140
GROW model   169
guidance   16, 168
Gunawardena, C N and Zittle, F J   169

Hall, B   117
Hambleton, R K   74
Hannafin, M J   34
Harp, S F and Mayer, R E   108
Hendrikx, P   152
Herb, A   39
Herman, J L , Aschbacher, P R and Winters,
    L   41, 42
Hermans, H J H *et al*   75, 82
hidden curriculum   40
Holding   168
Hom, J   116
Huisman, W *et al*   172
human resource development (HRD)   51–52
human resources management   160–61
human–computer interaction   28

IECLEs   26, 28, 29, 34, 36
    design guidelines   29–31
    research agenda for   36

IEEE (Institute of Electrical and Electronic
    Engineers)   141, 143
IELs *see* integrated learning systems
implementation   10, 11, 70, 176–86
    of ICT   158
    Open University of the Netherlands
        case   177–78
    organizational change strategy   181–83
    of performance assessment   48
    plan   161–2
improvement of e-learning   70–75
    development issues   70–72
    differentiated delivery systems   73–74
IMS   143, 144, 145, 148
IMS Learner Information Package (IMSLIP)
    74
IMS Learning Design (IMSLD)   71, 97, 129,
    145
individual accountability   31–32, 47
information and communication technology
    (ICT)   1–2, 5, 9, 158
    and virtual business e-learning (VBeL)   58
Inglis, A, Ling, P and Joosten, V   161
innovation   2, 153, 177, 178–79
input boundary spanning   66
instructional design   9, 13–23
    for complex learning   14–17
integrated domain model   64–79
integrated e-learning   5–7
integrated e-learning systems (IELs)   65–67
    assessment   74–5
    functional dimension   67–68
    organizational dimension   68–69
    production subsystem   66, 67–68
    technical dimension   69–70
integrated electronic collaborative learning
    environments *see* IECLEs
interaction processes   25
interface design, for digital courses   100–11
International Organization for Standardization
    (ISO)   113
interoperability   74, 201
    EML   82–3, 97
    specifications   69–70
Ip, A and Naidu, S   19
Itzkan, S J   178
Ivens, W P M and Sloep, P B   61

Janssen, J P W and van der Klink, M R   136
Jeung, H, Chandler, P and Sweller, J   107
'job profiles'   42
Johnson, D W   32
Johnson, D W and Johnson, R T   32
Johnson, D W, Johnson, R T and Johnson-
        Holubec, E   31

Johnson, J   101, 102, 103
Johnson, S   66
just-in-time information   1, 4, 15, 16, 18, 20

Kalyuga, S, Chandler, P and Sweller, J   107, 108
Kanuka, H and Anderson, T   169
Kauffman, S   66
Kaye, A and Rumble, G   127
Kensing, F and Blomberg, J   123
Kester, L et al   16
Kester, L, Kirschner, P W and Van Merriënboer, J J G   35
Khan, B H   13
Kim, D H   61
Kirkpatrick, D L   188, 191, 195
Kirschner, P   28
Kirschner, P A and Huisman, W   172
Kirschner, P A and Paas, F G W C   5
Kirschner, P A lans et al   165, 166
knowledge economy   140–41
Kohn, D   42, 144
Koper, E J R   66, 71, 81, 82, 83, 128, 129, 145
Koper, E J R et al   71
Korsten, A F A et al   20
Kraan, W   143, 148
Kraan, W and Wilson, S   145
Krämer, B J   73
Kreijns, K and Kirschner, P A   35
Kreijns, K, Kirschner, P A and Jochems, W   28, 173

Lansu, A et al   172
Larman, C   67
Laurillard, D   3
learner control   34
learning arrangements   7
learning artefacts   28–29, 66, 67, 70
   aggregation   73
   granularization   72
learning design see IMS Learning Design
learning environment   26–27, 34, 35
learning management system (LMS)   6, 126, 128
learning materials   203–04
learning network   67, 76
learning object economy   73, 142, 144
learning object metadata (LOM) specification 143, 144
learning objectives   87
learning objects   139–50, 144
   adaptation   145–46
   definition   141–42
   reuse of   143–45
learning task see task

learning technology   7–8, 10, 64–79
   standards   69–70, 148, 156
   standards see earlier   113, 203
learning value   7
Lee, S H   114
LeNoble, D F   144
Levi, M D and Conrad, F G   113
life-long learning   3, 9, 141, 200–02
Linn, R L, Baker, E L and Dunbar, S B   41
Littlejohn, A   8
Livingston Vale, C and Long, P D   69
Lockwood, F   40
Lynch, P J and Horton, S   101

McDonald, J and Gibson, C C   169
Manderveld, J M and Koper, E J R   82
Marcic   69
Marsick, V and Watkins, K   51
'mathemathantic' learning materials   24
Maturana, H and Varela, F J   66
Mayer, R E   41, 106
Mayer, R E and Anderson, R B   107
Mayer, R E et al   107
Mayer, R E and Moreno, R   107
Mayer, R E and Sims, V K   107
media mix   5, 6, 17, 199, 201
   and evaluation   189
   primary medium   17–18
   secondary media   18
Mehrens, W A, Popham, W J and Ryan, J M   47
Merrill, M D   3, 14, 154
metadata   87, 143, 144, 203
Miller, P   83
Mitroff, I I, Mason, R O and Bonoma, T V   33
Moore, M G   170, 1173
Moreno, R and Mayer, R E   106, 107, 108
Morrison, D and Collins, A   33
Mousavi, S Y, Low, R and Sweller, J   107
Moust, J H and Schmidt, H G   170
multidisciplinary teamwork   71
multimedia   18, 105–08
multiple modalities   107

Nielsen, J   113, 114, 123
Niesink, R et al   172
Norman, D A   26, 28, 29, 113

Occam's razor   197
Ohlsson, S   33
Oliver, M and Conole, G   195
Oliver, R   147
OMG   67
O'Neil, H F   41
Open University of the Netherlands   11, 27,

56, 58, 96, 132, 134, 172, 176–86
  implementation case study   177–78
  Public Administration Course   20–21
organization   56
  of e-learning   151–63
  evaluation   194
organizational change strategy   181–83
organizational dimension, integrated e-learning
    systems (IELs)   68–69
organizational learning   6, 61
organizational level   153
organizations   66, 68–69
output boundary spanning   66
overload   106, 107
Owston, R D   112

Pantano, V and Cardew-Hall, M J   177
Park, I and Hannafin, M J   100
Parsons, J A   34
Patrick, J   168
pedagogical perspective   13, 152, 159–60
pedagogical meta-model, EML   83–85
pedagogical models   6, 19–21, 22
'perception–action coupling'   28
performance scoring rubrics   3, 44, 46
performance-based assessment   4
personal development, and quality control
    60–61
personal development plan (PDP)   54, 61
personalization   1, 73, 85, 139, 140, 145
  see also adaptation
positive independence   31, 32
positive interdependence   47, 48
Preece, J   115
Preece, J et al   28, 113, 116, 117
Preece, J, Rogers, Y and Sharp, H   113
Prietula, M J, Carley, K M and Gasser, L   66
probabilistic approach   25
probabilistic design view   26
problem solving   16, 33, 41
problem-based learning   31–32
project work, and quality control   59–60
project-centred learning   21
project-oriented problem based learning (PBL),
    and virtual business e-learning (VBeL)
    53, 55
promotive interaction   32
Public Administration Course, Open University
    of the Netherlands   20–21

quality control
  and personal development   60–61
  and project work   59–60
quality performance criteria   43
Quellmalz, E   43

Raskin, J   117
Ravet, S and Layete, M   189
Rawlings, A et al   80
Reeves, T C   34, 39
reference architectures   69
Reigeluth, C M   14, 83
repository   67, 73, 144
Rescher, N   142
reuse   8, 10, 13, 70, 72–73, 146
  of learning objects   143–45
Rittel, H W J and Weber, M M   33
Robinson, D G and Robinson, J C   82
Rogers, E M   177
Romiszowski, A J   17
Rosenbaum, S, Rohn, J A and Humburg,
    J   117
Ross, S M and Morrison, G R   34
Rosson, M B   116
Rourke, L   174
Rubin, J   116, 123
Rummler, G A and Brache, A P   188, 191

Salmon, G   144
Salomon, G   18
scaffolding   16, 21
Schellekens, A, Paas, F and Van Merriënboer, J J
    G   4
Schlusmans, K et al   82
Schmidt, H G and Moust, J H C   170
Schneiderman, B   28, 102
Schön, D A   61
Scott Grabinger, R   82
Senge, P   62
sharing see reuse
Shavelson, R J   41
Sholtz, P   144
Shyu, H Y and Brown, S W   34
Silius, K and Pohjolainen, S   177
Sim, S   69
Simple Sequencing   145
simulation   17–18, 41, 204
  and virtual business e-learning (VBeL)   53
Singh, H   188, 194
skill decomposition   42
skills training   167–68
Slavin, R E   31, 47
Sloep, P B   142, 148
Sluijsmans, D M A   47, 48, 61, 74
Sluijsmans, D M A et al   48
SMS messages   156
Snyder, B   40
social constructivism   1, 14
Söderberg, J   144
Söderberg, U   114, 117
Spector, J M and Davidsen, P I   2

Spiro, R J et al   32, 166
split attention   106–07
staff training   183–84, 185
standard see learning technology
Stephenson, J and Weil, S   166
Stiggins, R   41
Stolovich, H D and Keeps, E J   83
Strijbos, J W, Martens, R L and Jochems, W M
    G   25, 31
structural models   16
Suber, P   144
substitution   152
supportive information   15, 16, 18
Surgue, B   48
Swanson, R A   188, 191
Sweller, J   106
Sweller, J and Chandler, P   107, 108
Sweller, J et al   106

Tabbers, H K, Martens, R L and Van
    Merriënvoer, J J G   107
Tapscott, D and Caston   176
Tarmizi, R A and Sweller, J   106
task
    authentic   19, 32, 33, 40
    character   2–34
    class   45
    control   34–35
    ownership   31–32
    part task practice   15, 17, 19, 33, 46
tasks   14, 15, 16, 17, 19
    for performance assessment   43
teacher's perspective   202–03
Tindall-Ford, S, Chandler, P and Sweller,
    J   107
trainer's role   172
transfer of learning   14, 22, 33–34
transformation   153

units of learning   71, 72
usability   28, 102, 113–14
    attributes   113–14
    design approach   28, 123
    engineering   123
    evaluation   112–25
    goals   115, 122
    inquiry   116, 119
    inspection   116, 118–19
    testing   116, 120–21
user interface   70, 201
    graphical user interface (GUI)   10, 28,
        101–05
Utterbeck, J M   177

Valdez, G   188, 189

Van den Berg, R and Vandenberghe, R   160
Van Den Boom, G and Schlusmans, K   127
Van der Harstt, G and Maijers, R   102
Van der Vleuten, C M and Driessen, E W   74
Van Merriënboer, J J G   14, 42, 46
Van Merriënboer, J J G, Clark, R E and De
    Crooc, M B M   3, 14
Van Merriënboer, J J G and De Croock, M B
    M   14
Van Merriënboer, J J G and Kirschner, P A   14,
    25
Van Merriënboer, J J G, Kirschner, P A and
    Kester, L   16, 168
Varela, F J et al   66
Vermetten, Y et al   74
Verreck, W et al   136
virtual business e-learning (VBeL)   1–63, 189
    characteristics   52–55
    compared to gaming   3
    compared to project-oriented problem based
        learning (PBL)   53, 55
    compared to simulation   3
    compared to work placement   55
    continuous development   55–57
    and ICT   58
    InCompany   56–57, 58, 61, 62
    initiation and implementation   57–58
    quality control   59–61
    setting conditions   58–59
virtual company concept   10
virtual reality (VR)   18, 41
Vygotsky, L   171

Wagenaar, A et al   170
Wagner   7
Waldrop, M   66
Walker, S   188, 197
Warmer, J and Kleppe, A   67
Wegerif, R   174
Westera, W and Sloep, P B   139, 141, 178
Westera, W, Sloep, P B and Gerrissen, J   18
Whitmore, J   169
whole task learning   15, 16, 46, 47
    role of coach   170–71
Wichansky, A M   123
Wiggins, G   41
Wiley, D   72
Wiley, D A   142
work placement   55

XML binding   71, 85, 129

Yeung, A S , Jin, P and Sweller, J   106

Zhang, J et al   39